W9-BRB-676

3—

Goddess

Cris Alexander.

Martha Graham in Judith, *1950.*

Goddess

Martha Graham's Dancers Remember

BY Robert Tracy

LIMELIGHT EDITIONS

NEW YORK

First Limelight Edition April 1997

Copyright © 1996 by Robert Tracy.
All rights reserved including the right of reproduction in whole or in part in any
form. Published by Proscenium Publishers Inc., 118 East 30th Street, New York, NY
10016

Manufactured in the United States of America

Library of Congress Cataloging-in-Publication Data

Tracy, Robert
    Goddess: Martha Graham's dancers remember/
    by Robert Tracy
    1st Limelight Edition
        p.   cm.
    Includes index.
        ISBN 0-87910-086-9
    1. Graham, Martha. 2. Dancers—United States—Biography. 3. Choreographers—
United States—Biography. 4. Modern dance.
I. Title.
GV1785.G7T73   1996
792.8'028092—dc20
[B]   96-31310

Designed by Gloria Adelson/Lulu Graphics.

Typeset by Bryan McHugh.

In memory of
my father
and for
M. W. S.
and
Melissa

The beginning is everything

"I did not realize,
my friend, that though you have
only this one body, you have
so many souls."

—Lucian of Samosata

Contents

My dancing is just dancing. It is not an attempt to interpret life in a literary sense. It is not the affirmation of life through movement. Its only aim is to impart the sensation of living—to energize the spectator into keener awareness of the vigor, of the mystery, the humor, the variety, and the wonder of life—to send the spectator away with a fuller sense of his own potentialities and the power of realizing them, whatever the medium of his activity.

—Martha Graham, 1935

THE

1920'S

Eastman Kodak Company.

*Martha Graham and Trio in Arabesque, 1926-27. Left to right: Betty
MacDonald, Thelma Biracree, Martha Graham, Evelyn Sabin*

Betty MacDonald

Betty MacDonald in Scéne Javanaise, *1928.*

Betty MacDonald was born in Bradford, Pennsylvania, in 1907. In 1925, although MacDonald did not have any formal dance training, an aunt suggested that she audition for the film director Rouben Mamoulian, the head of the Eastman School of Music, Dance and Dramatic Action in Rochester, New York. In 1925 Mamoulian had chosen Martha Graham, whom he had seen perform in her last season with Denishawn and subsequently with the Greenwich Village Follies, to teach contemporary dance.

In 1926 Graham formed a trio of talented students and asked MacDonald to participate. MacDonald also performed with the trio as one of "The Graham Dancers" in the Greenwich Village Follies. She remained with Graham until 1930, when the Martha Graham Group developed out of the trio.

In 1935, she married the actor C. Robin Batcheller and had a career in the theater until their son was born in 1944.

Betty MacDonald lives in Stamford, Connecticut

I was so thrilled to *move*, but I wasn't interested in ballet. I never wanted to be a ballet dancer. I auditioned for Rouben Mamoulian, who was head of the Eastman School of Music, Dance, and Dramatic Action in Rochester, New York, where I heard they taught "modern" dance. He took me and within three months he gave me a scholarship. He said, "Betty, you've proven yourself. You're gifted."

When I came [to Rochester] that September in 1925, Martha Graham taught three days a week, and the other part of the week she was teaching in New York City at the Anderson-Milton School. Well, the first day Martha walked in the door of the dance studio she had on an East Indian sari à la Ruth St. Denis, because she had recently come from Denishawn, and I'll never forget it

as long as I live. It was as though something happened to me. Martha illumi-
nated this whole place by her presence and she hadn't even moved yet. The
minute I started to study with her I worshipped her.

Evelyn Sabin and I would meet Martha's train every morning when she
would arrive from New York City. We loved Martha dearly. Martha always spoke
about Ruth St. Denis as "Miss Ruth," even after she had left her, so we always
called her "Miss Martha." We always waited for Martha to teach. That year,
Martha was finding her own way of moving the body. The class was very big.
There were some men, too. Some of the dance students left the school because
they didn't like what Martha was doing, and they didn't care for Martha's way
of moving. They were ballet dancers. Martha was discovering her own identity
while she was getting away from the character, revue-style dancing of
Denishawn's influence. She wanted to find meaningful, significant movement.

In 1926, Martha was going to do her first concert and she chose three of us
to dance as a trio with her: me, Thelma (Teddy) Biracree and Evelyn Sabin. The
other two in the trio had both been studying ballet. In fact, they were both
lovely toe-dancers, so Martha had to get them to forget their ballet background.
I never studied ballet so I didn't have anything to throw away. When Martha
started to rehearse with us, she wanted them to stop being ballet dancers and
for all of us to move, really move the body. I didn't have any problem with that.

Martha wanted to say something in terms of movement. It was like she was
stepping out of this encasement of Denishawn. She wanted to move the body
differently. And she certainly did. Already Martha's technique was beginning to
explore contraction and release. The first movements she worked on were the
"Graham falls." It was percussive—it was as though someone hit you, and you
went back and fell. You were using the contraction when you got hit and fell.
When you came up, you came up with your entire body naturally, not like a
toe-dancer who came up with prettiness and beauty. Coming up with the
whole body, you would use the release. Martha would say to me, "Betty, you
have ballerina legs." Martha encouraged us to complete each movement fully
so that it wasn't fake or false. She used to say, "you must complete every gesture down to the fingertips." Nothing was developed, compared with how
Martha went on to move later or to how her company moves today.

Martha was breaking away from tradition in several of the dances she choreographed for us to present in her first concerts in 1926. Martha created everything in terms of the movement and we would follow along. In rehearsals,

Martha would get ideas and try different movements. She would see what was coming and if she was getting somewhere with the dance, if it was coming along, we wouldn't have any dinner. Sometimes we would finish at 4 in the morning because she didn't want us to break her concentration. She wouldn't stop, because her movement ideas were happening. Martha was feeling and seeing the dance through.

Martha had an awful lot to do with people choreographing their own roles in her dances. Of course, much of it was Martha. I am sure the dancers did a lot to help her by going and dancing some movements, but then Martha would say "Good," or "No. I'd rather this." Martha pretty well knew [in] what direction your talent should go. She brought out of you the best of what was there, and then she would mold you, too. In the process, you became as committed an artist as Martha was. Martha created a great many dancers, both male and female.

Louis Horst[1] was Martha's mentor. He was also a wonderful man and a beautiful musician. Louis believed in Martha Graham beyond any belief. He was Martha's taskmaster and very stern with her. Martha, of course, was in love with Louis, and they did have a beautiful love together. Louis had gone through everything with Martha from the time they were both with Denishawn. Through thick and thin, he made a great deal of what Martha was. Martha wouldn't have gotten where she did without Louis. I think Martha's success was through Louis Horst and his unshaken faith in her. Don't ask me about Erick Hawkins.[2] Martha married him. After two years of marriage though it was horrible for her. She was unhappy. I think Louis was hurt by Martha's love for Erick.

[1] Louis Horst (1884-1964). Composer, educator and musical director for Martha Graham. Born in Kansas City, Missouri, Louis Horst moved to San Francisco at age 9. He was Ruth St. Denis' company pianist and the conductor of her touring orchestra. In 1925, after 10 years as Miss Ruth's music director, Horst left. He encouraged Doris Humphrey, Charles Weidman and Martha Graham to break away from Denishawn as well, in order to develop their individual styles. Horst composed for Graham and was her musical director and accompanist. According to Charles Weidman, Horst and Graham became lovers in 1921. Dorothy Bird, on the other hand, believed that their relationship was never physical. Horst and Graham suffered a personal and professional rupture in 1948, due to Martha Graham's love for Erick Hawkins. They reconciled in 1955. In addition to regularly teaching courses on the fundamentals of choreography at the Neighborhood Playhouse, Horst taught at the Julliard School of Music, beginning in 1952, when the dance department was created. He was the publisher of *Dance Observer* magazine.

[2] Erick Hawkins (1910-1994). Dancer/Choreographer. He first met Martha Graham when a member of George Balanchine and Lincoln Kirstein's Ballet Caravan (1936-1939), which began its first season with performances at Bennington College. Two years later, he became the first male dancer to join the Martha Graham Company (1938-1951). After having lived together for 8 years, Hawkins and Graham were married in 1948; they separated in 1950 and subsequently were divorced. See pages 64-70.

Isadore Bennett Collection.

Martha Graham and Louis Horst at Bennington College, 1936

Martha wanted us to study at the Neighborhood Playhouse with her and Louis, who was teaching dance composition. We got all our training with Martha [but] Louis was really doing choreography, teaching us how to put movement together. There was one dance [where] we had to be off the beat. That was very difficult for me. I thought I was off the beat, but I wasn't. Louis was playing away at the piano yelling, "Betty, what are you doing?" He was looking the opposite way. But Louis had eyes in the back of his head...Martha did, too.

Martha and Louis were really like my parents. At one point, I was living with Martha at her studio. I didn't have any money and I didn't have any place to go so she let me stay in her dressing room. I slept on Martha's chaise lounge until I could get some money to live. We got paid nothing all the time we danced for Martha.

Martha always did our costumes. She pinned them on us, and we had to sew them together. It was all done in the spirit of Denishawn. Martha had come from years with Ruth St. Denis. Martha was so important there. She hadn't yet broken away completely. In one sense, you cling to it because you know it works, and on the other hand, you try something new, you wonder how it is going to be received.

The trio was with Martha for about five years. Teddy only danced in the first concerts in New York City. Martha discovered Rosina Sevilli when she was teaching at the Anderson-Milton School, and she put her with us. So Rosina, Evelyn and I were Martha's trio. The trio danced in the *Greenwich Village Follies*. We were called "The Graham Dancers." Actually, in the *Follies* we performed Martha's choreography from our concerts. The trio had a great deal of work. I performed in 15 of Martha's 18 dances in those first concerts.

The dances were very lyrical, which was Martha's Denishawn influence, but the composers Martha used to create dances to were very modern because they were Louis Horst's choices. Every number was different in its kind and type of movement.

Often we opened and closed together as "Martha Graham and Trio." *Danse Languide*, to Alexander Scriabin, for the trio alone, was very popular. Louis loved *Alt-Wien*, which was a duet Martha choreographed for me and Evelyn Sabin to Leopold Godowsky's music, arranged by Louis Horst. *Tanze*, to Schubert, and *Scherzo*, to Mendelssohn, were for [just] the trio while *Chorale*, to

César Franck, Debussy's *Clair de Lune,* and [*Prelude from*] *Alceste,* to C.W. von Gluck, were for Martha Graham and Trio. *Alceste* looked like a Botticelli painting. *Scéne Javanaise* was a Martha Graham and Trio piece set to Louis Horst's music, which we performed at a concert in Rochester, New York. Allen Clark, the sculptor, asked Miss Graham if I could pose for him in one of the movements from the dance, which Martha had based on Javanese court dances. Martha said, "Yes, of course." I still have the statue he made of me.

Martha was lovely in her solos, especially "Tanagra,"[3] to Erik Satie, and *The Marionette Show,* to Eugene Goossens. Martha created the dances on us. She did what she liked in terms of movement. Then we would hold it and go on to something else. Her transition from Denishawn carried over to her work in Rochester. She hadn't [yet] been able to do what she was meant to do, which was to create a whole different way of moving. But she finally did it. Many thought of Martha as a rebel, because she had gone far, far away from choreographic traditions.

In the meantime, I met my future husband [C. Robin Batcheller], who was an actor, and I became very interested in the theater. We had a wonderful life together, playing opposite each other on the stage. I was very much in love with my husband, and [being with him was] what I wanted most of all in my life. I don't think Martha was upset when I left and…did not join her group—which was created after the trio—[because] nobody is that important. Besides, she had beautiful dancers. [But] I know Martha loved me. One night at midnight she called and said, "Betty, will you do something for me?" I said, "Martha, I would do anything possible that I could do. She said, "Will you dance in my next concert with the group?" Ruth White [had] hurt her leg, so I had to replace her. I learned the dances. Being smaller than Ruth, I know Martha rearranged everything so I would be seen. That was the only time I danced with Martha's group. I went to Martha's concerts constantly after that, until the end. I saw her once [when] she fell onstage. It hurt me so much.

Martha danced too long, you know.[4] But I feel blessed to have been a part of Martha's beginnings, where she used the body differently and expressed her

---

[3] From *Trois Gnossiennes: Gnossiene, Frieze, Tanagra* (1926), performed by Martha Graham and Trio.

[4] Martha Graham, although crippled by arthritis and suffering from the effects of chronic alcoholism, continued to perform until she was in her 70s.

ideas differently. The greatness was there. I recognized something I had been yearning for, that I had been longing for, and this woman, Martha Graham, opened the world up for me. Everybody adored Martha because she expected us to perform and produce her work. Martha was trying to be what she was going to be, this great, great dancer-choreographer. Martha was a genius and she changed dance forever.

MARTHA HILL

Thomas Bouchard.

Martha Hill at Bennington College, 1936.

Martha Hill was born in East Palestine, Ohio, on December 1, 1900. She studied music, Dalcroze Eurythmics, ballet and modern dance. She received her B.S. degree from Teachers College of Columbia University and her M.A. from New York University.

Hill was a member of Martha Graham's Group from 1929 to 1931, but she dedicated herself primarily to the development of dance education in America. She taught and choreographed in colleges around the nation. Hill was a consultant for the United States Office of Education, writing the dance section of a manual for teachers in 1943. She joined the dance faculty of New York University in 1930, eventually becoming its director and establishing its graduate program. She left NYU in 1951 for the Juilliard School, where she established the dance department which she directed until 1985 and of which she was named Director Emeritus. In addition, Hill founded the Bennington School of the Dance in 1934 and was associated with its summer school and festival until 1942. She founded the Connecticut College School of the Dance and the American Dance Festival, which was held at the college until 1978 in 1948.

Martha Hill died at her home in Brooklyn, New York, on November 21, 1995.

I started out as an amateur musician in the Bible Belt of Ohio where they didn't have dance. In fact, there are certain pockets left in the Midwest where dance is forbidden. My family would take me to Cleveland and Pittsburgh to the theater during the Twenties. I saw some things at an early age and at an early age of the theater in America. I saw certain things that gave me some idea of theater. I think I saw a follower of Loie Fuller—a skirt dancer—when I was very young. I saw Denishawn probably first... I saw Pavlova on her last tour, I saw Fokine and Fokinova— that must have been in the Twenties, the mid-Twenties—[so] I probably didn't see the Denishawn people until the late-Twenties.

By the time I saw Martha Graham's solo concerts in 1926 and 1927, I was already a ballet dancer in New York. New York was very lively. A daughter of a friend of my father's, fortunately a young intellectual, although I didn't know her, just sent me a ticket to one of Martha's early concerts. I didn't know who Martha Graham was.... If you were a ballet dancer you were in a closed circle. One didn't even know any history. I hardly knew who Isadora Duncan was. You were taught steps and technique; you had barre. Ballet was at a low period when I came into it. The Russian ballet had been and gone, leaving very little trace. The 1920s was Diaghilev in Paris; Fokine and Fokinova had toured. In the studios it was pretty cut-and-dried.

I had been, because of my training in music, sort of branching out in my ballet. I didn't want to use just traditional music like Minkus and Delibes. I knew music literature, mostly piano. I wanted to do some contemporary dance and, although I didn't call it contemporary music, I wanted to use later music like Debussy.... I wanted to do things that were evocative for me. I continued to take ballet lessons but I went to Anna Duncan, Isadora's adopted daughter, for classes and I discovered a thing called Dalcroze Eurythmics.[1] [Eventually] I studied with Elza Fendley, a marvelous Dalcroze person and a dancer. I was with her after I had discovered Martha because I remember Elza saying to me, "You. You Graham dancer over there...." I said, "Miss Fendley, I wish Martha Graham would say that."

I was at Martha Graham's first studio, the John Murray Anderson-Robert Milton School of the Theatre, in the East 50s in New York City. She was also with the Eastman School [in Rochester, New York]. I was still getting out of my ballet habits with Martha. It was a complete conversion, from the ground up. I didn't do ballet at all. I just concentrated. It was an instant conversion [from the first time I saw her perform]. I had been looking, feeling, for something more. I had been doing some creative work of my own because if you were going to dance you had to make your own dances.

It was an emotional feeling that led me to Martha; it was not because [her

---

[1] A system of rhythmic exercises designed to foster music students' expressivity by creating a greater feeling for the movement inherent in music. Created by Emile Jacques-Dalcroze (1865-1950), who was born in Vienna but performed his major work in Geneva, Eurythmics was studied by early modern dancers in order to increase rhythmic sensitivity.

style] was so progressive. Martha was dancing feelings. She was still doing post-Denishawn and things like a little scarf dance à la Ruth St. Denis and Isadora but they were always her own. She hadn't started doing political statements like "Strike," "Revolt,"[2] or *Heretic*, which I was in yet. There was an atmosphere of emotion, even if there was not a stated emotional theme.

Like all young people in New York, I [ran] out of money. I never thought about applying for a job at Macy's or in a restaurant. I was a dancer; I hunted for jobs in my profession. I went to Oregon for two years, all the while writing back and forth, and saved my money so I could go back. At the end of the second year I returned to New York City and immediately went to Martha. Technically, everything had changed. It was very, very different. Before I left, she had begun to experiment with the percussive attack—a sharp attack and breath phrase—and work with the torso. While I was away, she had gone on to a different phase. You had to react sharply then because you feared that people would take this experimentation away and you would be back doing the same thing—a ballet barre. If Martha had continued to work and had continued dancing, her technique would have been changing to the end. She was a constant mover—her ideas were active.

Things moved very fast. There were great differences between the concert programs of 1926 and 1927, as well as between 1929 and 1930. The transition from the trio (1925-28) to the group, which I joined in 1929, was a big jump. There was another big jump when she imported Erick Hawkins and an actor named Housley Stevens for *American Document* in 1938. They were the first men with Martha.

That summer Martha invited me into the company I had to continue to work on my own from the principles I had learned from her. They had already begun to be her own, not Denishawn's, through Louis Horst and through experimentation with her own body.

The floorwork was already developed. It was very revolutionary, the floorwork, although there must have been some floorwork at Denishawn too. I can still see Martha in a sari sitting with us in the studio with her legs crossed. We did a barre too, but a barre with a difference. We didn't do tendu and the things that come into her technique now.

---

[2] A Martha Graham solo from *Immigrant: Steerage, Strike* (1928).

Martha's spinal work, that feeling of what she called "contraction and re-lease," developed in a big way later. It wasn't the fall and recovery of Doris Humphrey,[3] but a falling forward and going back and swinging the arm. It was quite different than anything that was done [then]. The physical education people used to get very concerned about *contract* because when you do release you are actually contracting muscle. I would say, "You must realize Martha is using 'contraction' in a metaphoric sense, not in an actual sense." Martha meant in the *sense* of muscle. They would get very worried about the scientific thing of the contraction of muscle.

I came to Martha just when Louis Horst came back from Vienna where he was during 1925-26. Martha started a great number of things but we didn't fin-ish anything right off. We raced around doing this and that. We had a great many different ideas. Finally, Louis said, "Martha, we have a date in the theater. You can't do all of these things. You have got to do one and do it thoroughly. You can't go around playing with all these ideas." That's when she made *Pre-lude to a Dance,* set to Honegger, and *[Moment] Rustica,* which was Poulenc. Louis must have started to fuss in November since the performance was in January. This was the first year I was in the company, 1929-30. The second year we did *Project in Movement for a Divine Comedy,* which didn't have music. That was the only time Martha didn't use music.

I remember that first year I was in the company because it was a very pro-ductive year for us. We had input in what Martha was doing. She let us impro-vise. All of that material that any of us remembers from that very productive period is that it was such fun. We would take an idea, Martha would do some-thing, and we'd do something.

---

[3] Doris Humphrey (1895-1958). Performer, teacher, choreographer and theoretician. One of the great, semi-nal figures in the development of the modern dance, Humphrey is frequently cited with Martha Graham as one of its two main influences. Humphrey began dancing as a child and was instructed in a variety of styles, including ballet. She opened her own school in Oak Park, IL, but left it to study at the Denishawn school in Los Angeles. After touring with Denishawn, Humphrey and Charles Weidman left to found a com-pany and a school. Like Martha Graham, Humphrey was a renegade from Denishawn, but she and Gra-ham differed radically in their ideas concerning the importance of experience. While Graham depicted the conflict of humans within themselves, Humphrey was concerned with the conflict of humans with their environment. Humphrey viewed the body in relation to space and she spent the first years of her indepen-dent career forming her approach to dance movement based on a principle of duality in the contrast of the fall from and the recovery of balance. Although she had to abandon performing in 1945 because of an ar-thritic hip, Humphrey continued to choreograph and teach, and she became the artistic director of the José Limón Company. Humphrey codified her technique in her book, *The Art of Making Dances,* published in 1959.

Martha's early movement seemed right artistically...what she was saying and the way she was saying it. *Martha* seemed right. I saw Mary Wigman[4] in 1929 or 1930. They were related, but Martha was not doing the same thing. In dance the way Martha would say things seemed right to me because she had a *passion* about things. I've always said about Doris Humphrey and Martha Graham that Doris was Apollo and Martha was Dionysus.

I was in the first *Heretic*. It was wonderful...but very badly revived. Yuriko[5] had revived it [and] she had a film of the piece, which I was in. I asked her, "What did you think you were doing? We were always in a tight-knit semi-circle." I can still feel the pressure of the shoulder next to me now. Then we would rise, relevé and burst out of that into the next movement. It was a tight, tight phalanx of people against the Heretic...you had so little space between the dancers. It was done during that period of German artists Kathe Kollwitz [1867-1945], George Grosz [1893-1959]—violent things they were doing...you have a spotlight coming down on the cadaver and everybody leaning over at this anatomy lesson....So I asked Yuriko what happened. She said she had had it tight but Martha came in and said, "Yuriko, you know you are going to have a bigger stage at City Center." I told Yuriko that you don't spread the dance out. It isn't the nature of the dance. You pull the lights in. You pull the stage in. I was so distressed when I saw [the revival] I won't go see it now.

Robert D. Leigh discovered me teaching at N.Y.U., took me up to Bennington and asked me if I'd come to start [the school of dance]. There was still hay in the barn....The college started in 1932...it became the Bennington School of the Arts in 1940. I never did slavish, verbatim teaching of precisely what Martha did. I taught what I saw as good training. Ballet was very deep within me...I had my early training in anatomy and kinesiology [and] I had done a lot of folk dancing on the side. I knew something about the human body. That is why when I started Bennington it was a little arts school, but in the summer it was everything across the board, except ballet.... The first chance

---

[4]Mary Wigman (1886-1973). German modern dancer and choreographer who trained with Emile Jacques-Dalcroze in Hellerau and Dresden, and began to work and study with Rudolf von Laban in 1913. She trained virtually the entire first generation of German concert dancers.

[5]Yuriko [Anemiya Kikuchi] (1920-). Member of the Graham Company from 1944 until the late 1950s, guest soloist with the company in the sixties and founder of the Martha Graham Ensemble. After Graham's death, Yuriko served as the co-artistic director of the company until 1993. See pages 100-111.

Soichi

Martha Graham and Group in Heretic, *1929.*

I got to do ballet and modern dance together [was at Julliard]. Bill Schuman[6] asked me, "What do you think about a dance department at Julliard?" He wanted to make it professional, like the music school. I told him there wasn't such a thing in America. Dance has always been part of Physical Education or Art, or at a studio. Bill said, "Whom would you want?" I said, "Tudor[7] for ballet, Martha for modern." Hanya Holm[8] came in later. The curriculum was conceived as what I had discovered in my own life of ballet, modern dance, music and what have you...I incorporated it all...as well as the whole scientific background that Hanya Holm had in her training.

The Bennington School of the Dance was a phenomenal time because the head of the college was interested in us. Nobody knew it would catch on like it did but it was the right place and the right time in the dance. We had giants in the dance. Tudor and Balanchine had come to America...Lincoln Kirstein had long conversations with me about his opening of S.A.B.[9] and mine of Bennington....I was a crusader for an art idea that Martha personified. She was the best exponent of something in which I believed. I organized Bennington partly with this idea of Martha's of concert dance in America. Martha said she would come with her company. Big hunks of me are Martha, and I learned a lot about music from Louis and continued to learn more. I was with them a great deal through all the Bennington years (1934-38).

[6] William Howard Schuman (1910-1992). Composer and educator. President of the Julliard School of Music, 1945-1961; Charter President of Lincoln Center, 1962-1969. He composed the music for Martha Graham's *Night Journey* (1947), *Judith* (1950), *Voyage* (1953), which was revised as *Theatre of a Voyage* (1955), and *The Witch of Endor* (1965).

[7] Antony Tudor (1909-1987). British dancer and choreographer. *Time Table* (1941), for George Balanchine and Lincoln Kirstein's Ballet Caravan, was his second ballet choreographed in America. His chief contribution to dance was choreographing for the American Ballet Theater.

[8] Hanya Holm (1893-1992). Born in Germany, Holm studied in Dalcroze schools in Frankfurt and Hellerau. A disciple of Mary Wigman, she studied at the Mary Wigman school in Dresden, joining the Wigman company in 1919 and touring with it for 12 years. In 1931 she founded the Wigman school in New York, but by 1936 Holm had decided to form her own concert dance company and she changed the school's name to the Hanya Holm Studio. She led the workshop group at the Bennington College Summer School of the Dance during the summer of 1937 and in 1941 she established a summer dance program at Colorado College in Colorado Springs which she directed for four decades. Her students included Alwin Nikolais, Glen Tetley and Valerie Bettis. Holm's interest in various forms of theatrical dance for other media led to a 1939 television broadcast entitled *Tragic Exodus* and she created dances for many musicals, including *Kiss Me, Kate, Out of this World* and *My Fair Lady*. She also worked on operas and film.

[9] The School of American Ballet was founded by George Balanchine and Lincoln Kirstein in New York City in 1934. It is the "feeder" school of the New York City Ballet.

I had to choose to either go with Martha, where we couldn't yet be paid, or teach. If we got a little, tiny bit for dancing a concert we were lucky. You never wanted to be paid but you had to live. Sophie Maslow had a husband who taught. Jane Dudley was married. They came in at the end of my period with Martha. I had to do one or the other. I talked to Martha and told her it broke my heart…. It did…it broke my heart to give up performing [but] in that period you had to; it was hard for people to make a living in dance. It still is. It will always be tough. There is always somebody to say you did it all wrong, somebody who wants to do it a different way. Now, you see, you still cannot make a decent living, but it's better.

Martha always had an influence. I think people resented her strength. You'll find people who say Martha was a deterrent to their creativity and ability. Not true. Martha was always encouraging. When I went off to Bennington [and] N.Y.U. instead of devoting my life to her company, Martha said, "Well, Bill Bales is at Bennington. Be sure to make some dances together and perform."

I don't know if Martha gave up a lot to be Martha Graham. Robert Frost has a poem about the road [not] taken—you never know what another road would have been. She had to be herself—Martha Graham. I think what Martha prized above everything was the ability to perform. She thought of herself as a performer, not a choreographer. However, her works are right up there with [the] art expression [of] any period—like Picasso—and art dance is more difficult. You can't just get up and dance. You've got to have a setting. You've got to have a theater around you. If you want to express many ideas you can't be a soloist. When Martha came in, we were just moving out of a solo period where Fokine and Fokinova [could] do solos interspersed with other things. But [then] you had to do ballet with a lot of people in order to make it real, an event. When you think what it takes for a dancer to get something onstage…Martha was amazing to have accomplished what she did—a theatrical empire.

#

1930's

Barbara Morgan.

Martha Graham and Erick Hawkins in Every Soul Is a Circus, *1939.*

ANNA SOKOLOW

Barba

*Anna Sokolow (standing in front, far right) with Martha Graham and
Group in* American Provincials, *1934.*

Anna Sokolow was born in Hartford, Connecticut, in 1910. At the age of 10 she began to study dance with Blanche Talmud; later, she studied with Martha Graham and Louis Horst at the Neighborhood Playhouse. She began performing with the Playhouse Childrens' Theater.

Sokolow was a member of Martha Graham's company from 1930-39, while also teaching at the Neighborhood Playhouse as assistant to Horst. In addition, she choreographed both solos and ensemble pieces for her own company, which she formed in 1934. Sokolow became one of the leading American choreographers of the 20th century—in concert dance, for both drama and musicals on Broadway, for television and for the New York City Opera. Her biography, The Rebellious Spirit, *was published in 1992.*

Anna Sokolow lives in Greenwich Village.

The two founders of modern dance were Isadora Duncan, an American, and Mary Wigman, a German who is considered the founder of the German Expressionist movement. When I give a class or a talk [nowadays] I have to explain how amazing it must have been for Isadora Duncan to go onstage barefoot—wearing not a tutu [but] instead a long Greek robe, with her arms flowing that way—and dance. She had the courage to do what she believed in. To me, that was more of an inspiration than [anything] else.

Martha Graham was my first "artist teacher" at the Neighborhood Playhouse. It was a very interesting revelation to me: I [had] never had that. But it was Louis Horst who said more to me than she did. When Martha and Louis Horst were teaching at the Neighborhood Playhouse I related to him; I didn't relate to her. They were saying the same thing, but the approach was different. Louis Horst was Martha Graham's musical director for years, writing music for her, choosing music for her, which was wonderful. But Martha was very concentrated on herself. Martha had Louis, and she had sponsors—even then she had sponsors, something we never had until lately. The idea was if you stayed with Martha and danced with her, you would become a disciple, which I never was and never wanted to be. Each artist does it their own way. I think you are born with certain qualities in you. I always propagated the tradition of nonconformity. Unfortunately, modern dance has become conformist. I think Martha realized I could never be her disciple. I wouldn't say anything, but I felt inside, "What the hell. I don't want that."

Louis Horst introduced us to the world of choreography, of making a dance about how you feel about things translated into movement. That appealed to me immediately. We had to show our solos to both of them. Louis Horst always liked everything I did. I just did what I felt. Back then—and I still do in a way—I did dances on Jewish themes. I did a dance called *Songs of the Semite.* Graham said to me, "If you want to be Jewish, why don't you use the Old Testament?" Her idea of being Semitic was not doing what I did—about the day—but the history. Martha never liked anything I did. Never.

Martha was more into the inspiration of the Greek legends [than the social realities of the day], which . . . was very beautiful, but they had no connection for me. . . . Another important thing was that in Martha Graham's time you were supposed to not like ballet. . . . I went to see the ballet because I wanted to see why Martha didn't want us to see it. I fell in love with the Ballet Russe de Monte Carlo. The next day, while I was changing for rehearsal, I said that I didn't know what was wrong with ballet. Everyone said, "Shhh." I said, "I don't care. I'm going to study it." And I did. I was one of the first modern dancers to go to the New York City Ballet's School of American Ballet and study with all of Balanchine's Russian teachers. I still love ballet—it has a beautiful, poetic quality. Mr. Balanchine was a genius. As a choreographer, I never copied it. It's like seeing a painting which is beautiful: it can inspire you, but you don't have to copy it. . . .

I was on the first tour that Martha Graham ever had. We went on tour through the United States. It was quite a big tour. I remember *Primitive Mysteries* (1931) and *Celebration* (1934). I don't remember other things. I don't actually remember any of the movement from *Primitive Mysteries,* but I remember the mood of it was very good . . . and Louis Horst wrote the music. It was a very American theme. That's all I remember. I don't remember ever being explained what it meant. We just did what we were told to do in movements and steps.

In my time there were no men in Martha Graham's company. Even when I left, there were no men in the company. There was quite a group of women artists though: Sophie Maslow, Ailes Gilmour (Isamu Noguchi's sister), Jane Dudley, Bonnie Bird, Dorothy Bird and May O'Donnell, who, I think, isn't given the credit she deserves . . . she was a beautiful, beautiful dancer.

Martha was very interested in using designs of things, like ropes and material, and she did it very well. Artists like Isamu Noguchi and Alexander Calder liked her dances very much because she could include their sculptures into what she was doing. It was very interesting.

Martha may have inspired and stimulated others, but certainly not me. I didn't really feel that involved with her themes anymore. I didn't have an American heritage, which is what Martha was developing. I had a very special Russian-Jewish heritage. No matter where I go today, nobody thinks I'm American . . . I have to explain that in America, you see all kinds of faces and people. My family came over from Russia. I was a displaced American Jew and I had my childhood in the ghetto. My mother thought I would be a *kurua*—Russian for a whore. She said, "Are you going to be a kurua?" I said, "No, Mama. I am going to be a dancer."

There were certain elements in Martha Graham's technique that I didn't feel any closeness to. I found a language of movement for myself. Martha never incorporated any of my solo material into her dances. Never. What I did was not close to Martha. Maybe Merce [Cunningham] did create his solo in *Appalachian Spring*—it is close to what Martha was doing. . . . When you see Merce's work, there is a connection between his style of movement with Graham's, except that Merce became very creative and found his own expression, which he uses. I continued to study with Martha Graham, but I left the group. One day I opened the door and closed it. And that was that. I was one of the first ones. I wanted to find a language of movement of my own. I think I was revolutionary to come out of Martha Graham because I was one of the first ones to become a choreographer There are those who say, "Yes, this is fine, but not for me." . . . I think that is what Erick Hawkins said; he had a lot of courage to rebel. I have a great respect for him.

In those days none of us had any money. I don't even remember getting paid when we performed with Graham —nothing. I had to earn a living, and a friend of mine suggested I go out to Great Neck, Long Island, to teach children's classes, so I earned a living that way. I didn't have any money but I formed my own dance company, Dance Unit. Working-class organizations sponsored culture then. They would organize a tour with a painter, a musician, an actor and dancers. We were sent to many, many cities. That is how we existed. There are other ways of working in dance—you don't have to perform. I taught a lot, and I still do. I earn a living so I can pay my rent [and] be independent.

The first thing I did when I left Martha and went to Broadway was *Street Scene*, by Kurt Weill. Then came Tennessee Williams' *Camino Real*, directed by Elia Kazan. He always loved my work—he saw my solo concerts and things. When he started the Actors Studio, he asked me to teach the actors movement. It was a wonderful revelation for me, developing a new way of expressing. Then, when they started the drama division of Juilliard, John Houseman asked me to give movement classes there, which I still do. To me, movement can speak as much as text. It is important to feel movement—the rhythm, the music and how it relates to drama.

I always knew what was right for me: to be independent. When I left Graham, I felt I had to find my own way. Doing choreography was not something for my ego—it was creating, being creative. I never cared about performing myself. The work, yes, but not performing. I had a company with Paul Taylor, Paul Sanasardo, Donnie McKayle—who all came out of Martha Graham—and Alvin Ailey—who came out of Lester Horton. I never said, "Do it my way." Perhaps that encouraged them to be individuals. Martha Graham encouraged the individual quest in those [who] she felt were going to be important. But she didn't think I was. The greatest compliment to Graham should be that she produced these artists like Merce, Erick and Paul. Actually, Paul Taylor danced with me in the beginning.

I saw Martha Graham two or three years ago when they had a special occasion at her studio. They called and asked me if I would come, and if I would say a few words. I did. Then this man asked, "Would you like to come back and see Miss Graham?" I said, "Of course," so I went back. And she looked at me, and she nodded her head with her eyes closed, and that was that. She didn't speak to me. I hadn't seen her in years. *Years.*

My obligation is to present the world of art to the new people in dance absolutely so there is a continuation. The more students understand structure and form, the freer it looks. Conformity, I was never part of that. In the beginning I was against everything, but not anymore. In the arts you can say, "I don't want that anymore," and deny it. I didn't deny it, but at times I felt uncomfortable being there at Graham—that is what made me feel I had to leave and find my own way. . . . Now, at my age, and with everything I've done, I [have] begun to realize what a great artist Martha Graham was. . . . There is room for everybody.

MAY O'DONNELL

Arnold Eagle.

May O'Donnell (right) with Martha Graham in Hérodiade, 1944.

May O'Donnell was born in Sacramento, California, in 1909. She studied dance in San Francisco with Estelle Reed, with whose concert group she made her debut, and with Martha Graham in New York City.

From 1932 to 1938, May O'Donnell was a soloist with the Martha Graham Company; she was a guest artist with that company from 1944 to 1952. Graham choreographed several roles for O'Donnell: the "Pioneer Woman" (Appalachian Spring), "She of the Earth" (Dark Meadow), "The Attendant" (Hérodiade), and "Chorus" (Cave of the Heart). *In addition, O'Donnell danced the principal roles in* Letter to the World, Deaths and Entrances, Punch and the Judy, Every Soul Is a Circus *and* Primitive Mysteries.

Since 1944 she has directed, taught, choreographed and been the soloist of the May O'Donnell Dance Company, appearing in New York and on tour in the United States. She married composer Ray Green, who wrote the score for Graham's American Document, *in 1938.*

May O'Donnell and Ray Green live in New York City.

Ray Green: I started a biography of May O'Donnell...I said that one of the favorite games she would play when she was a kid was "Statues." The kids would all run around in a circle and she would stand there and yell "Stop!" and they would all have to stop.

May O'Donnell: They would all have to hold that position...the one that I thought looked the prettiest would get a pat on the head....

Ray Green: Thus was born the choreographic career of May O'Donnell....

May O'Donnell: I had come to New York City in 1932. I had left Sacramento to go to Los Angeles for the summer. My brother and I were able to get a place together cheap. I had been struggling to find some modern dance because I knew I wasn't built for ballet. I didn't know who to work with. Estelle Reed was the first modern dancer I worked with. Estelle actually had gone to Germany and studied with Mary Wigman. I had seen Mary Wigman in Germany and I liked her solo dancing very much. She was very strong, very earthy. It seemed so true.

Somehow Michio Ito[1] showed up in Los Angeles, so I took some lessons with him. He was a wonderful little man who looked like a cat. Someone said, "You should study with Martha Graham in New York City." I did manage to get there, even though it was the Depression, and I [went] to Martha Graham's studio on Ninth Street. I actually had more training than I realized. I expected everyone to have tremendous technique since they lived in New York City. Martha immediately said, "If you study with one of my teachers, I can use you." I can see now that she wanted me to do extra study, to catch up.

Martha sent me over to Gertrude Schurr. Gertrude was basically a marvelous, wonderful teacher. She saw the potential in a person; I was her meat. Gertrude was a real New Yorker. She knew the ropes. The relationship among the women in Martha Graham's group was intense and Gertrude protected me. She had known Martha Graham when Martha was in Denishawn and [Gertrude] was also dancing with Martha. She never was intimidated by Martha. Gertrude could say things to Martha no one else could—you know, not just being cute, by any means. And Martha very often depended upon Gertrude, although quite often Martha would get annoyed with Gertrude, too. Gertrude didn't mind that either. Gertrude remained Martha Graham's best disciple even [after] she [had] left. And fortunately I was able to make a life-long friend in Gertrude.

I came in the spring to Gertrude and I performed with Martha in the fall. Martha got the Guggenheim Fellowship that first summer [1932] and she gave Gertrude the studio to teach. We worked like dogs. It was during that time [that] I was able to get into Martha's technique. I had the strength and the range of movement . . . especially in that small studio on Ninth Street—you

---

[1] Michio Ito (1892-1961). A talented Swiss-trained Japanese interpretive dancer, Ito was a Dalcrozian disciple who taught phrases in unison, in canon and with changes of rhythm. He talked about symbolism, imagery and the use of minimal thematic materials, and was looking for modern expression. According to Elizabeth Kendall, Martha Graham was featured as a dancing maiden in Ito's 1923 ballet ballad for the *Greenwich Village Follies*, "The Garden of Kama." (Kendall, *Where She Danced*, New York: Knopf, 1979. p. 179).

didn't have a chance to do leaps. You didn't have a chance to do extensions without hitting the wall. It was very concentrated work. Getting the shape of Martha's intense movement, going down to the floor slowly and coming up expanding the movement could pretty much be done in one spot.

Well, Martha had been choreographing *Primitive Mysteries*, pieces like that. They had a kind of solid body, those dancers, but I think she was interested in moving on. I think without realizing it that she needed other kinds of shapes. She began to be a little more lyrical, although at the same time, her themes were still very percussive and dynamic. Those dances were of the social time— all of the protest, the anger—those kinds of qualities. And Martha would choose subjects relating to that time of the Depression. The idea of men coming in [came from] the work. She had to have men. [At first] Martha just had all girls . . .

Ray Green: . . . that they called "Graham Crackers."

May O'Donnell: Martha's work needed variety and . . . she was being held back on thematics, some ideas. I think almost immediately she did *Letter to the World,* and she used quite a few men in that dance. Martha Graham's technique, the shaping of it, was being explored in the Thirties when I first joined Martha's group. When I came back in the Forties to be a guest with Martha I never worked with her technique again. Martha worked with me privately because the roles were very particular and not with the group. The thing is Martha was very conscious of the people that could give—somehow or other— the possibility of creating an atmosphere with the movement she gave us. Very often Martha would experiment with movement, try something, and if somebody gave it life—that is actually what it would amount to—if you did it and you did it as if it meant something, why then she would use it. Even in *American Document,* in the old programs, I think Anna [Sokolow] and I were singled out. It would say "May O'Donnell and Group" or "May O'Donnell and Anna Sokolow and Group." Sometimes Sophie Maslow, also. Mostly these people.

Ray Green: On that note, one should pay Martha Graham a great respect. I had a similar little experience when I did the score for her on *American Document* [in 1938]. After we had a couple of sessions, Martha and Erick called me to take counts [of the movement for the music]. Martha then said to me, "Look, Ray, you are on the right track. So why don't you just bring in the music and then we'll do the dance to that?" Martha knew I was a professional musician and a very experienced composer. Martha had faith.

May O'Donnell: Martha put me in *Primitive Mysteries.* That was the first dance I [was] in. . . . Martha had new people coming in like Dorothy Bird and Bonnie Bird. Then I came . . . Sophie was already in when I came and stayed. Sophie was very fine. Anna was in some of the things. I don't remember Anna in class so much. Before we knew it, we were busy rehearsing.

I loved to rehearse. I enjoyed that the most. If there was a rehearsal, I was there on time. It was in those rehearsals one could see how Martha developed a piece, not only in structure, but how she would re-work a dance to project her idea more fully. Sometimes she would throw out big sections. For some of the kids who didn't like to rehearse so much it was very much like being killed. I loved changing. If you loved to dance and loved the whole process of choreographing, well, that was part of it. Some of those gosh damn kids—excuse me—would come in between class and rehearsal with their stomachs hanging out as if they just had a big meal. I [would say] to Gertrude, "How are they going to jump?"

During the years from 1932 to 1938, when I was first with Martha Graham, Louis Horst taught dance composition. I found out how much I enjoyed choreography, and how excited I was by it. I worked very hard at it. In fact, I was Louis Horst's assistant in dance composition. That was 1934. During that time I was so enthusiastic I was able to stimulate the other people to work a little harder. I got very involved.

Louis had a way of working: He gave us something to work on, some kind of a premise, instead of saying [use] anything that comes to your mind. Louis felt that we should have in our background some of the historical, ancient, old court dances with their different rhythms and qualities. For instance, if you had a sarabande you had to work in a very stately way. There were different things . . . the allemande, the courant, the pavane. . . . After going through [them], Louis would ask us to do a dance of "now" in the same rhythm. The next section of Louis' composition classes were called the Modern Forms. Satie was at the beginning of the course. I went up to the museum. In those days, the dancers would go to the museum whenever there was a new art show in town. It was a whole exciting time of supposedly breaking through in all the areas of art. I remember going up to the museum[2] and seeing some of the early Greek

---

[2] The Metropolitan Museum of Art in New York City.

statues. There was one of this beautiful young athlete . . . I sort of based the dance on that. It was a quiet piece.

Before I left, from 1932 to 1937, Martha Graham [had] choreographed 11 roles for me in her dances, but I was going to leave anyway. I was getting restless. I wanted to choreograph and get my own group started. There [had been] a girl, Lillian Shapero, who began to choreograph things, but it was outside the studio . . . Martha really didn't like that at all, [and she] wasn't really very nice to Lillian. Martha did one of those things in front of everybody where she denounced Lillian so that she would never want to come back. Most of the kids in the group were very upset the way Martha got rid of Lillian. Later when we were doing things it was in relation to Louis Horst—Louis would do performances several times in the studio itself—and [they were] controlled by Martha's studio. Martha then felt it was in her domain. That is another reason why I was afraid of Martha. I thought I would never give her that chance.

Ray Green: Martha had this habit . . . sometimes she would haul off and hit somebody if they didn't believe what she was telling them, and then tell them to get out. Martha never did this with me.

May O'Donnell: I never gave Martha a chance to do it to me. It wasn't that I was standing around thinking, "I am not giving Martha a chance." It was just I worked so well. The first time I left, I had already been with Martha Graham for six years. I felt it was time. I think, too, things were beginning to change generally. Going up to Bennington each summer you could see different elements coming into the dance. It was time to leave.

Ray Green: May and Gertrude were out in San Francisco [during the] summer [of 1937]...doing a master workshop at Betty Horst's[3] private studio. I had [had] a two-year fellowship [for composition] in Paris from Berkeley University[4] from 1935 to 1937. I came back from Paris at the end of June 1937. That is when I met May. I realized I finally found the person I wanted to be with . . . we are still together. She wanted to do her first major work. It was a solo and it was called, very properly, *Of Pioneer Woman.* I wrote the score. May [took] the score . . . back to New York City and when Louis Horst played the music

---

[3] Betty Horst, née Bessie Cunningham (1891-1967). Betty and Louis Horst (1884-1964) were married on November 29, 1909. Although they lived separate lives, the couple never divorced.

[4] University of California at Berkeley.

he loved [it]. Martha Graham was looking for a young composer for her dance *American Document.*

Ray Green: Louis told Martha about this young guy, Ray Green, a friend of May O'Donnell: "He is a young composer, why don't you use him this time?" And she did. I composed *American Document* in 1938.

We went to Bennington because I had obligated myself to do the score . . . May and I had already decided we would get married. I did one section—the emancipation section—of the music for *American Document.* . . . They rehearsed it and. . . it was completely the root dance. We went up to Bennington and completed the work. I wangled a piano in my room . . . I could work right there. I got a whole room for myself. At the close of that [summer], May and I decided she would leave Martha Graham . . . [and] return to California where she would have a chance to work on her own technique and works.

I'll tell you a little bit of gossip . . .

May O'Donnell: Be careful, Ray. What you are going to gossip about?

Ray Green: When we went up to Bennington—May told me this when it happened, and of course we both had a good laugh—the first one who approached May was Erick. Erick and May went for a little walk after the evening meal and he asked her if she would be his girlfriend. Here Erick was, all mixed up with Graham. God, it was sex, sex, sex all night long with Erick and Martha. Old Bill Bales told me all about that. . . . Then, by God, a little bit later, one evening Louis Horst got May on a little walk and they sat down by the tennis court and he reached over and put his hand on May's knee. May reached over and gently took his hand off her knee.

May O'Donnell: Now that is just gossip . . .

Ray Green: Well sure, but the reason I am saying this is not even to be funny. But it is funny, because naturally these guys were mixed up in a great big tempest with Martha. Everything at Bennington was like a giant storm all summer long because of the competition among Graham, Doris Humphrey, Charlie Weidman[5] [and] Hanya Holm.

---

[5] Charles Weidman (1900-1975). Born in Lincoln, Nebraska, Weidman was accepted as a student at Denishawn by Ted Shawn. A few months after his arrival, he went on tour in Shawn's production of *Xochitl* with Martha Graham. Weidman remained with Denishawn until 1927. He and Doris Humphrey left to give a concert of their own works and establish their own company. Their company and studio was dissolved in 1945. He contributed to the formation of the Humphrey-Weidman technique which is based on the concept of dance as the result of restoring balance after an imbalance created by any form of movement. Weidman toured extensively in the Forties and early Fifties, and then taught on the West Coast and in New York.

May O'Donnell: The people who were running the program had to be careful. I remember, first of all, they didn't have enough places for people to rehearse because they were having everybody there. This was the "Big Round-Up." It was almost too big and too much for poor Mary Jo [Shelley] and Martha Hill to handle. If you had the best place one day, you wouldn't be able to have the best place the following day. One day we were all called together to be told there had been this disgraceful thing going on. Some of the people of one group were peeking in on the rehearsals of another group. I thought to myself, "What in the hell is going on here?" It was like a big family fight. It was after that, the following summer in 1939, that Mills College in California began as an extension of Bennington College.

Of course when I first was with Martha, there was lots of tension, with Erick and Merce screaming and yelling. The few times I would go to the studios, rehearsals would be late. That was another reason I was dropping out—I couldn't waste my time on that. As far as Sophie and Jane [Dudley] leaving, well, they had already formed their trio, the Dudley, Maslow, Bales Trio, and had to get it going. In fact, that is one of the reasons I came back to Martha as a guest artist: She needed me to dance their roles, which Martha had choreographed especially for them. Then there were the younger dancers coming in, like Pearl Lang, Ethel Winter and Yuriko.

I always stayed very friendly with Erick. Martha sent Erick over to ask me to return as guest artist. That was very cute. I loved that. At first I was very apprehensive. I said, "You know, Erick, I've been working on my own. I can't stop that flow." Finally he prevailed upon me, and he said, "Why don't you try?" I said, "Well, maybe if it is just rehearsals." So then Martha asked me to come over and she talked to me too. Martha knew I was a responsible person. She needed somebody of my caliber, and somebody that was a little more mature than some of the younger girls going around. I said okay. I went up that summer (1944) to Bennington and that is when Martha started *Appalachian Spring* and *Hérodiade*. In *Appalachian Spring* and *Hérodiade* I was kind of on my own with the movement. First . . . I worked with Martha on parts that had to be covered, like the parts that mainly Jane Dudley had done, like "The Ancestress" in *Letter to the World.* I even had to wear her costumes. One of them was terrible, the one from *Deaths and Entrances. Punch and the Judy,* I didn't like that, either. I didn't like *Every Soul Is a Circus* because that was just sitting. I was a spectator. I had a hat. I got in a little booth, and mostly I just changed my hat while I watched the dance.

Appalachian Spring was a little more dancing for me than the other roles. . . . In *Appalachian Spring* we would all walk in single file. I would walk up on the Noguchi veranda and then I would quietly sit. I was the "Pioneer Woman." No matter what went on in the dance, with all the hustle and bustle, beyond was the Pioneer Woman's seeing eye: the future, everything. Once in a while Martha would get bored: There was one place [in the piece, after] she had done the love duet with Erick, [when] she would come up, and I think I was standing folding my hands—suddenly, after the love duet, Martha gave me something. Martha was just improvising. I said afterwards, "Martha, you weren't married long enough to have had a legitimate child."

Martha was never embarrassed, but she thought maybe I would protest because after *Appalachian Spring* and sitting . . . Martha was telling me her general feeling about *Hérodiade,* [that] I'd be in white and this and that and the other. Of course, I ended up in that same wool black/dark brown dress. I knew I would end up wearing it [even] when Martha was telling me I would be in white. Martha would say, "Now, May, this is your music . . . maybe you would like to listen to the music and, you know, just feel it out." Martha would suggest something here and there. It was that kind of improvised process, but it was interesting. Actually, I enjoyed that part of it because I could use my own imagination. I knew if Martha was *here,* I would have to be over *there.* I realized with Martha [for me] it would always be the same part under a different name, so I wasn't surprised. Even then, I can see now, I was really a foil to Martha and also a contrast. When they say pillar of society . . . that's how Martha cast me.

Ray Green: May would take the pose of a statue. . . .

May O'Donnell: I remember Louis Horst saying to me once when he saw *Hérodiade,* "May, you sustain so beautifully."

I don't know if it was 1948 or 1949, [but] I decided not to go on one of those trans[-Atlantic] tours with Martha. I didn't want to go because by that time I really was involved with my own group. Martha . . . called me up and asked me to come over. I said, "Martha, I need my time. You have yours, and you don't have to worry about it, but I have to have my time." She was very quiet. She didn't say anything one way or the other. She was smart to be quiet because I don't think I would have ever got into a fight with Martha. I just would have felt she didn't understand and left.

Who did she send over but Erick, with some Sara Lee cake. Erick made it seem so important in their lives. Martha couldn't . . . sell herself as well as Erick. I knew from the beginning there would be a disaster [on tour], but I wasn't sorry [to go] in the long run. Finally I said, "I'm petrified to fly." They all flew over and gave me . . . passage on a ship. Well, I got to Paris a few days late and they were having press conferences.

There [had been] a last rehearsal before we left. I never rehearsed that much with the group because I knew my part and could come in almost at the last minute and do it. Martha had a lot of people watching that last rehearsal. The minute the elevator door opened at 66 Fifth Avenue I knew there were problems. You could just feel the waves. Martha was in a terrible mood and Erick could be exasperating. I am not kidding. Martha was rehearsing *Letter to the World*. There [were] a few props in that dance. One prop [was] a little bench Martha sat on. Suddenly she started to get up and she dropped to the floor, destroying her knee. All the rehearsals stopped. Nevertheless, the concert [tour] was going to go on and it did. We got to Paris and there was the one concert. Of course, it started late. Erick didn't get a good review and he was feeling underappreciated. In fact, I think one of the reasons for going abroad was that Martha felt Erick would be much more appreciated in Europe than he was in the States. Martha was married to Erick by then and evidently really adored him, from what I can gather.

Ray Green: Erick wanted to leave Martha by that point. He actually did—he walked out on Martha in London.

May O'Donnell: Martha choreographed this special piece for Erick, *The Eye of Anguish*, based on *King Lear*. It evidently was cumbersome. It didn't seem to work—it is a hard thing to put into dance. Martha wasn't in *Eye of Anguish* herself. She had a nice part for Pearl Lang as "Cordelia," though. We were supposed to have a two-week run in Paris. We would go every day to the theater and there would be the announcement: canceled for tonight. Then we were supposed to have a week in London. We got to London, got into the theater and started rehearsing the dances. Meantime, Erick had been worked up to a point [where] he just blew his top. He wouldn't go [on] with the company. He separated himself from Martha. Erick just didn't show up. Martha was more and more devastated. Her whole world was crumbling. The last morning, in the canteen of the theater, with all that dismal smoke one finds in London, Martha said [that all of] the performances were canceled. I walked over to her and said, "Martha, we understand." It made it quiet. I thought that was the least I could do, being a little older than those [other] dancers.

Ray Green: Martha always had a very deep respect for May. May was devoted to the dance.

May O'Donnell: I think if I had worked with another person besides Martha Graham—who was a very fine teacher—I might have come to the same end. I am sure I would have kept dancing. Being here in New York City, I got a perspective of what was happening in the dance—in the field, what the directions were.

I became more involved with myself in that sense . . . I had been through this period of social unrest here with the Communist deal—and it was a time when my first program was called *So Proudly We Hail.* That was always very difficult for me because I had no idea about politics. I didn't know what a Communist, a Republican or a Democrat was. Suddenly, I thought, they [were] saying terrible things about the country. Well, I like[d] where I [came] from and it made me think in those terms. Ray felt the same way also. Going back and forth across the country you would see the markers on the trails where these pioneers would have encounters with death or with jubilation, where something wonderful [had] happened, like getting over the mountains. There was a whole history, a whole life there, and in a way Martha had documented it in dance.

I was very shy in a certain sense, except when I moved . . . I had control. I was able to lend myself to [dance] movement without having to worry if someone would think this, that or the other. I kept my mouth shut—I didn't try to attract any attention. Except my main thing was completely the dance. Strangely enough, I began to attract attention in movement. That is what it was all about.

I had a very nice relationship with Martha. . . . It was very professional. I never worshiped Martha Graham and I was always very distant. It was much better that way. Never once did Martha question my distant nature. Most people were bolder and would talk to Martha in a different way. They would try to be chatty with Martha. There was Bonnie Bird and Dorothy Bird . . . [who] became like Martha's little slaves. Martha could impose on them, and they would be so happy if Martha would give them the littlest job to do, like run to the corner and do this, that or the other thing. I wanted to save my energy strictly for the dance.

I always saw myself as a disciple of the dance. Martha was opening this world of dance, but she was part of it. I loved the way Martha worked. She was completely dedicated to what she was doing and that is what I would be like. One had the feeling this was her life. Dance was everything for Martha Graham.

SOPHIE MASLOW

Arnold Eagle.

Sophie Maslow (right) with Martha Graham *(foreground) and Jane Dudley in* Deaths and Entrances, *1943.*

Sophie Maslow was born in New York City to Russian-American parents, on March 22, 1911. She studied dance with Blanche Talmud at the Neighborhood Playhouse (now the School for Arts Related to the Theater) and she appeared in the children's Christmas production. As a full-time student at the school, where she took a three-year course in theater, Maslow appeared in Irene Lewisohn's productions. She joined Martha Graham's concert group in 1932, eventually becoming a soloist, and remained until 1944. The last dance Graham choreographed her into was Deaths and Entrances (1943). Maslow worked on the reconstructions of Celebration, Primitive Mysteries and the last section of Chronicle, "Call to Action," for the Martha Graham Centennial program.

Although she had choreographed two duets in high school, Maslow choreographed her first professional solo, which was presented at a New Theater magazine concert, in 1934. She first appeared with Jane Dudley and William Bales as the Dudley, Maslow, Bales Trio at a 1942 concert presented by Dance Observer, a magazine edited by Louis Horst. The Trio performed together for the next 12 years. They also performed as members of the New Dance Group Company. Maslow was the artistic director and choreographer of the Sophie Maslow Dance Company, and she has choreographed works for other companies in the U.S., Canada, England, Holland and Israel.

Sophie Maslow has choreographed for the New York City Opera, for plays on and off Broadway, for television and for summer theater. She was president of the Board of Directors and on the teaching staff of the New Dance Group Studio and she guest-teaches at the Martha Graham School. Maslow is the recipient of an honorary degree from Skidmore College and of grants from the National Endowment for the Arts, the New York State Council of the Arts, the New York City Cultural Foundation and the Martha Graham Foundation.

Sophie Maslow lives in New York City.

I always felt that modern dance was a true expression of life. There was no question about it. First of all, I was brought up in a home that was very encouraging. My mother was all for Isadora, although she did take me to see Pavlova. I loved it, but not like [I did] Isadora. I really didn't want to go to college; I wanted to go to the Neighborhood Playhouse, so I did. We learned Greek and Egyptian mythology by going to the Metropolitan Museum of Art, which was a great entrance into the arts. After being introduced to the museum, going to the galleries became a part of my life.

Martha Graham wasn't a household name at the time. Martha had been working with three people from Rochester—Betty MacDonald was one of them—where she had been teaching. I was still in high school when my future husband took me to see one of Martha's performances. It was Martha Graham and Trio. (He also took me to see Helen Tamiris[1] and the Denishawn Company.) I was immediately impressed. Martha came to teach at the Neighborhood Playhouse when I began to study in the first full-time school there. I think there were nine of us. Jean Rosenthal (the lighting designer) and Anna Sokolow were also in that class.

When I started working with Martha at the Neighborhood Playhouse . . . I felt everything was right. Technically, there was no question about it. I thought it was terrific. I made that choice right away, that I wanted to be with Martha. This was for me. That is the way I felt then and the truth of the matter is that is the way I feel still about her technique and approach to dance.

Also, Louis Horst was a remarkable teacher. I know there were many things that he disapproved of philosophically, but he was always sensitive enough to understand what a person was trying to do in dance, to be able to look at it with a cool eye and say, "It isn't my taste. I like something a little more neurotic. But you are doing something very good."

I came into the group when Martha Hill left. I replaced her in *Primitive Mysteries*, which had been done for the first time in 1931. Even though I wasn't

---

[1] Helen Tamiris, née Becker (1905-1966). Tamiris (an adopted stage name) studied with Fokine and danced with the Metropolitan Opera Ballet for 3 years. Tamiris joined the *Greenwich Village Follies* in 1925, a year after Martha Graham had joined. Tamiris gave her first solo concert in 1927. A maverick in the modern-dance field, she was, nonetheless, never embraced by the three great modern dancers, Graham, Humphrey and Holm. She was the first choreographer to use spirituals for a concert dance production. Tamiris achieved renown for her work as a choreographer for Broadway musicals, including *Up In Central Park; Annie, Get Your Gun; Show Boat;* and *Touch and Go,* for which she won a Tony Award.

Barbara Morgan.

Sophie Maslow (far left, standing) with Martha Graham and Group in
Primitive Mysteries, *1936.*

there when she choreographed it, I think in the early days Martha told the dancers exactly what to do. Something like *Primitive Mysteries* is so structured and defined. It was so unusual in its kind of movement. *Primitive Mysteries* has one character—Martha as "Mary"—and the rest is a group. But when Martha was choreographing *Deaths and Entrances* (1943) it was different—there were characters in that dance. Martha Graham also choreographed a trio, *Four Casual Developments* (1934), to Henry Cowell, for me, Anna Sokolow and Dorothy Bird, which we did for only one season. Martha made white organdy dresses on us which were held together by safety pins.

I did work a lot, when I think back on it now. I was in something like 18 dances of Martha's from 1934 to 1941. The group danced *Ceremonials* with Martha in 1932. It was never revived, and I didn't understand the dance. We did *Chorus of Youth* (1932), which was a group dance without Martha, to music by Louis Horst. It had quick moving runs and triplets, and I did slow extensions with Dorothy Bird. *Celebration* (1934), to music by Louis Horst, required a lot of stamina and had a lot of continuous jumps. The revival was successful. *Integrales* (1934) had a difficult, percussive score by Edgard Varèse. At that time it was very avant-garde for a composer to create an orchestral piece for percussion. We watched the conductor for cues for the changes of movement in Martha's choreography. *Course* (1935) was for Martha Graham and Group; in *Perspectives* (1935) Martha did a solo, "Frontier," and the group did "Marching Song." Martha Graham and Group did *Chronicle* in 1936. It had many sections and was an hour and a quarter long. I worked on the reconstruction. The problem was that there is no film of it. When we revived "Call to Action" I had to reconstruct it from what I remembered of the technique of the class which Martha had dropped years ago. Terese Capucilli was the soloist—her contribution was remarkable. *Every Soul Is a Circus* (1939) was fun, and *Letter to the World* (1940) was a lovely dance. I danced, at different times, two parts in *Letter*. . . . I was the "Young Girl" and the "Fairy Queen."

I was choreographing my own dances all the time I was in Martha's company as well as dancing. I never thought about it—I just did it. At that point in modern dance if I wanted to dance any place aside from Martha's company I just had to choreograph a dance. I couldn't take something out of Martha Graham's dances and do it—we were just doing technique classes. It wasn't like ballet where you learned variations from the classical ballets like *The Nutcracker* or *Swan Lake*. So I had to do my own choreography. I was dancing in places by myself, working with Martha Graham, and I was teaching, too. Of course, we didn't have very long seasons with Martha. Sometimes we would work all year and perform just a couple of times. I was on the first tour Martha Graham gave with her group. It was a very leisurely tour all over the country. We traveled by train, and each of us had a trunk. We went south to New Orleans, across Texas, up the west coast of California to Canada . . . then down to Utah and over to Chicago and Philadelphia.

I worked with Martha until 1944. The last dance I was in was *Deaths and Entrances* in 1943. All the time I was working with Martha—and this goes for Jane [Dudley], too—I was doing my own work, as well as going on tour with Martha Graham. The three of us, Jane, Bill [Bales] and I, would go on tour. I would return and then join up with Martha and her company. [We'd do it] simultaneously, accommodating our schedule so it didn't interfere with Martha. It made me feel I was doing the right thing, that I was in the right profession. There is nothing like being successful at something. It makes you want to continue, go on. I didn't stop with Martha because I wanted to do my own work— I was doing my own work. I stopped in 1944 because I was going to have a baby. Even then, when I was pregnant, I went up to Bennington to teach . . . my part in *Deaths and Entrances* to May O'Donnell for Martha.

I don't remember Martha trying to get anyone away from any [sensibility], or get them interested in her thing rather than what they were interested in. Martha Graham supported me in terms of giving me a chance to perform in her studio. She presented members of her own company in their own choreography. To have an evening of the works of members of Martha Graham's company, that was support. I don't think that Martha thought just because people did their own work that they were going to leave, necessarily. The thing was we all studied with Louis Horst, so we were all doing our own work in classes with him. We would show certain works for him to use in lecture-demonstrations, which were like concerts. Of course, when we did Louis' things it was support from him, too. . . . Martha really cared about those evenings. Martha wouldn't allow anything to go on in her studio that she disapproved of, no matter what. If you choreographed a piece that Martha didn't think was good, you couldn't do it in her studio, period. She saw everything that was going to be done.

Martha wasn't always easy to work with, but anything that makes you feel what you are doing is worthwhile is good. However, it was possible to be snowed under and destroyed, too, by Martha. You had to take things with a grain of salt. Sometimes I'd feel that maybe she was right, maybe that was the direction I should go in, even though the things Martha said could be irritating.

Once Martha was annoyed with me in class. It was always hard for me to dance sharp, aggressive, neurotic movement. I was always interested in American folklore and I did many things using folk material. It's so human. It wasn't right to use straight folk material. . . . I did have qualms about it, but I felt it was the right thing to do, to use the words and music exactly as they were. Martha said, "You are so *agricultural."*

I had this very definite feeling that everybody should see dancing—not just an elite group of people should come to the performances. I also felt dance should be seen in all sorts of places: We went into union halls; during the war, we went to Fort Dix; we danced for sailors in hospitals. There was a nucleus of dancers who were very left-wing and interested in what was happening in the society of the time. They felt art was for all people. If art was for the people, well, they better understand what they were doing, otherwise it wouldn't be for the people. It certainly molded my way of thinking and looking at the world. I was very interested in being as clear as possible in what I was saying in a dance, not allowing it to be mystifying. I still feel that way.

One never thinks of oneself as being part of the American century. We just are. Whatever works were being done of Martha's, there were certain ones that I felt were great while they were being done. Certain others fell by the wayside. Some dances were done once or twice, that's it. *Panorama* (1935) was never done any other place but Bennington. *Horizons* (1936), to music by Louis Horst, was done by Martha Graham and Group, but it didn't last. *Land Be Bright* (1942), to music by Arthur Kreutz, was never performed in New York. To me, the four most important dances are: *Primitive Mysteries*—I reconstructed it 20 to 30 years later for Yuriko (in Martha's role)—which was a shock to people because of the severity of the percussive movement and the angular positions; *American Document* (1938); *Letter to the World;* and *Deaths and Entrances.*

American Document was a marvelous dance. It is dramatic and based on documents out of American history like the Declaration of Independence—"We hold these truths to be self-evident: That all men are created equal . . . "; the Preamble to the Constitution; and [Franklin] Roosevelt's speech to the American public about the ill-housed and ill-fed. The [revival in 1990] was scrambled and didn't resemble the original.[2] When I walked across the stage, only a walk, I felt very heroic and proud.

The first time Erick danced was in *American Document* (1938). There were only women in the company until Erick Hawkins came. I don't think it was so much a matter of choice on Martha's part as a necessity. It would have been much more difficult to deal with love if there [had been] just women in *American Document*. She had different characters in the dances once men were in the company.

I don't know if Martha developed anything, really, for the male dancer in terms of technique. They did the same things we did. The floorwork was developed by the time the men came into the company. Men usually have a hard time with it; it is not the same for the male and female pelvis when you are on the floor. It depends on how people are built: There are some men who are more flexible and very loose who can do things on the floor without much difficulty. In general, though, it is hard for men to get in those floorwork positions. It is hard for a lot of women, too. When I taught I did less floorwork because I thought a lot of the things Martha did on the floor, like contraction and release, could be done standing up at the barre. It didn't have to be done necessarily on the floor.

I don't think of myself as a disciple of Martha Graham. Technically, certainly, I was a disciple without reservation. Choreographically . . . I don't work like Martha. There are many things Martha did—the way she worked and the way she put a dance together—that I don't do. I've always come to choreographing a dance with movements and different things I wanted to try. I don't say to the dancers, "Take this music and go and develop it," like Martha did later. I've never done that, but I always left them sort of loose. I would look at the dancers as they were learning [the movements], and often I would receive ideas from them when they were doing something, [different from] what I gave them—doing it wrong, as it were—that I thought was better than something I had given them. I like to let things come out of individuals because I think the dancers can contribute something to the choreography. Once I started to do that, I realized whatever a dance needs, whenever you choreograph it, is valid in terms of movement. It could come from Graham or folk dancing or ballet.

---

[2] The revival of *American Document* in 1990 starred Mikhail Baryshnikov. Ray Green's original score was not used.

You use whatever material is necessary to make clear whatever idea you are putting through the dance. I assume I always used Martha Graham's emotional qualities. I assume I use Martha's technique because that is the way I was trained. It was natural to me to move that way, so it just went into my dancing and my choreography, even though I don't think I was like Martha. If you saw a dance of mine, you wouldn't recognize the fact that it was based on Martha Graham's technique, yet it is always there.

Martha Graham had discovered something in the way the body is used—her way of making the body an expressive instrument—that nobody else had ever discovered. I was trained by Martha Graham in her way. Even though as I went along afterwards, I felt there were a lot of things that were left out—like speed, intricacies of leg work. Nevertheless, I still felt that Martha Graham's way of training the body was the best.

Martha had a vocabulary, and the vocabulary is what we were learning. It was through Martha that I understood the quality of a gesture. Whatever you did had an emotional quality, and your body was being trained so that it carried that emotional quality in her choreography. With Martha Graham, everything was dance.

JANE DUDLEY

Barbara M

Jane Dudley with Martha Graham in Letter to the World, *1940.*

Jane Dudley was born in New York City on April 3, 1912. As a child, she studied dance with Ruth Doring, who had danced with Ruth St. Denis. She went on to study with Hanya Holm, then director of the Mary Wigman School of New York, and became a member of Holm's senior demonstration group. By 1934 John Martin of The New York Times *had recognized Dudley as a young choreographic talent for her dance,* The Dream Ends.

In the summer of 1935 Dudley went to Bennington College to study with Martha Graham and Louis Horst. As a student, she danced in Graham's work, Panorama. *She joined Graham's group of female dancers in 1936, becoming a soloist in 1937. From 1938 to 1946, Dudley was Graham's teaching assistant at the Neighborhood Playhouse.*

Jane Dudley created roles in eight of Graham's dances, most notably in American Document *(1938),* Letter to the World *(1940),* Punch and the Judy *(1941) and* Deaths and Entrances *(1943).*

At the suggestion of Louis Horst, Dudley, Sophie Maslow and William Bales, a former member of the Humphrey-Weidman Company, gave a joint concert benefiting Dance Observer *magazine. The Dudley, Maslow, Bales Trio performed throughout the United States until 1954. From 1948 to 1952, Dudley was a charter member, along with Martha Graham, Doris Humphrey, José Limón, Sophie Maslow, and William Bales, of the New London Summer School of Dance, in Connecticut. Due to an injury, Dudley retired from performing in 1954.*

Dudley married documentary film maker Leo Hurwitz in 1935 and their son, Tom, was born in 1947. They divorced in 1965. At the invitation of Martha Graham, Dudley became the artistic director of the Graham-based Batsheva Dance Company in Israel from 1968 to 1970. In 1970, she was appointed vice principal and director of contemporary dance studies at the London School of Contemporary Dance. The headquarters for the school and the London Con-

temporary Dance Theatre was known as "The Place."

As a dancer, teacher and choreographer, Dudley has promulgated the Graham tradition for more than 60 years.

Jane Dudley lives in London.

———————————— ◆ ● ◆ ————————————

The story goes, I always wanted to go study with Martha Graham, but my mother was against it because she wanted me to work with Hanya Holm. My mother, who had danced with Hanya up at Bennington, felt that anyone who studied with Martha became very "Martha Graham." In Hanya's teaching, I thought she seemed to work on a minimal basis. I found it not to be the training that was going to make me a professional dancer. I felt Hanya's approach was limited. But I see now that I was wrong, because Hanya moved so well. At any rate, my desire beyond anything else was to work with Louis [Horst] and to be in Martha's company.

No matter what anyone says, Martha and Hanya were not rivals. . . . Martha was never in a rivalry with anybody, except maybe with Balanchine—or the Ford Foundation or the Rockefeller Foundation—because Balanchine would get the grant money and Martha wouldn't. On the other hand, I think both Hanya and Doris [Humphrey] were both in rivalries with Martha. I think Hanya, from the very beginning, felt challenged and threatened by Martha and the American dance scene. I didn't like Doris' work very much [or] Charles Weidman's. I took a summer course with them and, I remember, Charles was so scattered as a teacher. He was a mess. I didn't get any feeling of Doris' lyricism. I don't know why I didn't like Doris' work.

You must not forget that Martha Graham had enormous charisma. She didn't work at it. She had this immense quality, intelligence and flair for being highly articulate. Listen, Martha would make the most outrageous statements. I remember her saying once that there is no such thing as a straight line in movement. The movement was to go out from the dancer like a boomerang and return. When you think of Martha's movement at that time (in the Thirties), it was true. Martha was fighting against the line of ballet. Martha felt the process was important in dancing the movement, not the end result.

When I went to my first summer course at Bennington to study with Martha, I was absolutely, completely, transported. We would have a technique class with Martha and then a practice class or a rehearsal. Martha would come in [wearing] white taffeta, a bolero jacket, a wraparound skirt and tights underneath—you know, Martha's legs were not very beautiful—and her black hair [went] down her back just below her shoulders. Then we would start class on the floor. The interesting thing about Martha's work is that it is not at all the work that is done at Graham now. But one must have hips that are made like butter to be able to work on the floor the way Martha wanted us to in the early days. It is not men's movement, so it is difficult for men.

We had a dance-history class first thing in the morning with John Martin. We always fell asleep in his class because Bennington is hot and sweaty in the summer. Martin finally complained that he didn't like talking to sleeping bodies. It was a six-week course, so he got fed up. Then we had technique with Martha, a course with Louis and then rehearsals in the afternoon.

In the summer of 1935, Martha created a new dance, *Panorama*, at Bennington. She didn't have any of the movements choreographed for it. Martha used a lot of the technique we were getting in class as the movement for *Panorama*. The music, by Norman Lloyd, was written as Martha choreographed the dance. What was exciting during that time was that Martha took a liking to me. Martha had a way of walking, and how I picked it up I don't know, but it was very quiet . . . the dance was very still. You would move, then you would be in a position and hold it. You would go from one pose to another. They were not really poses because they were too distorted and strange: You would walk up without any connection at all and put your hand on top of somebody else who was upside down with [her] foot in the air. It had that impersonal and distant feeling [throughout] the whole dance. I remember feeling very pleased with myself because Martha had chosen me because I think the other dancers were already company members and I was only a student at the time. [After] dancing *Panorama* up at Bennington, Martha asked me to join her company.

Panorama itself was quite a dance.[1] Martha had a knack for using the special

---

[1] *Panorama* premiered at the Vermont State Armory in Bennington on August 14, 1935. The dance was 50 minutes in length and had 3 sections, each with a specifically American theme leading to, in Graham's

(continued . . .)

qualities of a dancer—the qualities that they came with when they came to study Martha's technique. In this situation she really had to work that way because the dance combined her company members with the 35 students in the Bennington workshop. Martha got through that experience by the skin of her teeth. I know Martha went back to New York City swearing [that] she would never create a dance for that many students again.[2]

When I was asked to join Martha's company, I had to learn Martha's dance *Celebration,* which nearly killed me. The fact is, enthusiastic as I was, and with as well-endowed a body [as] I had, I wasn't prepared for the stamina a dancer needed for *Celebration.* [But] I performed it. After the first performance, I started to cry. Anna [Sokolow] came up to me and said, "You didn't do badly, Jane. That was pretty good." Of course, I always thought Anna was wonderful. I feel very bitterly about what has happened to Anna. I don't think people in England know who she is. She is such an important American choreographer.

The next dance I was in was *Chronicle,* in 1936. However, I was in the soup at the time because the New Dance Group, where I had come from, with Hanya, was starting a professional company. I felt [that] if I didn't devote all of my love and attention to the New Dance Group, [then] I was being disloyal. So I went to Martha—and she nearly ripped me up the backside. John Martin told Martha that I was not disciplined and that she couldn't rely on me. So I was out with Martha for the rest of the year. But I had learned *Celebration* and *Primitive Mysteries,* and I had danced *Heretic,* once.

Primitive Mysteries was also very difficult for me to dance. One had to be very strong in Martha's percussive movements and [also in] holding the positions. I think *Primitive Mysteries* is one of Martha's very great works. Now at the Graham studio the training is so different, and the *Zeitgeist* is so different, that people are not willing to put themselves on the line and become committed the way we did in the early days.

---

[1](. . . continued)
own words in the program note, social consciousness in the contemporary scene. One writer described one scene of *Panorama* as Mussolini's impending attack on Ethiopia and another as a scene of Negro exploitation in the South. The set by Arch Lauterer incorporated mobiles specially created by Alexander Calder.

[2] The dance incorporated 12 members of Graham's Group and 24 students from a Bennington College workshop. The summer dance festival had been established at the college the previous year. *Panorama* was presented on October 13, 1992, 57 years after its premiere. The dance was reconstructed by Yuriko (Kikuchi) based on an 11-minute film which contained fragments of Graham's choreography.

Finally, I did get to dance [in] two sections of Martha's *Chronicle*—"Steps in the Street" and "March to the Future." [In] the other sections I sat on some boxes in a frozen position. When William Bales saw me sitting he said, "Somebody is in the doghouse." Martha got her revenge. It really wasn't until Martha choreographed *Letter to the World*, in 1940, and I was "The Ancestress," that I really emerged as a soloist with Graham.

Chronicle was about imperialism and/or the Spanish Inquisition. [There were] many brilliant images. I remember the intensity of the movements Martha choreographed for us in *Chronicle*, but I don't remember Martha's choreographic process. I was surprised when I saw the reconstruction of *Chronicle* [by] how much of the technique we did at that time—how much of it she used in the dance. Martha [would] set a pattern for a class and we would stay with that material maybe for one or two months. I always say it is better to do one movement eight times than eight movements one time. Your whole body had to be spun to such a high level to execute Martha's technique, which she then choreographed into her dances. The technique we kept repeating was extremely valuable and challenging.

In 1937, I danced in Martha's *American Lyric* to the music of Alex North, who, at the time, was Anna Sokolow's husband. But that was a potboiler. Again, it was one of Martha's dances that was built out of her technique. I don't think it amounted to very much. Now with *American Document*, in 1938, on the other hand, Martha's choreographic process was very vivid to me because I was very much a part of that process. Martha choreographed most of the dance in New York City so that she wouldn't be hung up the way she was with *Panorama* when we got up to Bennington. Of course that was the first time Erick [Hawkins] joined the company. I think Martha's love for Erick developed in the course of time. Actually, I think it was over the rehearsal time for *American Document* while we were at Bennington. And we all hated Erick. Eventually, Martha became madly and sexually in love with Erick up at Bennington. Erick was beautiful, but he was a bull in a china shop. I don't want to take down Erick because I have a great admiration for him. Later, when Erick arrived as a dancer, he did foolish things, like demand equal billing with Martha. So then it became the kind of circus that happened with Ruth St. Denis when Ted Shawn demanded equal billing with her.

Martha choreographed the big dances for the ensembles for *American Document* in New York. Those dances came out of documents [and speeches] such as

the one that Lincoln gave at Gettysburg—I think it was the Emancipation Proclamation for the freedom of the slaves. The [document] Martha used for the
Group was the Declaration of Independence. [It] was very stylized, but a very
jubilant dance. Sophie and Erick were in the center, and then there were
groups on two sides. The whole piece had a series of "walk arounds" which
came out of the minstrel shows. The "Emancipation Proclamation section" was
beautiful, and quite jazzy in a funny way. Martha never choreographed any
dance that was jazzy up until 1990, when she choreographed the Scott Joplin
piece, *Maple Leaf Rag.*

I remember there was a turn in *American Document* where you brought your
leg up and then twisted your leg like fouetté, pressing way forward with your
hip out into your hand. We had to do it three times, and I used to have to
work like hell by myself to master the technique of that turn. Martha wasn't
concerned with the patterns that Balanchine was so adroit with. . . . What was
so important to Martha were the movements themselves. Martha would always
use her technique, and every year it was growing and would change. New
material would be added to Martha's technique and curriculum each year.
Martha would work for one month in the summer by herself and in the fall
she would come up with new movements. *American Document* had quite a jazzy
pulse, with the way Martha wanted our bodies pressed into the movement and
rhythm. Martha was able to develop with any class she worked with—but particularly with the company—a way of walking, with such dignity, quietness and
a sense of self. I will tell you, these are the things I taught out of my own
experience, and it is so hard to translate this and get a result from students.
I don't think the students realize how important walking is in the Graham
technique.

I wasn't cast in Martha's *Every Soul Is a Circus* in 1939, and that broke my
heart, because there was Jean Erdman[3] doing that part of "Ideal Spectator." But
Martha liked Jean Erdman because she had that well-bred certain kind of look.
When I asked Martha why I wasn't cast in *Every Soul . . .* , she said, "I didn't
think you were suitable." In a way, I really wasn't. I certainly wasn't suitable

---

[3] Jean Erdman (1917-). American modern dancer, choreographer and author; widow of Joseph Campbell.
Born in Honolulu on February 20, 1917, Erdman danced with Graham from 1938 to 1943 and created roles
in *American Document* (1938) and *Punch and the Judy* (1941). She is best known for her role "One Who
Speaks," in *Letter to the World* (1940), in which she recited the poetry of Emily Dickinson.

to be one of the little ponies that came in holding the rope. That dance had very little movement in it. It was no loss for me, really.

In *American Document*, though, the dances Martha choreographed before we got up to Bennington were the Indian dance, the Slave dance and a trio for Sophie, May [O'Donnell] and myself. Then she choreographed a solo with the same idea for Erick. Our trio was entitled "Three Women"—"We are three women. We are three million women." It was a dance of protest and anger. This, I will tell you, is the way Martha would work. She would be lying on a couch or a chaise longue, with the dopey little dachshunds around her, who were always peeing on the floor. She would get up, and for this trio she would improvise, and she started on the walk. She went straight through it. The three of us would follow as best we could. Then she [would go] to the couch and lay down, and say, "Now let me see it." It was a question of retaining the sequence of movement Martha [had] improvised. The most important thing for a dancer was to catch the mood Martha danced in. Martha trusted us, and had confidence in us, as dancers. We would take what she gave us a step further and clarify the movement. I remember that the intensity of Martha's movement was so strong that you couldn't do it without getting exhausted. You weren't being tense, you were just involved in her process physically. One became physically committed to Martha's movement and her choreographic process. Martha . . . would rarely warm up. [Very often] she would come to the theater, put on her stage makeup, get into costume and dance. But Martha could also dance pretty sloppily, perhaps because she didn't do warm-up exercises. I am not sure Martha wanted us to feel the effort of her movement, but one did.

Letter to the World was the first break I had in Martha's company—when she created "The Ancestress" role for me as a soloist. By then, Martha knew me pretty well and what she could do with my height. When Louis played the Hunter Johnson score and Martha danced it with Erick and Merce [Cunningham]—no one else really counted except the little ones, Helen [McGehee], Pearl [Lang] and Ethel [Winter]—Martha, at the time, was beginning to develop roles for the company members. The dances were becoming more and more dependent on Martha and a few characters around her. What was fascinating about working on my part was that Martha got me alone and it was the first time I had any idea about what I had gotten into. Martha gave me my opening gestures, which was really a statement that was sketched in by her. I did about five gestures, and then I stepped downward and did the "Mysteries Walk" forward, with my arms out. I think that was as far as she got in the first rehearsal. I think Martha was overwhelmed when I showed her the movement because I don't think she expected my dance to be as strong as it was.

The next thing I remember about working with Martha that was interesting was how important her accompanists were to her creativity, especially Helen Lanfer and Ralph Gilbert, both of whom played a large part in Martha's creative life.

At one point in *Letter to the World* I followed Martha and then I sat down on this bench—and it really was as if I were pushing Martha forward out of my own power, my own determination. I will tell you how I analyzed my figure of "The Ancestress" for myself. Martha tipped back into my arms, and I held her there, like an infant, and I rocked very stiffly forward. Martha didn't tell me to rock stiffly forward, I just did it—in that period of Martha's work, the dancers contributed to Martha's choreographic process. I rocked Martha in a very detached way, and I let her slip down to a kneel. I put one hand on one knee and one hand on my chest, as though I [was saying] "I reduced her to a child again, and she won't leave me." I felt it was important to work out what my figure meant from the beginning to the end of the dance. "The Ancestress" in *Letter* had several roles. One had to add onto what Martha gave you to dance. The dancer had to find the resonance in the body—the physical and psychological attitude to her gestures—in order to develop in her roles. It was a wonderful experience [by] which Martha developed many choreographers—because they had to develop and grow in the movement sequences that she had choreographed. From this period of time with Martha, what I learned in terms of performance I draw on over and over again, as a dancer, teacher and choreographer.

For the "Ancestress" role, I started looking at early American portraits of women, of matriarchs. I mainly looked at the early American artists. I kept one portrait, and I would look at it before I would perform. . . . I got an image about what this ancestress, or matriarch, was, and I felt that her role was not to let Martha grow up and have love and sex with Erick—whose role was "The Lover"—in the dance. I thought Erick's role was a ridiculous, naïve piece of choreography, but all right. The Ancestress wanted to keep Martha a baby. In some places, I was like a governess. The climax of *Letter* came when I destroyed the relationship between Erick and Martha with a great downstroke with my

Barbara Morgan.

From right to left: Jane Dudley, Ethel Butler, Jean Erdman and Erick Hawkins in Punch and the Judy, *1941.*

arm—my arm like a sword. In the end there is a struggle between Martha and me, and she defeats me. Jean recited the words of Emily Dickinson as she walked across the stage. She said, "Glory is a bright, tragic thing that for a moment means dominion." Then she stood behind Martha, who . . . sat on the white bench, and said, "This is my Letter to the World." Jean was really beautiful, with the most amazing voice. What was really important about these early years was our tremendous belief in Martha and our individual commitment to her.

The next dance I was in was *Punch and the Judy,* in 1941. I was one of the three Fates, with Jean and Ethel [Butler]. Martha hated *Punch and the Judy* because it was a vehicle for Erick and Nina [Fonaroff]. Martha couldn't stand that at all, so she didn't take the dance on for very long. All we did was sit around a globe and pose. We did triplets with our legs in the air—that was fun—[but] it was not an interesting dance for us dancers. Martha didn't really put herself out very much. We were like extras, or supernumeraries. And the next dance, in 1942, *Land Be Bright,* was not a very important dance, either. It wasn't very good, and we only performed it on one tour, and then Martha dropped it from the repertory.

Now *Deaths and Entrances,* in 1943, about the Brontë sisters, was an enormously important dance of Martha's. *Deaths and Entrances* was a departure into an area of movement and feeling that Martha hadn't hit ever before—totally personal states of being and finding the movement, gesture and images that matched it. For me, *Deaths and Entrances* is that from top to bottom, [such] a subjective piece that one didn't know if it was the way Martha's family was, or the way the Brontës were. At any rate, the Brontës were certainly the background for *Deaths and Entrances,* and they were a weird family. With Martha, a new dance was a huge event. Sophie and I were the other two sisters with Martha. Martha sketched out what she wanted us to do in the first rehearsal, while she was lying on the couch. The next day we showed Louis the movement. Louis said, "Martha, it's terrible. What do you think they are doing? They look like ghouls. It's no good." We were left alone for awhile, and then Martha called us again. The new movement was on a completely different wavelength. There was a solo entrance for Sophie, and a solo entrance for me. Again, Martha did it once, and we picked up the movement and deepened and defined it.

I feel very deeply that Louis was Martha's conscience and, in a way, her taskmaster. There is no doubt about it: Louis held Martha in line. When Erick came onto the scene, Louis did not like it because Martha was in love with Erick. Now, the thing that was good about Erick was that Martha eventually involved men. Erick had a sense of how the men should be dressed. He insisted upon there being some kind of décor, usually by Noguchi. Erick was responsible for the décor and how it was packed when we went on tour. Erick got three commissions from Elizabeth Sprague Coolidge so that Martha could create *Hérodiade, Imagined Wing,* and *Appalachian Spring* in 1944. Martha Hill, who ran Bennington, was never stingy in her praise for what Erick contributed to Martha. Of course, Bennington was very geared to Martha Graham, and I think both Doris and Hanya felt that very keenly.

The trio of "Dudley, Maslow, Bales" was formed the year before I danced *Deaths and Entrances.* The trio was Louis Horst's idea. It did kind of break my heart to leave Martha Graham when we formed the trio, but I managed to do it. Louis invited Sophie and me, and then Bill Bales, who was in Charles Weidman's company. The only time I felt Martha Graham's fury was really when I finally decided to leave for good in 1944. I did return to dance as a guest artist in 1954, in *Deaths and Entrances* and *Letter to the World.* I then stopped dancing.

As a teacher, I have always taught the Graham technique. In fact, I have never taught anything else, because I believe in it. I was important as a Graham dancer, but I am also a very good Graham teacher. I love teaching the old Graham technique. Once [when] I was teaching at Martha's school, while she was still alive, the dance critic for *New York* magazine, Tobi Tobias, asked to watch. In the middle of class, in marches "His Royal Nibs" (Ron Protas), who says very loudly, "Martha Graham hates Tobi Tobias. Get that woman out of here." I didn't know what to do. That evening I called Martha Hill, and she said to go directly to the source. The next day in the dressing room, I told Martha the story. Martha didn't say anything about Tobias. She only said, "I owe Ron everything. He saved my life." So Martha sold her soul to Protas, and now he runs the company.

At any rate, through it all Martha remains the master. It is interesting how her role changes [in this oral history]. In the very beginning years [when] she was dancing [the fact of her dancing] demanded certain things from her dancers. As she stopped performing, the dancers were called on for more role-creating. Also, what this oral history reveals of the dancers who worked with Graham—those who wanted to be choreographers, and those who just loved to dance. I think Merce is very interesting—his very conscious craftsman's approach to dance and technique, using what he felt was important in Graham's technique, and [knowing] where it was lacking, and where ballet was stronger. And then Pearl Lang, with her strong identification with Martha. . . .

I am delighted to have been part of Martha's scene in her best days. It was a remarkable experience that I continually utilize to this day.

ERICK HAWKINS

Barbara Morg

Erick Hawkins with Martha Graham in American Document, *1938.*

--- ◆ ● ◆ ---

Erick Hawkins was born in Trinidad, Colorado, in 1910. A graduate of Harvard University, where he studied Greek literature and art, Hawkins began his career as a ballet dancer. He studied at George Balanchine and Lincoln Kirstein's School of American Ballet, and was a member of their American Ballet, from 1935 to 1937, and Ballet Caravan, 1936-1939, both forerunners of the New York City Ballet. He also began to choreograph at this time.

In 1938 Hawkins joined the Martha Graham Company as a guest artist and was the first male dancer to do so. He became Graham's leading male dancer and danced with her company until 1951. He was briefly married to Graham (1948-1950); the couple subsequently divorced.

From 1957 he ran his own dance company in order to pursue his avant-garde principles, working in close collaboration with musician Lucia Dlugoszewki. His book, The Body is a Clear Place, *was published in 1992.*

Erick Hawkins died on November 24, 1994.

--- ◆ ● ◆ ---

I was born in Colorado. [George] Balanchine's aesthetic was towards St. Petersburg. So for me there was another ambiance when I was dancing with his American Ballet and Ballet Caravan (1935-39).

When I started dancing with Balanchine, I knew already I wanted to be a choreographer. It was the choreography, the music, and the visual arts all put together that interested me. I choreographed *Showpiece* in 1935 for Balanchine's American Ballet, and he did say, "Erick Hawkins is my most promising choreographer." In any case, after about four years with Balanchine, I knew I needed to go on and that is when I went to work with Martha. I danced with Martha in 1938 and by 1940 I choreographed my first New York solo concert. During the summer of 1945 I choreographed *Stephen Acrobat*,[1] then I separated from Martha for about one year. Unfortunately, I went back to her. Naturally the differences in our ages were a big problem, too.[2]

It was liberating, the change from Balanchine to Graham, but that is why I consider my time with Balanchine and with Martha as my apprenticeship as a choreographer. It was a wonderful apprenticeship. For me, they were two very important people who [served as] my teachers.

Martha was one station on my own odyssey, which she didn't like being. You can hang onto something where you have found something and it can be very valid, but the whole problem is how to keep arriving at the truth. Nobody knows it all. Nobody has said it all. Hopefully, you learn and grow all the time. That is where the avant-garde is always edging along against the clichés.

The difference between Merce's and Martha's ideas, and of course Balanchine's earlier ideas, and mine, is the concern to go back to what the body really is—that is what I am after. One does not distort what the body needs to do. Merce does the same thing as Martha. Merce never studied at the School of American Ballet long enough. I don't know whether he picked it up from Balanchine or what. The point is, the tension is wrong in ballet or Graham for proper virtuosity. When it comes to skill or dance training, you can't base a training against what the nature of the body wants to be. My goal is to have all the brilliance without the forcefulness of the ballet. I want it done naturally. There are some other problems here. Have you ever heard of Jacques Maritain?[3] He said, "Virtuosity is an escape for the artist." To train people to be like trained dogs, to do all kinds of tricks, is not at the service of the art. On the other hand, Stanislavski says, "The more talent you have, the more technique you need." You have to put those two statements together, but they have to be at the service of art. The technique has to be at the service of the art by itself.

---

[1] Erick Hawkins' ballet, *John Brown*, was performed with the Martha Graham Dance Company at the New York National Theater on May 16, 1945, with Hawkins in the title role. *Stephen Acrobat* was performed with the Martha Graham Dance Company at the Ziegfeld Theater on February 26, 1947.

[2] Martha Graham was born on May 11, 1894. In her memoir, *Blood Memory*, Graham admits to consistently taking 15 years off her age (Graham, *Blood Memory*, New York: Doubleday, 1991. p. 171).

[3] Jacques Maritain (1882-1968). French philosopher and diplomat. Maritain regarded the metaphysics of existence—the study of being—as the highest expression of human intellectual activity.

A Japanese man said, "The natural state of a man's mind is delight." That delight is seeing the wondrousness of the world. I question some of the agony and tension that both Martha and Merce sometimes have. There is no ugly tension and it is only delight. There are big questions here that just haven't been answered and looked at.

What was most important to Martha was her emotional life. Without any question that was her strength, and also her limitation. She could tap her own emotional roots for those solos, but it was very hard for her to convey those feelings to another dancer. Martha enjoyed wallowing in the ambiguities of neurotic emotions. We have neurotic emotions but you want a resolution. Martha enjoys the titillation of this negativity instead of rising above that mediocrity.

Martha worked on the dance *American Document* [in] about July (1938). Just as I had sat on the floor and watched Balanchine work, so I sat on the floor and watched Martha, and Martha would say, "Erick and I will come along here." She put me into *American Document*, so it became another kind of dance instead of being a straight mime.

Dark Meadow (1946) was one of my favorite roles, but Martha never choreographed that well. I remember once down in Philadelphia—it had already been done in New York—I said, "You've got to go to the studio and fix that movement for us to do tonight." I don't think Martha ever totally invented the movement for my part, but it did have some other magical quality because of Isamu Noguchi's sculptural space. *Dark Meadow* was very mysterious. There was a place [where] I stood behind one of Isamu's sculptures and branches fell out of it.

The last performance of *Eye of Anguish* (premiered 1950) was at the Champs-Élysées in Paris. She never worked on that dance so it never came off. Because Martha wasn't the center of that dance, she never worked at making it right. Here was another person, me, who was at the center of the dance. Martha wasn't interested in that.

Martha hurt her knee the opening night in *Every Soul Is a Circus* in Paris. The next night we canceled. The next night after that we did my *Stephen Acrobat* and Martha's *El Penitente* and *Eye of Anguish*. But as I said, Martha never worked at *Eye of Anguish* seriously enough.

You notice in Martha's later works, when she had stopped dancing, she usually had the heroine remain the main figure. Maybe that is natural. A choreographer who doesn't get caught up in her or his emotions could then see a lot broader picture of men and women. Martha always turned the modern woman,

Arnold Eagle.

Erick Hawkins, May O'Donnell and Martha Graham (fore-ground) in Dark Meadow, *1946.*

or any woman for that matter, into this psychoanalytical drama.

It was hard for the men because Martha was very self-involved and that was her power. Martha was a marvelous performer in terms of her own intimate emotional life. She wasn't able to give the men or the women that personal power that she had. She came onstage electrified. In terms of choreography that was also her limitation. Once she stopped dancing significantly and she got other dancers to interpret her roles, you could feel her choreographic limitation. I have said [that] after I stopped working with Martha, in one sense I don't think she did a truly original work. . . .

Martha went around saying things like, "Erick tried to kill me." That was Martha's problem. In terms of her ego she always had to create a tremendous drama around herself. So if I was her love affair, it had to be [National] Enquirer level. It was very difficult for me. Martha blacklisted me for I don't know how many years, when I couldn't perform at the American Dance Festival. I was shut out of Juilliard. It is really a tribute to one's talent that one could transcend all that and come out strong. I almost didn't survive Martha Graham. The emotional was very hard for me. Martha had the critics in the palm of her hand, so they always panned me totally.

Martha had a tremendous ego which helped her career immeasurably. But anyone who is the head of something they say is tyrannical. I don't think she was anymore so than anyone else who runs something. Balanchine had a tremendous ego also, but he wasn't a performer. That was Martha's fragile thing; that was also her greatest treasure. She wasn't going to have anyone interfere with that. So whatever that took . . . I don't know whether Martha nurtured dancers—men or women—except as they could be foils for herself. I was an equal and that created a lot of tension, and that is why I left finally.

The whole goal of human experience is to see what you call the "workable truth." This is what I am after, and this is where my study of the Greek comes into it, and this is why Isadora Duncan went back to the study of the Greeks, in the sense that it was the first time the body was not disturbed or not distorted. Rodin fell in love with the body because it was an embodiment after 1,500 or 2,000 years of showing the loveliness of the human body. You can't place a training for the body against what is natural for the body.

When Martha said, "Movement never lies," she was talking about emotional truth. I, however, am speaking about a kinetic truth: having that formal, concrete, lovely, beautiful, poetic . . . just creating the beauty of the movement.

That is choreography. You can infuse it with emotions if that is your choice. Both me and Merce decided, in different ways, to find everything that wasn't that because it does interfere with just the art of dance itself. Martha's particular artistic contribution is strongly emotionally-centered. It was inherent in Martha's nature.

MERCE CUNNINGHAM

Barbara

Merce Cunningham and Martha Graham in Letter to the World, *1940.*

---◆●◆---

Merce Cunningham was born in Centralia, Washington, in 1916. He studied tap, folk and exhibition-ballroom dancing before enrolling for two years in the Cornish School of Fine and Applied Arts in Seattle, Washington.

From 1939 to 1945 Cunningham was a soloist in the Martha Graham Company, where he created "The Acrobat" (Every Soul Is a Circus), "Christ Figure" (El Penitente), "March" (Letter to the World) *and* "The Revivalist" (Appalachian Spring). *He was the second male dancer to join the company. During that time he began to choreograph independently, presenting his first New York solo concert with composer John Cage in 1944. He formed the Merce Cunningham Dance Company, for which he has choreographed more than two hundred dances, at Black Mountain College in the summer of 1953.*

Cunningham is the recipient of numerous awards and honors, including two Guggenheim Fellowships (1954 and 1959), the Samuel H. Scripps/American Dance Festival Award for Lifetime Contribution to Dance (1982), and a MacArthur Foundation Fellowship (1985). In 1982 he was made a Commander of Arts and Letters by the French Minister of Culture; he was made Chevalier of the Legion of Honor by President Mitterand of France in 1989. He has been a recipient of the Kennedy Center Honors and in 1990 he was awarded the National Medal of Arts by President Bush.

Merce Cunningham lives in New York City.

---◆●◆---

I probably had heard Martha Graham's name, but I knew nothing about her work. You know, I never saw Graham dance until I was in her company [in 1939], until those first performances later in New York. I met her for the first time at Mills College [in California] where a summer session of dance was held. All of the modern dancers then prominent in New York were there to hold classes. It was toward the end of the summer session that Graham said, "If you come to New York I will put you in a piece." I went back to Centralia, Washington, and told my parents I was going to New York. My mother was properly shocked.

I was lucky. I wasn't a ballet dancer so there were few places I could go, even if I wanted to be in a ballet company. From that point of view, I was very fortunate to be with Graham.

Martha already had a company, for several years. There weren't many performances for anyone during that time, compared to the possibilities that have arisen. Certainly for the modern dancers. Maybe there would be a short tour, two or three weeks at the most, and one or two programs for New York.

After I had been in the Graham Company for a year, perhaps it was two years, I began to think about making dances for myself—solos. I wasn't involved with any other dance than the Graham work, and we weren't constantly rehearsing or performing, so one begins to be involved in other possibilities. I remember thinking very clearly one day, maybe it was the third year I was with Graham, that this is not what I want to do. I didn't know what I did want to do, but this wasn't it. If I don't do that, what am I going to do? I realized at that point I would be leaving the Graham Company. I did stay about two more years. Once I started to make solos, I made lots of them.

One takes what one has learned, what has been in one's experience. But from the beginning, I was more prone to use my legs, primarily, than Graham [was]. That was my instinct even when I started. I had come out of the Graham work, which included the exercises on the floor, but by a certain time I don't think I used that anymore. I know I dropped that Graham floorwork at some point. I didn't see the point to it for me. What I kept seeing were those women able to do all those shapes on the floor with their legs, but when they stood up it was not at all the same.

I had gone to the School of American Ballet earlier. The second year I was in New York, Graham said something to me, something about studying at the American school, and that she knew Lincoln [Kirstein] and would phone him up. I remember going up there and being terrified. Lincoln said, "What do you want to study ballet for? You are a modern dancer." I said, "I really like all kinds of dance." He said, "Oh," and went out and spoke to the woman who was the registrar at the school. It was then on Madison Avenue and 59th Street. I did not go consecutively, because of working with Graham. But I went as often as

I could—sometimes three times a week.

Possibly in the first solos I made, I used Martha Graham's vocabulary. One, *Root of an Unfocus*, was based on the emotion of fear, and certainly that could have expressive connections with my Graham experience. But even in that solo, the structure was based on time, that is, the compositional procedure was in a rhythmic structure that John Cage and I used, he in his way, and I in mine. John's music was for the prepared piano, and beautiful, the sounds.

Graham let one develop characters. She worked that way, at least when I was there. She would suggest something. I would be hopping around and she would say, "Oh, let's put that in." Originally the movement—even in *Every Soul Is a Circus* (1939)—what this particular solo would be about, it was not pedantic nor fixed. . . . You see someone doing something and you think it is interesting, so you use it.

I was quite willing to participate in that kind of endeavor of choreographing my own solos with Graham. Partly because of that working atmosphere I could absorb from Graham. I could see other people in the company at that time were confused by that responsibility. Not greatly perhaps, but something like finding out what foot are we on? Then, I have a tendency to think that way anyway, to be sure a dancer knows what foot he or she is standing on. The Preacher's solo in *Appalachian Spring* (1944), I remember making. Graham said, "Well, you work at it." Then she left the room, so I made the dance.

With Graham, one had class and there wasn't a great amount of rehearsal every day. I had to think of something else to do. If I went out on my own, that meant I had to find not only a means of support, that I had to do anyway, but [also] how to do one's own work. What is class? What kind of daily discipline could I devise? What does it mean? From the beginning John Cage and I had a way of working together that allowed for a different idea about the relationship of music and dance. The structure and basis on which we put the music and the dance together was not either through psychology (like Graham), certainly, nor through the use of 19th-century forms, but through the use of time, the one common denominator between them. Immediately it was different. I remember clearly that first performance we gave together, when I presented five or six solos and John had composed the music for the dances using the prepared piano. One of those European painters whom we knew came to our program and said to me a remark I remember as, "You and John Cage are doing something that has not been done before and you may or may not be

Barbara

From left to right: Merce Cunningham, Martha Graham and Erick Hawkins in El Penitente, *1940.*

successful." I am not sure I knew then what he was talking about, but I went home saying it. I knew later, when John and I worked with chance procedures and other kinds of possibilities that can open your imagination too—I felt the involvement with these ideas seemed enormous.

By the time I did leave Graham I had a terrible loft on 17th Street which was mostly unheated. However, I worked there by myself. And eventually I began to teach. The first class had one student. In my initial teaching experience the steps and exercises would have been much less complicated than now simply because I hadn't thought that far yet. Not only in my own thinking, but how to execute those steps. I would spend hours trying to figure out how to do steps in my loft.

Perhaps I did contribute to Graham's male syllabus. If so, it wasn't a conscious act. And I should think Erick Hawkins would have had a great deal to do with it, as he came out of working with Balanchine at the American School.

I don't think of my class work, the exercises and [movement] phrases that are given in our classes [at the Cunningham Studio] as being a specific technique. But what we do give is different from what I remember of the Graham technique. I accent the legs, because I think one moves on one's legs. For instance, I found no reason not to use the turn-out of the legs which is associated with the ballet, since without it an enormous area of movement possibilities is eliminated. That is, the flexibility and variety of movement is less wide. I am prone to emphasize the use of legs, but what interests me in working on technical exercises is to find a physical approach that uses both the legs and the torso. With Graham I remember, particularly on her, astonishing movements with the torso. But when I began to look at ballet and take classes at the School of American Ballet, I was amazed at the activity with the legs. I remember watching [Alexandra] Danilova in class, and the woman was beautiful in action, with the most incredible legs.

My experiences with the modern dance led me to feel there was something lacking; seeing ballet and working at it brought in another movement area. It was necessary for me to work with both areas: the weight and shape of the torso, and the dexterity and openness the use of the legs gave. I hoped to push it a little. I thought it would be a way to enlarge dance technique. I don't know if it has, but that was my thought. And whatever else, the continuous search into different movement possibilities has been a rewarding, if exhausting, action. It also furthered the experiences of making dances not based on linear continuity, but field, where a number of dance actions could take place in the same time, no one of them dependent upon another; and having the durations in time in seconds and minutes, rather than metric beat, could give to each separate dance action an elasticity—with several going at once that brought up a new kind of adventure as to how one dances, and how one sees dance. It was risk. It still is. It is probably the reason why the work of Elizabeth Streb[1] is lively to me. She risks in a large way. It is exhilarating. You know, she feels strongly we should be able to fly. She seems to be well on her way toward doing it.

Anyway, I realized that what Graham did was what she was and obviously strong, but there was another whole area. So as I continued working by myself my search went on with the torso and the legs.

---

[1] Elizabeth Streb (1950 -). Dancer-choreographer and artistic director of Streb/Ringside. Creator of "Pop action" movement.

◆ THE ◆

1940's

Arnold Eagle.

*Martha Graham and Erick Hawkins with May O'Donnell (seated),
Nina Fonaroff, Yuriko and Marjorie Mazia in Appalachian Spring,
1944.*

PEARL LANG

Cris Alexander.

Pearl Lang in Diversion of Angels, *1948*.

Pearl Lang was born in 1922 in Chicago, where she began her dance training as a child and also studied acting at the Goodman Theater. She came to New York to study with Martha Graham and Louis Horst in the early Forties and was a soloist with the Martha Graham Company from 1942 to 1952.

Lang danced many important roles in Cave of the Heart, Deaths and Entrances, Punch and the Judy, Night Journey, Letter to the World, Diversion of Angels, Canticle for Innocent Comedians, Ardent Song *and many other creations. She was the first dancer ever to take over a Graham role when she danced "The Three Marys" in* El Penitente *and "The Bride" in* Appalachian Spring. *From 1954 until the late Seventies, she danced as a guest artist with Graham's company.*

In 1952 Lang formed her own company for which she has choreographed many works. She was a featured dancer in a number of Broadway productions, has choreographed and danced in many musicals in summer stock and has frequently appeared on television. Lang has taught at Jacob's Pillow, the Juilliard School and the Yale University School of Drama. In addition, Lang was granted a fellowship from the Guggenheim Foundation.

She is on the faculty of the Martha Graham School for Contemporary Dance.

Pearl Lang lives in New York City.

I just always loved to dance. I had no idea what kind, or when, or who or anybody. Actually, I saw Harald Kreutzberg[1] first. Later, I saw a series of American dancers and choreographers. Doris Humphrey came. Martha Graham came. Hanya Holm came. I saw them but I had no idea what I was going to do. I

---

[1] Harald Kreutzberg (1902-1968). Czechoslovakian dancer who studied with Rudolf von Laban and Mary Wigman. He appeared in solo concerts of his own works and with Yvonne Georgi, his principal partner, and Ruth Page in Chicago. He danced in the United States throughout the Thirties and Forties.

just loved to watch dancing and to do it. I think I liked to do it more than to watch it. I saw Martha Graham when I was only eleven or twelve years old.

The Graham Company I saw in Chicago was a big ladies' company. I loved one dance of Martha's, *Chronicle* (1936). The girls leaped in a circle and Martha ran against that circle. I loved that. I thought that was marvelous. Many years later, I read Martha Graham was giving a June course. I saved money and I went to New York City and I took it. That was that!

I was dancing before I came to Martha Graham. I had my own little company in Chicago before I ever came to New York. When I came to study at Martha's, Louis Horst was teaching composition. The "Y" dance series always opened with a lecture-demonstration by him. He would talk about various studies and the Graham dancers—the company—would demonstrate. It turned out that I did almost every other study on that program.

I think the thing that attracted me to Martha was the inner-ecstatic thing that we have in the Hasidic dance. I had seen the Graham contraction when the Hasidim danced. It was a revolution in Jewish religion. They considered the act of dancing and singing more holy than reading biblical text and participating in the ritual. If you jumped, and jumped high enough, you were closer to God. If you sang, you sang with a *niggum,* a melody without words. The spiritual quality is holier if you are not using the tongue and the lips. It is a very strange kind of puritanism. The dancing now has deteriorated into happy dancing. It is not Hasidic for me unless it has an ecstatic inner tension. That is what I saw in Martha's contraction.

It has to do with imagination, the teaching of Martha's contraction. I know some teachers teach it on a breath. The technique is based on breath—it is not pulling out of the breath, it is the pulling in of the breath. I give the Graham class, I believe in it. I teach the Graham technique because I feel it prepares the body for a dynamic eloquence that can satisfy many different choreographic demands. After a real involvement in that discipline, a dancer's movement takes on a muscular depth, resonance and vibrato that no other technique seems to produce.

When I came, and when I was taken into the company, Martha taught us every day. She *taught.* When she choreographed a work, she would get up and show some movement and we would do it, and then she would look at it and say, "Now do this over here, and take this part of it, and you wait, and you, do this." Martha really danced the movement. She didn't tell you what to do, she did it. So that made a difference. Then I toured for 10 years with Martha Graham, and watched her dance every night.

I was in Martha's choreographic process. What was wonderful was to be around when she choreographed. When I came, they had been working on *Letter to the World* (1940) and *American Document* (1938), which was already two or three years old.

Originally in *Letter to the World* I was one of the . . . two little girls. Then I did "Young Love," which was a duet with Merce Cunningham. When we went to London on our second European tour we opened with *Letter* and I did "The Words" —the one who speaks the Emily Dickinson words—and Martha danced "The One Who Dances" with Bert [Ross]. When Martha couldn't dance anymore—it was 10 or 15 years later—then I did "The One Who Dances" with Bert. So I really know that work all the way through from beginning to end. I was also in *Deaths and Entrances* (1943) when Martha choreographed on me as a child in Bennington.

Celebration (1934) was not performed anymore but they used to teach it because the technique in it is very difficult. They used to teach the difficult jumps from *Celebration* in class. Then Barbara Morgan photographed the repertoire for [her] first book,[2] and I had to learn those dances in order for her to be able to photograph them. I had to learn parts of *Primitive Mysteries* (1931) and *Celebration.*

With *Primitive Mysteries* you lift the soul higher and that is the story. I think one of the reasons I may have been more successful in doing some of Martha's roles is that that is my image of her contraction. It is an inner-ecstatic tension. It is not just the muscles and the pelvis moving. Martha was not a practicing religious person; however, her dances are really religious pieces. Part of that ecstatic tension has to be in the body when Martha's dances are performed.

I watched Martha rehearse *El Penitente* (1940) in the studio when she was still performing it. It was a remarkable experience, *El Penitente.* Later, in 1975, we did *El Penitente* together, Nureyev and myself. It was wonderful to dance with Nureyev. Talk about rehearsal. He was on the Nile. He had two weeks to learn it. I, of course, had done it for years. Then we got this telegram that he was not coming in for another three days. I thought, how is he going to know what to

---

[2] *Martha Graham: Sixteen Dances in Photographs.* Duel, Sloan and Pearce—New York, 1941.

Arnold Eagle.

Pearl Lang (far right), Yuriko (foreground), Helen McGehee (seated) and Jane Dudley in Letter to the World, *c. mid-forties.*

do? I prepared all kinds of books of New Mexican Indians talking about penitence and so forth. I brought these to the first rehearsal and he didn't show. But nobody—not even Erick—has done the whipping solo in *El Penitente* the way Nureyev did it. The Russians have this thing of beating themselves. I said, "We better learn everything he does and coach him all the way through." I remember as he was about to enter the stage from the wings that Rudolf said to me, "Which foot I start on?"

Every choreographer is a sculptor, actually. For *Appalachian Spring* (1944), Noguchi created this sculpture that I was to sit on, but I was sliding off of it. The dancer has to be very proper. It is a very Shaker kind of piece. You have to keep the weight in your legs and then you have to get up and jump. Then in his set for "Joan"—*Seraphic Dialogue* (1955)—we stood. The Saints and St. Michael stand on rungs—a brass rung under your feet. Noguchi never considered what the physical problems were for dancers. He was a darling, though. It is [in] the way Martha uses space that she is a sculptor herself, which has a great deal to do with the Japanese idea of uncluttered space. For a sculptor, that is very important because whatever he shows should have space around it.

When Martha choreographed *Night Journey* (1947), I was leader of the chorus. There are long sections where the rest of the corps leaves the stage. But I stayed there and sat on one of Noguchi's rocks. So I saw Martha's interpretation of "Jocasta" firsthand. What was fascinating was that I did the leader of the chorus in *Night Journey* in the Forties and it wasn't until the Seventies that I did the lead role as "Jocasta." I had gone away with my own company and then returned a number of times as guest artist. In fact, I danced *Clytemnestra* first, before I danced "Jocasta" in *Night Journey*. One certainly couldn't get a better repertoire than with Martha Graham—beheading, jealousy, murder, incest, lust. It was very hard for me to do that killing in *Clytemnestra*. I would never lift a dagger in my life with such power.

The technique changed with the choreographic ideas Martha had. We worked on a very different kind of movement for *Diversion of Angels* (1948). In class she worked on how to pull the body out in space. You never stood on your foot and lifted your arm, but the body pulled up. "I don't want you to be on the ground," she kept saying, "I want it to look like a Chagall." You don't take a step and a balance—you take a movement and find your balance in the movement. You don't lift your arms up and lift your knee—your body pulls the whole leg up. This is a very ecstatic dance. Now you say "ecstatic" and the people look at you with such blank eyes. There was a body plunge in *Diversion of Angels* that was very hard, now that I think about it. It was a plunge down, but you had to come up in a high spiral double turn, or three [turns] if you could get around, depending on how sticky the floor was. It is easy to turn on a ballet shoe, but not on a bare foot that has already perspired on a wooden floor. They are doing it still, but it doesn't have any attack. What it doesn't have either is a vision, a thrust.

Diversion of Angels was very hard to come by [choreographically]. It was a piece Martha was not going to be in. From February until August, when we did the premiere at the American Dance Festival at Connecticut College, she sat with her face in her hands. You warmed up three times. Then you got cold, then you warmed up again. You had to keep yourself warm in case Martha asked you to do something. I once did this second-position extension, just playing around because she was working with Natanya Neuman. I did a contraction and I heard Martha say, "Do that across." That became it. We were three or four days away from this premiere and she hadn't finished this dance yet. "The White Girl" was at the time the "Blue Girl." Martha wanted the three primary colors—blue, yellow and red. Martha had seen our choreographic work in Louis' courses. So Martha said, "I can't do this now. We are going to divide the stage with the couples. You take the right, and you take the left, and just come up with some movement. It will be a dialogue. Let me see it tomorrow." So we did. So I started and Martha would say, "Hold it there. Now let's see Natanya." Then she would hold it. "Now you hold it. Now you continue." That is the way the dance was choreographed in the end.

Martha would not do a piece without consulting Joseph Campbell, the mythology man. Martha would come in and tell us the story or the myth. There is a funny story about Mary Hinkson and me. For *Ardent Song* (1954), Martha wanted us to be goddesses. I saw Mary was reading this Haitian book about a "queen for a day." I was reading the same book. Martha had done a very Miss Ruth [St. Denis] thing: She gave us both the same story to read because she knew we would be, or make, different goddesses out of the same story. Martha read all the time. When you looked at her books you knew what kind of piece we were going to do. Martha's dance *Adorations* (1975) was a classroom work put together for the stage. *Adorations* is what we call a "technique piece," like Martha's *Acts of Light* (1981), which she made later. Only *Acts of Light* is a better dance, and it has that beautiful duet. Martha's technique is so theatrical that it should be seen onstage.

It wasn't traumatic for Martha at that point, dancing and running a company, because Martha was dancing in most of her repertoire. She would open with *El Penitente*, then came one large work, either *Deaths and Entrances* or *Letter to the World*. We would close with *Appalachian Spring*. Or Martha would dance *Night Journey* or *Dark Meadow*. Those were the large central works.

I always say now in order for you to maintain this repertoire, you have got to bring somebody back who was in the company when Martha was choreographing the dance, not somebody who has learned it from somebody else who learned it from a video. You look at a video and it is three times removed from the actual physicality of the movement.

I am 75. I have been dancing for over 60 years. The joints have done more than they should. It is very hard. We are not doing to our bodies what we are supposed to be doing to them. The little bones in your feet are not supposed to land from jumps. Not even animals do that all day long.

It was very exciting to work in Martha's camp. Martha never said this, but if you made it on Broadway you knew you had a solo in Martha's company. What Martha trusted was theatricality. If other people in the theater saw your talent and used it . . . [Martha] would go to see anything anybody did—it was the only time Martha could see you on the stage when she wasn't involved in her own dancing in her own concerts—so she could really see what your possibilities were. I have a hunch about this, it may be far out, but I think Martha would light up when I would speak Yiddish because she heard it in the Yiddish Theatre. She would always say, "What have you been reading?" Then, "Say it in Yiddish." I said, "Martha, you are not going to understand." She said, "I want to hear it." "Okay." Martha saw the [Yiddish Theatre] and because they had a wild passion, even if it might have been melodramatic, but it had such a theatrical energy, that is really what she learned there. I think that is one of the reasons she trusted me with one of her roles. She knew I would deliver something that would come out of that theatricality.

I think without Louis Horst, who knows what would have happened at Graham. One choreographs about things one is concerned with. You must have some sort of clue to a living, human experience. I am very concerned with the air we breathe, the water we drink, the land we stand on, how we live on this earth. There were other people who were around at that time who didn't somehow choreograph, and those who had to do it because we had to do certain studies for Louis Horst's work. Some people hated it and didn't want to continue with it. I am not a linear abstract choreographer. Shape alone does not interest me. I would never choreograph a sequence of movement just for the line of it. If I want to see line, I'd rather look at Noguchi's work. At least I can use my own imagination to fantasize where these lines come from. I am dismayed when I see modern dance companies today. But I must say you don't throw a dance together if you have been working in new works with Martha. You just don't do that. I tried to have a vocabulary. I try to have a certain kind of movement for every work and then comes time to choreograph yourself into the dance. It is horrendous because there is nothing left. I always say, "I am going to start with myself," because Martha always started with herself. But she had Louis Horst watching for her. He would say, "No, Martha. That is wrong. It doesn't work with what you did before. It was better yesterday. Try to get it back."

JOHN BUTLER

Cris Alexander.

*John Butler (right) with Martha Graham and Erick
Hawkins in* Deaths and Entrances, *1945.*

---◆●◆---

John Butler was born in Memphis, Tennessee, in 1920 and was raised in Greenwood, Mississippi. He danced with Martha Graham's company from 1945 until 1955. During this time Butler earned his living by experimenting in the commercial theater, and performed the choreography of Agnes de Mille in Oklahoma! *and of Jerome Robbins in* On The Town.

He formed his touring company, the John Butler Dance Theatre, in 1955. Its members included Carmen de Lavallade, Glen Tetley, Mary Hinkson and Arthur Mitchell. In 1958 he was named dance director of the Spoleto Festival, in Italy, and in 1959 his company was the first dance troupe to perform at the Newport Jazz Festival.

Butler choreographed dances for televised opera productions, including Gian-Carlo Menotti's The Consul *(1947) and* Amahl and the Night Visitors *(1951), as well as for programs such as* Omnibus, The Bell Telephone Hour *and* The Kate Smith Evening Hour. *He also choreographed for Broadway and Off-Broadway shows. Many of his dances are in the repertoires of dance companies around the globe, most notably with the Alvin Ailey American Dance Theater.*

John Butler died in September 1993.

---◆●◆---

I knew I always wanted to be a dancer. I loved being a dancer. I loved being onstage. I came to New York [when] my family cut me off without a cent because I was going to become a dancer. I got a job teaching ballroom dancing for 15 dollars a week. One day, by sheer accident, I picked up the [Barbara Morgan] book on Martha Graham.[1] I had never heard about Martha Graham. It didn't look like the other dance pictures I had been seeing. I thought, "That looks like pretty good

---

[1] *Martha Graham: Sixteen Dances in Photographs.*

stuff," so I looked Martha Graham up in the telephone book.

I went down to Fifth Avenue and asked to see Miss Graham. I suddenly appeared in Martha's studio. I think out of pure astonishment Martha allowed me in and started to talk with me. In high school I was the "Blue Prince," so I had brought my "Blue Prince" costume with me to New York City to try out. Martha sent me into the dressing room and I came out in the Blue Prince outfit. Martha never let me forget it. I flew around that room and she said, "Sit down, young man." Martha talked to me for about an hour and a half —I had a scholarship. I was in the company within a year.

I went there in the winter [1943] and Martha took me in the company when we went up to Bennington for the summer. Martha always took the company up there for the summer. But my training was to get me into her dances and to get me onstage. I didn't stay with Martha all [10] years. I was in and out and in and out.

Martha had Merce and Erick and that was it. It really was. When Merce left I took his place. There were very, very few men. At first I was one of those that leapt across the back of the stage. The first work Martha choreographed that I was actually used in was *Deaths and Entrances* (1943).

Almost immediately, like the second or third year with Martha, I knew I wanted to do my thing. Jerry Robbins picked me out for *On The Town*. Then *On The Town* closed. I needed a job. I was cast to dance "Curly" in Agnes de Milles' [ballet in] *Oklahoma!* [while] Agnes was in London doing a film. She was furious I was dancing "Curly." She didn't know who I was. She came and saw me dance Curly and didn't say one word to me except "I'll see you tomorrow at 10 o'clock," which meant rehearsal—a product of death. I dreaded working for Agnes. Three months later, Agnes, who worships Martha Graham and always has, came to see Martha's concert, and there I was dancing. All of a sudden Agnes de Mille had discovered John Butler and she put him in *Oklahoma!*. There are so many of these stories one shouldn't tell because they are so convoluted.

Martha was such a total demonic artist. She admired you as an artist, a dancer, but she was too powerful; if you had your own thing that you wanted to do—like Merce had, and I had, and Glen Tetley had—well, you had to get out of there. You as an artist wouldn't submit to that kind of dictatorship.

Martha was that funny woman who was always lying on the floor. From the beginning, my training was in acquiring technique. I had been in the world's worst, as far as ballet dancing is concerned, in Greenwood, Mississippi. It took me 2 or 3 years to get over that bad training. Martha sent me over to Balanchine's School of American Ballet . . . the only man from Martha's who put on shoes and learned how to study ballet. Martha was using me purely as a guinea pig. I know the other dancers laughed and asked me what it was like with those people that wore shoes. In those days, people were always one or the other, ballet dancer or modern dancer, and never should the twain meet.

Erick was with Balanchine's American Ballet. Merce went over to teach modern dance for Balanchine. It was a strange time for dance because you were branded a modern dancer—barefooted. Martha, who had always spoken like a prophet from year one, took it for granted, your seriousness and concern for dance. It was not the same atmosphere at the School of American Ballet. They learned the steps. And then there were the god-given artists, the wonderful ones that turned out, like the Melissa Haydens, that just evolved in spite of Balanchine's technique. Balanchine thought the dancers from the neck up just didn't have anything. Martha was just the opposite. If we were going to have time to dance and do ballet we would be dancing from the neck up and down, the way we were taught at Martha's.

I *use* dance. I use the ballet and I use the modern. You use dance especially if you work as a person in the theater idiom. All of my ballets are dramatic and require a theater technique and a theater presence. I never lean toward a dancer because of a wonderful technique. I think of the artistry more than the technicality. Martha's emotional qualities influenced me a lot. We got into real trouble a lot of times on TV. I was always invited to do work on *Camera Three,* or *Adventure,* or *Omnibus* or *NBC Opera.* I did television only to a certain degree to keep my dancers alive. My dancers would be dancing with me all day long in a television studio, and then they would give their evenings to do my work. It was another kind of exchange. Martha came always to my dress rehearsals. We would talk afterwards. She never gave me corrections, but she would talk about . . . the work, something to do with the costumes, etc. She faithfully was there at every one of my premieres until I did *Carmina Burana* at City Center (1958). I will never forget this: I took Martha, [then] I took Martha home, and she still lived down on Ninth Street. It was so warm and special. She took my face and held it for a very long time, and kissed me on the cheek, and said, "I tell you goodbye," and she never came to another premiere of mine again. That was her stamp of approval: "Welcome to the club."

It was wonderful for us because we had the freedom to dance with Martha.

I was a natural. Merce was a natural. I guess Bertram [Ross] was a natural. I know Merce and I were very much our own creatures. We were given such freedom and wonderful encouragement. Martha would give to you so completely that she could let you go out in those dances to make up your solo, but you were using her sense of theater. You were using what Martha had given with love and somehow it was all so unselfish and so ungaining.

I danced *Punch and the Judy* (1941) and *Every Soul Is a Circus* (1939), all of those things. It was just the beginning of *Punch and the Judy*. All for Erick. I swing both ways. I was the "Romantic Beloved" and I'd do Erick Hawkins' role. Then I would do the "Poetic Beloved." I don't think Martha knew what she wanted. She was, of course, completely in love with Erick. She gave Erick everything. I don't know whether or not Merce felt left out to the point that Merce finally had to leave and I took his place. But the focus was on Erick— The Beloved. But he would be the "Dark Beloved" and we would dance the "Poetic Beloved." At that point Merce was so young I don't think he had really formed his own opinion of himself. The roles that I inherited from Merce had that light pixie quality that Merce was so brilliant doing.

Almost immediately after me, Bob [Cohan] and Bert came. Bob danced my roles like I danced Erick's things. Then Bertram came sandwiched right in between there. Then, of course, Bertram stayed longer than anyone with Martha. It is very strange. I was really with Martha for, like, two years. I was always back and forth, back and forth. Totally was I influenced by Martha Graham's dramatic narratives.

The first time anyone except Martha danced *El Penitente* was Pearl Lang. Erick Hawkins danced his role. I danced Merce Cunningham's role. We were all kind of easing into it. But really when I first went there Martha was with the company. She had had people like Sophie Maslow, Anna Sokolow. May O'Donnell was still with Martha and the company. It was amazing to see how all of us odd ones with Martha, who kind of had our own thing going, that no one who ever went on to do his work or her work stayed very long with Martha. I danced Martha's solos with her for about two or three years. Then I went into a nightclub act with Alyne Ann McLerie. Martha did my costumes and an unheard-of man called Dick Avedon took all our photographs.

It is very hard to explain without sounding bad. Martha didn't steal, you didn't choreograph her ballet for her, but she dramatically explained who you are and where you are in the dance work. [Then] you would go to another studio and you would do your solo. I would go there with Pearl Lang and work on a pas de deux. You were on your own but you were so under Martha's influence there was no other way you could move. It was so give-and-take that you almost couldn't separate it. Being given that freedom from Martha, there is nothing to inhibit you from being creative in doing your own thing. And using the Graham technique as a basis for your body and how you use it is the same way you use the ballet barre in your training. I would go and take class at the American School regularly. I'd take my ballet class and then go downtown and take modern with Martha. So I had both worlds going for me.

When Martha rehearsed with you, actually, you were not learning dance, you were learning theater. She was using you as a performer while she choreographed [for] you. It is hard to explain. People could explode with Martha. You could just begin and suddenly be doing a solo with Martha. What she was looking for was the performer or the creature on the stage, not a Martha Graham dancer. She dealt in terms of dancers or what they could do with a role. She would give you a beautiful introduction dramatically to what it was and then shape you. *You* did a lot, but in all fairness to Martha, *she* always gave you your sense of theater and your direction. It was not like Tamiris or other people where they used you to do something and said, "Do that again." That was not Martha. Martha always dealt with you . . . and I didn't know what the hell she was talking about. She did it with such conviction and such belief, it rubbed off. You become as committed because of her total commitment.

You would kill for Martha. I miss that. The dancers then danced with a different reason. Now it is a job and progression . . . how much to get promoted or how much money to make, what roles, etc. That never entered our heads. It was a very unselfish time of creativity. We were really lucky to be in that, totally free. You were respected with total evenness with Martha Graham. You always felt on the level of an artist—you were never the student or a subordinate. That was something so beautiful. God, when I worked with other choreographers, I had the rude awakening about being treated another way. You soon appreciated [her way]. Martha didn't ask for credit. She didn't ask for recognition. She gave you her genius because that was the way she was.

I remember [when] I went in to learn *Letter to the World* (1940). Martha always did the duets at night—in the studio downtown and uptown and all that. I always remember going into those evening rehearsals with just Martha and myself. It was like a beautiful seduction. She would be in a wonderful long black dress, her hair would be loose. She had on a nice cologne. She had prepared for a performance and she seduced you into the role. I swear it was that. You had a strange kind of love affair with this woman which had only to do with dance. It was so beautiful. She was giving you your takeoff into theater. As a woman she wanted to respond to the men. It is hard to put that in words. It's so powerful. . . . Seduction with no sex. It is very strange.

It was an incredible closeness and need for real people. It is not that bitchy competitive thing which seems to be the whole reason now. There is a funny continuity [when] you find [an] artist [who] wants much more to dance than [to make] money. It is still there, but, boy, you wade through such crap to [find it]. But the real ones will show up. The real ones will work night or day for you and talk to you at 2 o'clock in the morning. They know I'll pick this phone up at 2 or 3 in the morning, that it means that much to me. There is a curious continuity. The artists will always give you [their] extra. It is an unspoken recognition of each other. You don't even have to talk about it. You just go to work. The dancer has to, and will, give everything in spite of . . . money, and all of that. What I am saying is, I'll go all over the world, whether I'm down in Caracas or in Tel Aviv . . . I can walk into the studio and recognize the real ones in the first rehearsals. There is a recognition of the one who will kill to dance that role and who will suggest, "Why don't we work evenings?" or "Why don't we work on the day off?" They are hungry people. Hungry people recognize each other. And the hunger is just as strong in the choreography. It really works out. From my first meeting with Martha, I realized [there was a] family of artists. You need the same sustenance and the same seriousness of purpose, a love and a mutual respect for each other. You buy that very dearly—with great costs sometimes—and it is more than worth it.

We didn't get paid for dancing with Martha. You got paid for one week and rehearsed for the rest of the year. I was lucky because Dick Avedon kept me working [as a model] for years, and that was how I ate when I was dancing with Martha.

Me being an overly Southern gentleman, anything Martha told me to do I would do. Martha invented for each person his own area of theater where he was potent. Her dancers influenced what she was choreographing. She learned from you, your dance quality, which she really taught you. Martha was wonderfully generous.

I always managed to live near Martha, down in the Village where she lived.

When the divorce with Erick [happened] I lived with her through that time. Glen [Tetley] and I lived together for a while. I can't tell you, it gets so convoluted, these relationships. Glen, all along I think, knew that he wanted to choreograph—but I was the choreographer, he was the dancer. It is all like incest. It made for some very difficult times, but very exciting times. Martha, of course, was smack dab in the middle and loving every minute of it.

YURIKO

Philippe Halsman.

Yuriko with Erick Hawkins and May O'Donnell in
Cave of the Heart, *1946.*

Yuriko (Anemiya Kikuchi) was born in San Jose, California on February 2, 1920. An American of Japanese descent, at the age of 9 she went to Japan, where she was educated and where she began her dance career with recitals and a tour of the Orient. She returned to the United States in 1937. She was a member of Dorothy Lyndall's Junior Dance Group in Los Angeles until 1941.

In February 1944, Yuriko received a scholarship to the Martha Graham School, and she was asked to join the Martha Graham Company by May of that same year. Immediately after that she created roles in Appalachian Spring, Dark Meadow, Cave of the Heart *and* Night Journey. *In 1946 she was a YMHA audition winner in choreography, performing a concert of 10 solos. From that time on, Yuriko gave concerts of her own work at least once a year while continuing to dance for Graham. From 1951 to 1954, Yuriko danced the role of "Eliza" in Jerome Robbins' famous ballet,* The Small House of Uncle Thomas, *in the Rodgers and Hammerstein Broadway musical,* The King and I. *She reprised the role for the motion picture version in 1955.*

In the late Fifties, after performing in Graham's film, A Dancer's World, *Yuriko created the roles of "Eve" in* Embattled Garden *and "Iphigenia" in* Clytemnestra, *after which she left the Graham Company to form her own troupe. Yuriko returned to the Graham Company in 1967 to dance the role of "Helen" in* Cortege of Eagles. *In that same year she received a Guggenheim Fellowship for choreography, left Graham and shortly thereafter retired from performing. Yuriko returned to Graham in the Seventies to remount* Dark Meadow. *She went on to establish the Martha Graham Ensemble, a touring repertory and lecture-demonstration company.*

Yuriko has had a 50-year association with the Graham establishment, as a dancer, teacher, coach and choreographer. After Graham's death, she served as co-artistic director of the Graham Company. She resigned from that position in 1993.

Yuriko lives in New York City.

I went to Japan at the age of 9. I studied European dance with Konami Ishi. In Japanese, "ballet" means European, or foreign, dance. It was not ballet, no toe shoes, [although Ishi] put in a lot of balletic steps. It had everything, including Mary Wigman. Ishi had been in Europe, so she picked up Mary Wigman and all those other people around that time. I started touring with her company from the age of 10 until I was 17. Out of 20 numbers, I was in 15 or 16. . . . We had to put on our own makeup and do all the backstage things—taking out the costumes, ironing the costumes. It was the greatest experience. It was fabulous!

I came back to Los Angeles from Japan when I was 17, in 1937. I studied with Dorothy Lyndall, both modern and ballet. She was a ballet teacher originally, then she moved [into] modern. I started to know about Martha Graham from her. I got invited to the UCLA Dance Club where I saw Hanya [Holm], Doris [Humphrey] and Charles [Weidman], and Martha's company. Martha did *American Document* (1938), I think. It was all new to me, every one of them. I had seen [Harald] Kreutzberg in Japan and La Argentinita. As a matter of fact, [Martha] didn't impress me that much. I had much more of an impression of Hanya Holm and Doris Humphrey. . . . I saw some of the technique being taught and the one I didn't like was the Martha Graham technique! Doris was much more fluid, and Hanya . . . both were the two that impressed me. [What] I do remember is that after I came back it was 1937, and then [World War II] started. I was [in Los Angeles] a very short period of time. At least I saw all that.

There was no doubt in my mind that I was a dancer—that I was going to become a dancer. The first time I taught was in the relocation camp.[1] In the barracks it was 110 degrees in the summertime. It was hard. I taught modern [dance], but really it was a combination of things. I had over 100 students . . . [ranging from] children, 3 or 4 years old, up to [their] mothers. Then I did choreography; I did concerts. I did a whole *Nutcracker Suite* with the children. I had the nerve! The costumes were made of crêpe paper or curtain materials. I just thought it would be fun for the kids to do. I don't know how I managed to do it financially. I got $19 a month. I think I got assistance from a recreation department, or something. I just didn't want to see the children go nuts. Besides, I didn't want to go nuts, too.

---

[1] In 1942, Yuriko was sent to an internment camp for Japanese-Americans, in Arizona.

I applied for relocation to Detroit, [where] I had a friend who was studying ballet. She wrote, "Come out. We will take care of you. . . . You can study whatever you want." To get permission you had to get clearances from Army and Navy Intelligence, the FBI, the relocation people . . . I mean name it—everything we had to get cleared. Clara Claymen was the person who helped [people] apply for relocation. Many years later, Clara became the manager of my dance company. . . . It didn't last too long because financially I couldn't swing it—I had two children and a husband. I got the Guggenheim, but I was overwhelmed by financial problems. I'm sorry about that, because I didn't really get my creativity going.

I went to the office to apply [for relocation] and Clara interviewed me. She had seen my concert. She said, "Yuriko, don't go to Detroit. Go to New York. Think about it." Clara was going to New York to open a resettlement office. Then she said, "[New York] is the center. You have a great talent. You're a dancer—you shouldn't be in Detroit. You've got to [go to New York]." She helped me get the clearance. Clara said she had secured a domestic job for me and that she would sponsor me. In other words, she sent a telegram and I got cleared and a one-way ticket to New York. I arrived in New York on September 23rd, or something, 1943. The war was still on. Clara said, "I don't have a domestic job [for you]." She had just written it to get me out. That is how I got to New York, instead of Detroit.

I wanted to start [dance] classes right away. By the Monday after I arrived, I had a job [as a seamstress]. I was making $25 a week, and at that time I just couldn't believe it. Anyway, when I was assured of a job, I started looking in the telephone book [for the studio addresses] of Doris Humphrey, Hanya Holm and Martha Graham. Martha was still at the bottom of the list. She was "three"—one, two, three. I carried that [list] all the time. All of the studios were downtown: Doris was on 16th Street, between Sixth and Seventh Avenues; Hanya Holm was on 10th Street, between Eighth and Ninth Avenues; and Martha was at 13th Street and Fifth Avenue—66 Fifth Avenue.

I went downtown by bus and plunked myself at the northeast corner of 14th Street. I was standing there with my list. It was around 7:30 or 8:00 p.m. Of course I wanted to go to Doris first, but Martha was the closest. So I went to Martha's. I go up the elevator two or three floors, then I knock on the door. A lady opens the door and says, "What can I do for you?" I said, "I would like to inquire about the schedule of the class." I planned to do this at all the different studios. She said, "Come in," and started [by] asking where I was from. Then she said, "I'm Martha Graham.""Oh!" I didn't even know. That is how I met Martha Graham. I met Martha Graham because she opened the door—that was my opening of the door!

I didn't have the New York psychology of "the Great Martha Graham, teacher with a company." None of these people did I put up on a pedestal: It could have been Dorothy Lyndall [at the door], but a little bit more [so]. Of course, after I got to Martha, I stayed there for over 25 years. So I am a disciple of Martha Graham.

I didn't know [about] audition[s] at that time, either. Martha said, "I have a leotard. Why don't you change and show me what you can do?" I said, "Oh, no. I can't do that. I'm out of condition. I have not been taking classes. I can't possibly do that." Martha said, "I just want to see you move." I said, "Before I can dance for you I have to know your technique. You are the master. I just can't jump in and come to your class without knowing your technique." You don't just come to the master right away. This is the attitude of respect to the master which, of course, is very Japanese—[when you] come to the master to study. Martha, Doris and Hanya Holm were the masters of their techniques. Martha said, "Why not? Everybody else does. . . . Come tomorrow and take my evening class." Martha was teaching all three levels then every day. In any case, I refused Martha's audition and finally she gave up on seeing me dance. I asked, "Do you think you can send me to one of your students or company members?" Martha sent me to Sophie Maslow and Jane Dudley, who were renting a studio from the Neighborhood Playhouse on West 47th Street. They would alternate teaching in the evening, and Marjorie Mazia, Woody Guthrie's wife, play[ed] the piano.

That was not enough for me. I [found] another teacher downtown. I would have class with Jane or Sophie . . . and dash over to the other class. . . . I would take two classes with just a bowl of soup. When I go into something, I just go into it and I don't consider anything else. I just do it. I wasn't impressed with anything. I was just learning a new technique [and] I didn't even make any judgment. During this time—this was in October and Martha was going to have a concert around December—I heard Jane Dudley say in the dressing room that Martha needed a seamstress. I was working in alteration at a very fancy store on 57th Street. Clara Claymen [had arranged] an appointment for me there the week I arrived in New York. She had said, "I want you to crack the union . . . because they are discriminating against the Nisei—second generation Japanese-Americans." They liked me so much that the union accepted me. So I cracked the union. I was in the newspaper. From there on the door was wide open. I said [to Jane], "Oh, I'm a seamstress."

Martha remembered me. We had a lovely conversation. . . . I worked on Martha's *Deaths and Entrances* (1943) costumes—yards and yards of skirt. For four or five days they killed us, but I was working for Martha Graham—as a seamstress. I got to know Isamu [Noguchi] that year, too. He wanted me to make the sail for *[El] Penitente*.[2] They are still using it. I remember sewing the corners and all those things. That is when I got to know Noguchi. Looking back, [I see that] everyone was scared of Martha. People were distant from Martha. I didn't know a thing about her, so I was able to talk naturally with Martha about a lot of things. I kept calling her "Miss Graham." I wouldn't have thought of calling her "Martha."

I was the last one to close the door and take the last costume for *Deaths and Entrances* up to the theater where Martha was going to premiere the dance. I [stayed and watched, sitting] way up in the balcony, and that was my first, very first impression that lasted. Merce, Erick, Jane, Sophie, Pearl and Ethel Butler were all in it. It wasn't [the dancers] who impressed me, it was the whole impact, especially of Martha Graham.

I suppose Martha was waiting for me to come [to her], but I didn't come. While they [were] all rehearsing, Jane and Sophie would [speak] about this amazing Oriental dancer, a Japanese dancer: "She [can] do anything." Martha was very, very curious. Time passed. . . . Towards the end of January or February 1944, Martha called me and said, "Yuriko, I want to give you a scholarship." She hadn't even seen me dance! I will never forget it.

At my first class, Martha was sitting in the front and I was way in the back, near the piano. We did the bounces, then we did the contractions. I said, "That is what I want in my body. The way Martha was doing contractions . . . it was totally different from anybody else's. I kept watching her. For 23 years I watched Martha Graham. And I stole it, that contraction.

That first day Martha called me into her dressing room. She said, "I have never said this to anyone, but I want to tell you—you are a born dancer. If my

[2] *El Penitente* premiered in 1940 at the Bennington College Theater with a set design by Arch Lauterer. It was redesigned by Noguchi in 1944.

technique doesn't agree with your body you must leave and go someplace else." I said, "No, I'm fine." She said, "I want you to think about it." I said, "Please give me one week." You know, I never thought about it. At the end of one week she called me in again. Martha said, "How do you feel?" I said, "Fine. I would like to stay." She said, "Oh, fine. I would like you to come to repertory class."

I was very, very naïve. I didn't know the politics; I didn't know anything about the situation in New York. What Martha said was, "Would you like to learn some of my dances?" That is how Martha put it. I said, "Oh, yes." She didn't explain to me what was happening or what was going on. She was doing *Primitive Mysteries* and *American Document*. Ethel Butler was doing *Primitive Mysteries* and somebody else was doing *American Document,* but they were all there doing it. I thought it was a repertory class. I just did it. And then once in a while Martha would call me in, and all these other dancers would go "Uhhh!" I couldn't understand why they were so nervous. I was so happy learning her repertoire.

It turned out it was going to be a selection of augmented dances from these two pieces, which I didn't know. Martha came in after three weeks and . . . I heard that [at] a company meeting she [had] said, "To my sense and my eye, I think Yuriko is the best. But I would like to get the opinion of the company members, since the war is on. [Does] anyone have any objection?" I think either Sophie or Jane [had] said, "I think it is wonderful to introduce Yuriko to New York with *American Document* and *Primitive Mysteries.*" I had started in February and by the end of March I was dancing in Martha's company. I believe we had Needle Trade School and YMHA concerts and then we opened sometime in May. Right after that, Martha called me in and said, "I would like you to become a permanent member of the company. I am going to Bennington. I can't give you any pay. You have to support yourself." That was the summer Martha created *Hérodiade* (1944), *Imagined Wing* (1944) and *Appalachian Spring* (1944), which were for the Library of Congress concert . . . I believe . . . in September.[3] They found me a job with a principal [at Bennington], and I took care of the children and the house. They gave me room and board as well as $10, perhaps. I could rehearse any time. Then I totally quit [my job]

---

[3] The Library of Congress concert took place on October 30, 1944.

and started sewing for Martha's company. I did all the *Document* costumes. Edythe Gilfond was the designer. I changed the scenery for the different solos or duets, whatever, in *Imagined Wing.* I did all kinds of things, which is how I was able to survive. No one got paid for rehearsals.

Appalachian Spring and *Imagined Wing* were my first creative works with Martha. I danced in the chorus, "The Followers," in *Appalachian Spring.* It has such a brilliant set—[the use] of the space with the fence—it has the sense of a Japanese house with a rock garden. I was "The Page" in *Imagined Wing.* After we left Bennington, I didn't have any money so I took a job as a domestic in New Jersey. I came back with $100, which kept me going until the Library of Congress concert. Then I started working again; I did private sewing.

Martha was hard to work with, but she didn't have the personal digging to hurt a person like [some] choreographers. Around that time, Martha was very much in love with Erick. There was the difficulty between Erick, Martha and Louis. Martha always got along very well with women. But she could be very hard on someone by saying, "Don't you dare think you are a permanent company member." As long as you produced, Martha Graham was not difficult. Martha wanted me to do "For Moon" in her *Canticle for Innocent Comedians* (1952). I [had] opened on Broadway in *The King and I,* in 1951. I didn't come out until the second act . . . in Jerome Robbins' "Uncle Tom's Cabin," so Martha put *Canticle* first on her program so I could dance in both productions. I was very impressed with Jerry [Robbins], but he is very hard to work with. Martha and Jerry are both geniuses. I knew that even then.

I began my solo career in 1946. I was not seasoned, but at least I had experience firsthand. Even though it was nothing, at least I did it. That was a very important experience. I was an audition winner at the YMHA that year—that was my first acceptance into the dance world—and I gave a solo concert at least once a year from then on. I choreographed *Tale of Seizure* in 1947, but I did it with Martha in 1948. She had seen [the piece] and wanted to put it on her program. This was the first [time] Martha . . . put some of the choreography of the company members on her program. Merce did his piece, I did mine and Erick did his piece. I had a weird-looking set which I designed myself. Martha needed a set which was a little more elegant than what I had put together: She got Isamu to design a set for me. Isn't that wonderful?

It was very interesting the way Martha worked with a set designer and a composer. With a composer, Martha gave a script; with a set designer, she out-

Courtesy of Yuriko.

Yuriko dancing "For Moon" and Bertram Ross dancing "For Sun" in
Canticle for Innocent Comedians, *1952.*

lined vaguely what she wanted and what she had on her mind, like in *Cave of the Heart*: the serpent, the wire dress, the throne and the garden effect—[the rocks] representing islands.

The way Martha worked [with the dancers]—you can't really say that you yourself choreographed your own role, because Martha would start out [with] something and then kind of leave you alone. Martha would say, "I will be back in 10 minutes. See what you come up with." Then Martha would say, "That's good. But can you do this or can you do that?" Martha was selfish and generous at the same time because it was to her good that each one put their own little something into her choreography. So Martha didn't have to drag it out. Martha would do this with the principal roles. But [for] the chorus, like in *Night Journey* (1947), Martha did everything. She would do a sequence and then say, "Now do it." Martha would do it only once and seven of us women would have to follow. Then Martha would look at it and say, "That is good, Pearl." Then we would all follow Pearl. Then, "That is good, Ethel." Or, "That is good, Yuriko."

I did "They Who Dance Together" in *Dark Meadow* and "The Princess" in *Cave of the Heart*, both in 1946. I had an input into the choreography of my role in *Cave* when I was "The Princess" and Martha was "Medea." Martha explained to me the myth about Medea. It was the same thing with my role of "Iphigenia" in *Clytemnestra* (1958). Martha said, "This is it and this is your music. You are completely different from the other characters because you are very innocent and very young. [Your part] is in Clytemnestra's mind. It is [what] Clytemnestra is [imagining] Iphigenia went through when she was sacrificed by Agamemnon." Martha sat there as "Clytemnestra" thinking, "What an awful thing that I allowed Agamemnon to sacrifice her." She said, "That sacrifice is what turned Clytemnestra against Agamemnon." It was a turning point: Clytemnestra must have suffered, allowing this to happen.

We all chipped in to choreograph *Clytemnestra* for Martha. I had to choreograph my section as "Iphigenia" from Martha's ideas . . . this whole imagination thing. . . . What is in the mind [of Clytemnestra]—if you actually saw it, then you saw it—when you imagine what might have happened to [Iphigenia]? . . . I was on the spearhead and [for the death] I turned over [on it]. The first thing that came to my mind was that this spear is here like from a cloud. In Clytemnestra's mind, Iphigenia is calling through the clouds, "Mother." Finally, she comes through [the clouds]—that is when Clytemnestra sees in her mind

Iphigenia's sacrifice. All of her imagined things [were] Iphigenia's struggle with death.

Eye of Anguish (1950) obviously wasn't important enough for Martha, or dramatic enough for her. I was "Regan." If it [had been] somebody else besides Erick playing "King Lear"—like, say, Bertram Ross—it would have been more dramatic. Already, [by] Martha's *Night Journey,* Erick was not quite "there." Bert was so much better than Erick as "Oedipus" in *Night Journey.*

Right after [the film] *A Dancer's World* (1957), Martha called me. She wanted me to do something and . . . to use Bert [Ross] as my partner. She liked what we did [in the film]. [That was] the way *Embattled Garden* (1958) happened. Glen [Tetley] was the serpent with Matt [Turney]. Bertram Ross partnered me. I was "Eve." The role is very jagged, the whole thing. Martha [had] asked me what kinds of things I wanted to do. Katherine Cornell, who had been visiting Martha backstage, had [once] said, "Yuriko, you are like a willow tree that comes down and never breaks." That was [supposed to be] a compliment—in other words, you are in absolute control. Boring! With human beings—there is a breaking point— there is always a breaking point. [My dancing] was too smooth, too this, too that. So I said to Martha, "I want to conquer awkwardness." That is how "Eve" started.

After "Iphigenia" and "Eve," from 1958 to 1967, I was doing film [and] I was with Martha. [But] Martha was touring and I didn't do any of her new creations then. I can't remember exactly what I was doing. I returned to dance "Helen" in *Cortege of Eagles*[4], in 1967. It was a very, very difficult time for me. . . . There were a lot of internal politics going on. This was just before Ron [Protas] came in, I think. I was in some ways starved, and I felt it was time I left. Fortunately, I received the Guggenheim Fellowship for choreography [in 1967]. That was good because I didn't want to part from Martha with anger.

I came back in the Seventies, after being absent for about seven years, to teach. Of course, I am a very good teacher, as far as the Graham technique is concerned. After teaching . . . I remounted *Dark Meadow.* I worked with the company. I revived dances. The Graham Ensemble started when I gave a course. By then Ron was there. [I gave] a three-week course and at the end I gave a demonstration. It was technique and repertory. At the end of that someone said, "Wouldn't it be nice to get some of these dancers to work in Martha's pieces in a

---

[4] *Cortege of Eagles* was originally performed as *Hecuba.*

second Graham company?" Ron agreed, and said, "Why don't you start it?" After Martha died, I became co-artistic director with Ron of the Graham Company. Ultimately, I resigned because I felt there were philosophical differences between Ron and me in terms of where the Graham Company should be taken in the future. There was no discussion. I decided it was time to leave.

[When I started with Graham], I really didn't think about [my identity]. I was not looking back at what effect Martha had—I was going forward: I choreographed; I got married; I had two children, Susan and Lawrence. There were times when Martha and I didn't get along at all. Somehow or another, there was a time when she didn't trust me. [Then] she [did]. There were things that everybody knew, of course. Everybody knows Martha drank a lot, so she couldn't really control her dancing. But with something like *Clytemnestra* . . . she was just magnificent. No one could duplicate what Martha Graham did, even when she couldn't dance.

ETHEL WINTER

Anthony (

Ethel Winter as "Aphrodite" and Martha Graham as "Phaedra"
in Phaedra, *1962.*

———————◆—●—◆———————

Ethel Winter was born in Wrentham, Massachusetts, on June 18, 1924. She graduated from Vermont's Bennington College, where she studied dance and became a student of Martha Graham.

Winter became a member of the Graham Company in the mid-1940s. From that time she danced a large repertoire of important roles. She has the distinction of having been chosen by Martha Graham to re-create a number of Graham's great, early roles in works such as Salem Shore, Hérodiade, Frontier *and* Night Journey. *She also has been a choreographer. Winter retired from performing in the early 1970s and she was on the faculty of the Graham School until 1993. She teaches at the Juilliard School of Music.*

Ethel Winter lives in New York City and Florida.

———————◆—●—◆———————

I graduated from Bennington College in 1945. I went there specifically because I wanted to dance. Previously, I had studied ballet, classical Spanish and a little Indian dance in Boston. I didn't know what contemporary dance was from beans. Well, I knew what beans were—I came from Boston! I just knew I wanted to dance. My family insisted I go to college, and in those days you really could only choose Bennington or Mills—those were the only places that had dance—so this was a compromise on my part.

Martha Hill and Bill Bales were at Bennington. . . . During the war years the summer school of dance at Bennington didn't take place, so Martha Graham came up with her company for the last month of our school year. It was the month of June. We studied with her, along with Louis Horst. That happened my second, third and fourth year. Somebody from Martha's company couldn't come up my third year so Martha put me into [*Every Soul Is a*] *Circus*. I didn't have that much to do, but I learned my first lesson from Martha. She made me go out and take a bow with her; I felt so very embarrassed because I felt I hadn't done that much. She made me understand that that was a false vanity—the other students wanted to clap because they were proud of me. It's like saying "thank you" when you bow, it isn't an ego trip. It was an interesting lesson to learn.

Martha didn't like to teach that much. I demonstrated for her at the Neighborhood Playhouse, which is where I really learned a lot about her technique. But I think she enjoyed teaching there very much because it was from a motivation. She loved using images. She would get them doing things you wouldn't believe. They didn't have the muscular capacity, perhaps, to do it all the time, but they could do it because of the motivation. Sometimes you get students who are so overly technical they don't know how to make it meaningful. That's not good either. I think Martha got bored with that, and I don't blame her. In those days, we always taught in the school. That's really why Martha had the school: Because we weren't able to perform as much . . . you made your living by teaching. I really enjoy teaching. The younger kids now don't teach that much because there is more performing and rehearsing. Maybe they don't want to teach.

I hadn't set out, necessarily, to be part of Martha's company. I fell into it, so to speak. I knew by that time I wouldn't be a ballet dancer—I'd lost too much time, in a sense. I also found something else in dance that, in terms of communication, was very, very satisfying to me: what Martha Graham was saying in movement. Martha was using movement to communicate on many levels. This was an entirely new concept for me.

Because of World War II and a lack of fuel, Bennington had something called "Winter Period," during January and February, when the students worked. My senior year I was allowed, as part of my dance training, to go on tour for six weeks with Martha and I did a New York season, too. I earned dance credit at school. It's been said that I joined the company in 1946, but I had already learned the repertory before I came down to New York to join the company. When I first went into the company I did Pearl [Lang's] parts in [*Appalachian*] *Spring, Deaths and Entrances, Letter to the World. . . .* Pearl was in one of Agnes de Mille's Broadway shows and couldn't get out. You know, I really don't remember whether *Dark Meadow* came before *Night Journey*. Actually, Martha created *Night Journey*—the Oedipus and Jocasta story—in 1947. I did the "Chorus" in *Night Journey*. We were a smaller company then. . . . Martha created for the whole chorus of girls. That was the beginning of the Greek works. Then came *Cave* [*of the Heart*] (1946), *Errand* [*into the Maze*] (1947) and, later, *Circe* (1963). However, *Dark Meadow* would have been the first piece that was choreographed on me when I first went into the company, in 1946.

Dark Meadow was an interesting development . . . an interesting working process that kind of went where it had to go. As far as I know, Martha had given a script to Chávez—the composer for *Cave of the Heart*—for the Medea legend, but she couldn't make Medea to that music. Martha intended *Dark Meadow* to be very Greek, but it really had a pagan quality, all about the earth and blossoming. There was a beautiful, primitive, ritualistic dance for girls which opened the piece . . . and Noguchi's rocks intensified the dance space beautifully. Very often Noguchi would do something that would send Martha off creating and vice versa. There always was an exchange of ideas. The "Sarabande," of course, became quite well known. Sometimes Martha would take a long time to choreograph and then she would throw everything out. The "Sarabande" was different. We worked one evening and she practically finished it right then. When the dance was first performed it was considered quite unique.

I performed *Salem Shore* and [*El*] *Penitente*. Martha relinquished her role in *Salem Shore* to me in 1948 because I was to do a tour with Erick and Stuart Hodes. You know, I was probably a little naïve: All of a sudden then I was to do *Salem Shore* in New York and that was a little bit of a surprise! It was hard for Martha to relinquish her roles. I had to learn it by myself. She didn't spend any time teaching or coaching the women in her roles when we did do them. You had to do it yourself. You were going to either sink or swim. Personally, I had great help from Eugene Lester, the musical director at the time. But I'm not putting her down for it. I understand: These roles were her creations, her "babies." Looking at it a different way, it meant that she gave you a certain amount of trust. I saw Martha do *Salem Shore* at one rehearsal and from then on I worked on it with the accompanist, Helen Lanfer.

Martha never saw me do "The Bride" in [*Appalachian*] *Spring* until I performed it and she was offstage. But that didn't matter. I had seen Martha perform . . . *Spring* enough to know the depth of it. In some ways I think that was just as well because I had to dig into it and find my own motivations. I wasn't Martha so why try to imitate her? I think in one of the reviews that was one of the things they brought out. All right, it was not Martha, it was a young girl, but the choreography stood. This was something that way back then people questioned. Would this choreography stand with somebody else dancing the role besides Martha Graham? It certainly has been proven again and again that it does. Later on, when I took over "Jocasta" in *Night Journey,* the critics felt I was too human. I will agree with them. The problem with taking over a role from Martha is that when you're performing a role you learn about the role: You're probably learning for the first time what you are really going to do with that part when you're out onstage. There is something about the stage where all the little holes show up. . . . Unfortunately, you're usually reviewed on your first try. Now Martha spends time with the dancers. But sometimes I think she fiddles too much. By that I mean it takes a while to grow in a role. Of course, she has a perfect right to change a phrase for a certain dancer, but if you do it too soon. . . .

I had to take an enforced break from Martha's company because I had gotten tuberculosis. It was one of those things where the doctor, negative as usual, said I would not be able to go back to professional work. I couldn't accept that. I tried to re-join the company in 1950 but it was too soon and I had another breakdown. Of course, they didn't have the medicine they have today. I had to lie flat on my back for over a year . . . so the next time I tried to do it slower. To get started back I thought I would try a Broadway show. I did *Ankles Aweigh* with Tony Charmoli. I needed to see if I could do the demanding rehearsals— that certain amount of money per week didn't hurt, either. I re-joined the company in 1954 when we went on the Asian tour. I did "Joan as Maid" in *Seraphic Dialogue* and I took over the main role in 1955. The Asian tour was an amazing period with Martha's company. We were very enthusiastically received in the Far East. But more than that, Martha was such a poetic speaker that as an ambassador for the arts she was truly brilliant. It was a great privilege to be part of that.

When we returned, Martha settled into working on *Clytemnestra* (1958). Martha enlarged the company for *Clytemnestra.* For her own purposes when she danced these tragedies they were always taken from the female's point of view. She always took the Greek tragedies, say *Agamemnon,* and said let's see it through Clytemnestra's eyes. Or like she did with *Night Journey*—let's see it through Jocasta's eyes. Hippolytus she saw through Phaedra's eyes. Why do it if it were only going to be an exact retelling of the story? Once someone asked why she chose this particular material so consistently. Martha said she felt it to be very current. One picks up the newspaper every day and reads about a jealous wife, a rape, a broken marriage. But these are just ordinary people. By taking the epic stories of kings and queens, of gods and goddesses, one identifies, but since it is larger than life, it can be done very theatrically.

We did read the play. Martha always spoke of revealing the "interior land-scape," and that's exactly what she did. In *Clytemnestra,* she saw the role of Helen of Troy—which was done for me—as a victim of the circumstances, not the instigator.   Already at that time Martha was telling us what qualities she wanted in the dance. . . . You would do a phrase of movement and she would take what she wanted and throw the rest away. In other words, you knew the vocabulary well enough and you could change its coloration to meet a quality that she wanted. Martha wasn't out in the studio doing every single step. We, as company members, had worked for so long with her that we knew both her verbal and dance language.

People say, "Oh I choreographed my own role," but Martha wrote the script and she molded it into shape. We were used the same way Noguchi would use a piece of wood. The sculptor knows what he can do with that kind of wood. Martha molded you that way.

I think with *Clytemnestra* there was a lot of controversy when it was first done because people wanted to think of it like *Night Journey,* which is 25 min-utes long and packed with a lot of dancing. *Clytemnestra* is a total theater expe-rience. There are passages that are not going to knock you out from the danc-ing, but as theater and how things are put together, it is brilliant. So some people were disappointed. I hadn't seen it from the front . . . until much later, and I was very impressed with the beauty of its theatricality. I do wish people wouldn't get so intellectual about dance. They don't care let it just happen—instead, they try to get it all in at one time. You don't get lots of things in one time. You listen to music many times before saying, "Oh, I love that section." Sometimes I think people are too quick to judge dance.

Episodes (1959) was a very interesting experience . . . Bill Carter and Sallie Wilson[1] joined us. . . . Martha gave Paul [Taylor] to Balanchine in exchange. Bill and Sallie are dancers everyone knows. That was about the extent of the inter-change. It was so funny. I was sitting in the audience one evening—we got tickets . . . to all the performances—and I was listening to a couple of people

[1] William Carter (1936-88) and Sallie Wilson (1932-). Principal dancers with both the New York City Bal-let and American Ballet Theater. Carter also performed as a guest artist with Martha Graham's company into the 1970s.

Arnold Eagle.

Ethel Winter as "Helen" in Clytemnestra, *1958.*

talking. Somebody asked the difference between modern dance and ballet and how would someone know between the two. So the other one said, "Oh, they will be in bare feet in modern dance and they will be flexing their feet with just tights on—no costumes." Of course, *Episodes* was completely the opposite. Martha's company were the ones in shoes and full costumes; Balanchine's New York City Ballet [dancers] were in tights, flexing their feet and arms. Somebody must have been very confused!

I loved the chance to be evil. I think it is much harder to be "good" onstage and have an impact than it is to be nasty and evil. Martha didn't really know that I could get evil—except once she did see me get angry. It happened when we were on tour in the Far East, after a performance of *Ardent Song*. I was supposed to be "Dawn." It was one of those performances where . . . everything went wrong. I got off that stage, ripped my costume off, and started stamping on it and cussing violently. I had forgotten we were all in the same dressing room. Martha was right beside me. I thought I was going to get it. I literally stamped on the costume—and it was a mud floor. Martha looked at me and I looked at her. All she said was, "Good girl, Ethel." I thought I was going to get a tongue-lashing, at the very least. I think that is when she knew she would give me a different kind of part. That part was "Aphrodite" in *Phaedra* (1962).

Acrobats of God (1960) wasn't going to be such a comedy when Martha started choreographing it. We were told the first night not to play it for laughs. But it started to come off that way and Martha went with it, so everybody went with it. Martha was already having difficulty by the time she choreographed *Alcestis* (1960). Even with *Acrobats of God*. It is very difficult when you leave performing. A very difficult thing. But it can't be your total life forever. Martha was really suffering. She found the transition to be something she couldn't face.

The last role Martha created for me was "Andromache" in *Cortege of Eagles* (1967). Martha played "Hecuba." Her role was choreographed more from a dramatic point of view. She didn't make herself do maybe some of the physical things she would have done for herself if she had been younger. Maybe it was too intricate. Yet she had this incredible ability to hold the stage. It was at a time that Martha didn't go back to re-work the piece like she did so often—which was a shame, because I think it could have become another great work. It was amazing to see her perform during this time. We dancers were still effected by her charisma and dramatic power, even though some of the public felt that she stayed on the stage a little too long.

Martha's work made so much sense to me. What Martha did was demand everything of you—a wholeness of activity of mind, body and spirit. She made one realize it wasn't just a lot of stunts. The principles of the Graham technique . . . each individual can use depending on what is being communicated. That is what I find so fascinating about her technique. It can be used to say so many things.

Martha wanted us to be individuals but at the same time, when in a group, to be able to dance as one. In my eyes, Martha had tremendous stature as a choreographer. Many of her dancers in turn became choreographers in their own right. The strength of her genius is demonstrated by the fact that her vision so influenced others that they felt they had to rebel and use their imaginations for their own purposes. Most of us working with Martha took courses with Louis Horst, so we knew the *craft*. But to really stay with it, there has to be an unquenchable burning desire, and not everyone has that gift or, perhaps, I should say, burden to bear. The dancers got a lot from Martha, whether they wanted to do something different or not. She laid a solid foundation. That was exciting. Merce [Cunningham] and Erick [Hawkins] found entirely different esthetics. Sophie [Maslow] and Anna [Sokolow] went their way; Paul [Taylor] went another. I did choreograph a little, but it was not a priority.

I did enjoy my years in the company. Martha's works were always a challenge, whether we were creating or re-creating a role. As a dancer, I loved—much like an actress finds her character in the written word—making movement phrases speak. To have been there during Martha's most creative years makes me feel very privileged. It was my choice to leave in the end. I could have gone back, but I didn't want to be in that position again as a dancer—where your life was so devoted to Graham that there was little time for anything else—like making a simple dentist appointment.

The situation now for the company seems very tenuous. So many of the earlier dancers and appointed directors have left because of differences with Mr. Protas, the artistic director appointed by Martha. Consequently, the supervision [of the dancers] cannot help but be less vital. Tapes are a valuable tool, but not everything can be learned from a video. One can see the outline [of the dance] and who goes where, but the heart and soul will be missing. At this moment, I'm the latest to be banned from the Graham studio.

Helen McGehee

Arnold Eag

Helen McGehee dancing "For Water" in Canticle for Innocent Comedians, *1952.*

Helen McGehee was born in Lynchburg, Virginia, in 1921. She graduated Phi Beta Kappa from Randolph-Macon Woman's College with a degree in Greek and Latin. She studied dance there and later with Martha Graham.

McGehee was a member of the Graham Company from the mid-1940s. One of her early leading roles was one of the "Three Remembered Children" in Deaths and Entrances. *She went on to dance in most of the Graham repertoire, creating roles in* Acrobats of God, Clytemnestra *(Electra), and* Phaedra *(Artemis). She designed costumes for Graham's* One More Gaudy Night *and the women's costumes for* Clytemnestra. *McGehee resigned from the Graham Company in 1971.*

McGehee also presented programs of her own choreography and was choreographer for the Ypsilanti Greek Theatre production of Aeschylus' Oresteia. *She retired from performing in the early 1980s and returned to Randolph-Macon Woman's College to establish the Visiting Artists Program in Dance, from which she is now retired.*

McGehee is the author of two books, Dancer *and* To Be A Dancer, *and was married to the artist Umaña (1917-94).*

Helen McGehee lives in Lynchburg, Virginia.

Eleanor Struppa was the head of the Fine Arts Committee at Randolph-Macon Woman's College, [which] was really a very vital institution. Eleanor had studied with Charles [Weidman] and Doris [Humphrey]; she went to the Bennington summer courses and studied with Martha Graham. She was in the first performance of *American Document,* probably one of the "walk arounds." Eleanor had returned to Randolph-Macon as a teacher soon after graduating. My exposure to all these dancers—Hanya Holm, Doris Humphrey, Charles Weidman, Martha Graham—was through her.

Eleanor was so fair she would never choose an artist for anybody. She would just say, "Well, there is this, this, this and this." She was so enthusiastic about all dance. . . . We finally realized that Martha Graham was the one she really was interested in. Eleanor wasn't really teaching Graham technique, but we did all those basic things like contractions, some bounces, some turns, fourth position seated on the floor. . . . I had been fortunate not to have studied with anybody in Lynchburg, where you turned your feet out, learned social dancing and making patterns and carrying roses—things like that. I didn't have to bother with all that. It just never occurred to me that I could dance. When I was probably 10 years old, I read an article about Mary Wigman. I thought that it was wonderful that she could do that. It never occurred to me that I could do it too. When I got to Randolph-Macon I was stunned that I was good at it, that I could do it. It was amazing.

I studied with Martha Graham during my first June course between my junior and senior years. I had seen Hanya Holm during my freshman year. Then I had seen Doris Humphrey and Charles Weidman and I thought, "Oh wonderful," so I wrote to them asking about their summer offerings. I got back this mimeographed thing that didn't make any sense, so I wrote Martha, who sent back a very precise, glamorous thing. For $100 for four weeks they offered two [dance] classes a day, one taught by Ethel Butler, the other with Martha; one class with Louis Horst; and one rehearsal with Nina Fonaroff. It was just fantastic.

I went back the summer after I graduated [in 1942]. Martha had said to me, "You must not get stuck teaching Latin"—I had a degree in it since we didn't get any credit for taking dance. We still had to do all those things in gymnasiums, like swinging on the rings. I got a scholarship because I had taken the June course the previous summer. Ethel and Martha taught every day. There was an 8 o'clock class and a 2 o'clock class. Ethel had been in the company for maybe three years when I first went to New York. I think she moved to Washington around 1945 or 1946.

During those early years—'42, '43, '44, '45—Martha was teaching a lot, and teaching wonderfully—all these images and how you must listen to the movement. Throughout the time I was with Martha, she would choreograph these beautiful sequences and if they didn't fit, she would throw them away. Noth-

ingness would be in their place—nothingness was it. But it was not an emptiness, it was a focus. Martha always said that the steps were the least of it.

I took Pre-Classic and Modern Forms (composition classes) with Louis Horst.
He was a wonderful man. I learned about so many different things from him,
not just music and choreography, but painting and sculpture as well. I think he
had quite a lot to do with Martha's choreographic vision. I think he had a tremendous influence on everybody: modern dance could be considered Louis
Horst's achievement. He had strength of character to tell Martha off when she
needed to be. I remember there were some rehearsals when I first joined the
company—we had gone to Washington for a performance—and Martha was
just blessing everybody out. Louis looked up from the piano and said, "There is
nothing wrong with the girls. It is just you and your dumb partner [Erick
Hawkins]."

Martha Graham was so terrifying when she taught, I couldn't believe it. I just
thought I would do whatever I could do. Martha came up to me, took my arms
and, with those green eyes looking into mine, said, "Do you understand?" I had
not the slightest idea what she was doing but it was magic. I never thought of
departing to study modern dance with anyone else. It was always Martha.

Pretty soon I was demonstrating for Martha. I was still not absolutely sure
of everything. I remember once when I was demonstrating for Martha at the
YMHA . . . that was fun. . . . When we did the back extensions, we used to sit
and then just stretch the leg and bring it in, and stretch it and bring it in. That
particular morning in class Martha decided that the hip should sit on the floor
when the leg came in. Well, I hadn't been there. I had taken the afternoon
class and then gone to demonstrate that night. So I didn't know. Martha kept
saying, "The hip goes down." My hip didn't go down. Martha shouted, "Put it
down!"

Martha herself had some strange kind of ballet training, whatever it was,
along with the Denishawn. She always incorporated some of that into her technique. Once when Dan Wagoner was at rehearsal doing brise volés . . . she
poked her head in the door and said, "Ahh. Volinine beats." She said they were
named after Alexandre Volinine. I didn't know who [that] was. But really
Martha's technique all came out of what she was choreographing. Martha
would say, "Well, I've been working on this. Let's nail it down and teach it." It
was interesting, fascinating. I'm sure she just got bored as hell teaching, as we
all finally do.

One of the first things I did was to rehearse the role of one of the children in *Letter to the World* for a film [that was to be made of it]. Nina Fonaroff was the other child. In 1945 I went on tour doing just the child in *Letter to the World*. On the 1946 tour, I was in *Appalachian Spring* (1944), *Every Soul Is a Circus* (1939) and *Deaths and Entrances* (1943). I got into *Dark Meadow* (1946) in 1948. The first role that Martha created for me [when I] was with the company [was] in *Night Journey* (1947). It was marvelous. I knew exactly what I wanted to do: spend my life dancing *Night Journey*.

Night Journey even works in the film (1960). Although that was another situation where Martha Graham ruined the costume: In the film that is not the costume she was supposed to wear. Martha had stayed up all night and came in with these long things hanging off her costume. So when she does the wonderful "leap dance" there are those things hanging down. She was so bad . . . terrible! During the 1950 tour of England, Bert's costume had copper loops around his buttocks. He was arrested and had to go to court: Bert had been at the beach with his bathing suit all rolled up so he could get a suntan [because] he didn't want to have to wear so much body paint. He told them it was because he had to do a performance of *Night Journey*. He wanted a suntan because the costume didn't cover his butt. Oh, thank you, Bert!

I remember when we were working on *Night Journey*, toward the end of the "wild dance," Martha said, "We've just got to top this." She wanted something parallel to the bed. I just stood up, fell parallel to the bed, and went [down] to the shoulders. That was the invention of the "shoulder-fall." Otherwise [you would have to do] the very difficult "back-fall," where you had to hang there forever [in the air], parallel to the floor. Bob Cohan said he saw Pearl [Lang] in the dressing room later trying to do the shoulder-fall that I had invented.

There were six or seven of us in the chorus including Ethel, me, Yuriko and Joan Skinner. Dorothea Douglas got sick and couldn't do it. Pearl was the leader. Mark Ryder was the Blind Seer. We worked separately—Mark had been working with Martha alone—then we put the whole dance together in the studio at 66 Fifth Avenue. One of the first times we put it together . . . we were arranged in that "sit," waiting for Mark's entrance on the pogo stick. That was fine and he got into position. He did his back-fall, got up to do the turn with the stick and hit everybody in the head with it. We finally figured out what was wrong: Mark was being blind by closing his eyes. Martha was furious and Mark was very stubborn. He insisted that he needed to close his eyes if he was supposed to be blind. Martha became so furious that she stamped out of the room and slammed the door. It split in two, from top to bottom!

I remember when we got to Boston and it came to the final orchestra rehearsal of *Night Journey*—we had miserable room to get dressed in—there on the floor were a million of little pieces of a metronome. Martha had thrown it at Helen Lanfer, the pianist.

Martha gave us the movement for the "Daughters of the Night" in *Night Journey*. If she got stuck for a movement, like the shoulder-fall I did . . . but she did mostly all of the movement. It was exciting—and scary, too—that Martha was having the dancers participate in her choreographic process. You just had to throw yourself into it. Martha Graham did encourage the individual quest. I would say I realized my identity through the act of dancing, the doing of it. I remember after the first performance of *The Archaic Hours* (1969), Martha, who had been watching from the wings, said, "Whatever you may think of the piece, your performance was masterful." I didn't know what to say because I really didn't think too much of the dance. It was a little . . . confused. It was the last dance Martha choreographed for me. All I remember [now] is having to balance on Clive Thompson's and Bob Cohan's very slippery backs. I guess I was the "Moon Goddess." I stood there, waving a coat hanger around, making the moon rise. I never did know what it was about.

I don't remember being amazed at the freedom she gave us. I remember thinking that it all seemed part of the process. You [would] go in to rehearse and Martha would say, "This is your music. What can you do here?" [And] you would do what you had been doing most recently. My movement in *Cortege of Eagles* (1967) came directly out of a duet that I had recently choreographed. *Cortege* was a very good work and I think it works very well on film, too. It is very modern, whereas some of the other pieces don't look so modern on film. The simplicity of Noguchi's set was remarkable. There was just that one curtain that "flies"—you couldn't really lean on it—and the two slabs at right angles. The slabs stood up. They could be twirled, they could be turned over and become tombs.

I was one of the four Marys with Ethel [Winter], Linda [Hodes] and Akiko Kando, and the four men in *Episodes: Part I* (1959). I don't remember it too well. Mainly, I remember we had to put the red dress that Martha was beheaded in on her. Akiko and I couldn't make the snaps meet. . . . We kept pulling and pulling until we finally got it together. Afterwards, we realized that

Arnold Eagle.

Helen McGehee as "Electra," Bertram Ross as "Orestes" and Martha
Graham as "Clytemnestra" in Clytemnestra, 1958.

we had pulled it too far together! Poor Martha, she probably thought she was being squeezed to death. Actually, Martha was in pretty good shape then. *Episodes* was supposed to have been a collaboration with George Balanchine, but Martha couldn't collaborate with anybody. With the company it was different— we were part of her company. . . .

For years we denied that we had done anything [choreographically]. Suddenly, though, we realized that yes, we had done a lot. When you see "Aegithus" do those funny little walks on the side of the foot—those are Paul's. I choreographed most of my "Electra" role. Bert [Ross] may have choreographed most of his part in *Clytemnestra* (1958), but he didn't choreograph the whole dance. Bert talked to Martha constantly about all of the aspects of it; Bert thought so much about it. Maybe that's why he thinks he did choreograph most of the dance, and perhaps Bert had a tremendous influence over the shaping of the dance, not necessarily the choreography, but the shaping of it. But I think *Clytemnestra* was, of course, Martha's. Really, Martha used Bert as a springboard for her own imagination. Martha said it herself, "I steal from the best: Plato, Picasso and Bertram Ross."

Later, Martha let us finish her dances, because they were so bad we had to finish them. Martha was so drunk. We would go to her apartment and beg her to come [to the studio], but she would not come. That began with *One More Gaudy Night* (1961). I think Paul and Ethel were disappointed that it was not going to be an attempt at doing a *Clytemnestra*-like *Antony and Cleopatra*—it was very lightweight and kind of funny. But going to get Martha from her apartment was to no avail.

All during that time, Martha's favorite trick was to finally come to a rehearsal, open the door, scream "one" and leave. The count was "one." She did that to show us that we didn't know what the music was. It had nothing to do with the music, though. She had to make a statement: She was there. Then Martha would either come in to rehearse or go home again and drink some more.

There would be times when we would be working on *Alcestis* (1960) when Martha would say, ". . . and don't forget the mandolin players are right over there. Right there." She was mixing *Alcestis* up with *Acrobats of God* (also 1960). *Alcestis* was not as lightweight as *One More Gaudy Night*. It was more like the play, a celebration of spring. It was a good role for Martha and it was something that I had gotten sort of sick of doing, all those same old things, being a backdrop for everybody. I didn't care much for Martha's *Alcestis,* but I don't care all that much for it as a play, either.

Anybody dealing with a Greek play in terms of movement, dance, has to re-arrange it. You cannot just use the play: All the things the messengers tell you about [in the play] have to happen onstage so the audience knows. It is a very natural kind of rearrangement. The two myths in *Cortege of Eagles,* "Hecuba" and the "Trojan Women," were appropriate, occurring at the same time. By itself, *Alcestis* doesn't stand, and the music was really dismal. Vivian Fine was the only woman Martha had compose for one of her tragedies. Her score was okay as an audible backdrop, but it was almost like doing a dance about the triumph of life in spite of this dreary kind of diddly-sounding music.

I found *Phaedra* (1962) to be more interesting than *Alcestis.* They had a big Congressional fuss over it—it was too erotic to be exported on a State Depart-ment tour. However, it had already been exported. Martha had such wonderful taste—she could do anything because it was never in bad taste. It was uncom-fortable to see Martha flipping her legs up and sliding off the bed and all that, though. I did think that it was kind of silly to be standing there forever-and-ever as the goddess Artemis, but after a while I liked standing there. I liked my breathing to come alive. I stood, with hardly any breathing and my eyes dropped, until Bert got out of his piece and began the worship of Artemis. I really enjoyed just breathing, raising my eyes and then stepping onto his shoulder. It was terrifying because I couldn't look at him—I was just doing it. It turned out to be a nice part. I loved the end, in tiers, getting on top of Bert when they bring in his dead body, like the cover of a sarcophagus. . . .

What was so wonderful about dancing an evening in the theater of Martha Graham was that you could do *Cave of the Heart, Appalachian Spring, Acrobats of God,* and *Seraphic Dialogue*—all totally different works, all totally different char-acters. You could be "Medea" or "The Bride." *Acrobats of God* was Martha's com-ment on her work. I haven't seen *Maple Leaf Rag* (1990), but I understand it is a comment on *Acrobats.* . . . Martha never decided what *Acrobats* was supposed to be. She would say, "I can't decide whether it should be heartbreakingly beautiful or just a riot of laughter." It is funny; Martha's part was funny. It had one of Noguchi's most wonderful sets but, my god, what a pain that set was. Martha did a very inventive solo in *Legend of Judith* (1962): Bert's body was behind a net that the angels held. The net had a hole in it and when the an-gels exited, Bert's head rolled out, as though he had been decapitated. . . . Such

Jaacov Agor.

Helen McGehee with Clive Thompson in Errand into the Maze,
c. 1960s.

theater . . . all those things to do of Martha's—that's why it was so great, and so exciting.

During the Asian tour (1955-56), Martha had done *Errand into the Maze* (1947) and I was in *Ardent Song* (1954). Donnie McKayle had come into *Ardent Song* to go on that tour. His part did not exist until Martha created it—just for him. He was just sort of stuck in there. When I did my solo "Moonset," or "Deep Dark," he was just lying on the ground whenever they fit it in. It was a wonderful part that really came out of me. Ethel danced with blue streamers— that was originally Pearl—and she looked like Loie Fuller. Yuriko was the "New Moon," or "Early Moon." She wore a kind of transparent jersey and did a dance with a shell. I came in the middle. Pearl was "Dawn." Then came the group sections. It really was a very beautiful dance, but they never picked it up again after the Asian tour.

Then, in 1959, I did *Errand* . . . I loved doing it. That was a marvelous role. Martha taught it to me. It was her way of getting back into it herself. She was very giving of all of her images, all of her help and advice, in rehearsals. It was a beautiful experience. I don't think Martha was thinking in terms of relinquishing the role . . . but I don't believe she ever did it again. She was completely different about it than she was with "Medea" but, you see, it was a lot earlier.

People ask, "What was your favorite role?" I can't say. I didn't feel comfortable as "Medea" in *Cave of the Heart* (1946) because Martha didn't teach it to me. [It was] around 1965 when I first did "Medea." Yuriko was to do *Primitive Mysteries* (1931), Ethel was to do *Appalachian Spring,* and I was to do *Cave.* . . . I was determined to do it. I reconstructed the role from Martha's notes, which she did let me see, and with very generous help from Bob [Cohan], Bert, Yuriko and Eugene Lester, the rehearsal pianist; there was no film of it. Martha never took a look at it to see how it was going. Finally it was time for dress rehearsal. We always reversed the order of the program for dress rehearsal because it saved money. The last dance on the program was done first, then the middle dance and then [the opening dance]. *Cave,* which was to open the performance, was the last dance to have a rehearsal.

I saw Martha go out front to watch. There was nothing I could do except . . . perform what I had rehearsed. The curtain was at 8:30 p.m. Around 6:30 p.m. Martha called me into the dressing room. Now, if she was calling me in to say that I should do this, that or the other, it was too late to change anything. I didn't know what it was [she was going to say], but I was going to dance "Medea." But Martha shocked me. She said, "That was wonderful." I cried.

"The Bride" in *Spring* had been relinquished to so many people before me, but it was nice to do a different kind of role. I was never too pleased to be a goddess: I'd rather be a human being. I was "The Warrior" in *Seraphic Dialogue* (1955). The first time I was in it, it didn't make any sense to me. The original version of *Seraphic Dialogue* had been done as a solo, *The Triumph of St. Joan* (1951). When Martha expanded it for the company, I was cast as "The Warrior." I was just a warrior fighting [with] the air: there were no images other than stabbing and dueling. I felt like I was this small. I said, "I'm not doing this well—I can't really do this." So Mary [Hinkson] did it.

I went back to doing "The Warrior" on the Asian tour. I am "The Warrior" in the film also. It hadn't been working out the way Martha had hoped and it became necessary to take out one of the dancers. Martha asked me if I would try it again and I said of course. She re-did the role with St. Michael—and then it made all the sense in the world: All the fighting images fell into place and the dance had a continuous, logical sequence of images. "The Warrior" was valid as a small woman inspired by St. Michael to take up the sword. The whole thing was that Martha put Bert into it as "St. Michael"; it made sense by his urging "The Warrior" on and her wanting to, but not being able to, then finally taking the sword and winning. I wouldn't have minded doing the other roles in *Seraphic Dialogue,* but I loved "The Warrior": It is a triumph to have gotten over that inadequacy of being too small!

Yuriko called me when they were going to revive *Canticle* [*for Innocent Comedians*] (1952) recently. It didn't do that well [originally] and had been put off. It had been out of the rep for a long, long time. The dance died partly because of the music. The vocal, which was later changed to a violin, had no lead-in. It was very hard for the performer—he couldn't get his pitch. It was a beautiful dance, though—a celebration of the world. I was "Water" and "Stars" with Bob Cohan. Dancing with him was marvelous, wonderful! "For Stars" happened because while the music was composed with themes of water and of wind, Martha had sense enough to say, "No, you're stars." So, Yuriko asked, "How did you get in?" They didn't care what the dance was—it was the "magic" of how you got in and got off [the stage].

It seems to me that *Diversion of Angels* (1948) has changed—just judging from what I saw on television. It is the quality that has been distorted. I am sure, basically, that all of the movement is there, although what they did is not what I did. All of the women seem to be the same now. I was the "Girl in Yellow"; she was young, wild and uncatchable. What is so disappointing is the "Girl in Red." She, as her first entrance, is supposed to do the tilt across the stage, right after the "Girl in White" sits. After she got all the way across the stage, one of the men put his arm around her. On a chord she used to contract, and disappear from under his arm, leaving him with nothing. On the next chord, he would turn and see the "Girl in Yellow." Now, he puts his arm across, then [retracts it] on the chord, as though he has touched a hot stove, and [they've] added three turns to his movement. It is totally different—there are so many little meanings that are gone. There is no sense of loss. I said to myself, the last time I saw it, "Why did I used to love this dance?"

During the 1950 tour to Paris and London we—Bert, Stuart, Bob, Pearl, Natanya, Ethel and me—had the funniest costumes for *Angels*. [The women's] were chiffon, with long sleeves that were gathered and hung straight to the floor. Every time you bent in any direction you stepped on everything. If you tried to bend the other way, or just to stand up straight, you would hear rip, rip, rip. Finally we had to have gold harnesses to pull them together. The men had the saddest-looking costumes you have ever seen: union suits cut off at the elbows and at the knee—not below the knee, or above the knee—at the knee, so it all sort of frayed out. They had to have some green tape sewed onto everything.

Martha made up things to say about the 1950 tour, like "I want to show Europe Erick Hawkins." Erick and Martha were the only ones that got any notice at all. They had wonderful reviews, but that tour was one big mess.

We were really terrible about blaming Erick. We fell for Martha's manipulation—we *fell* for it. I have figured it out in the years since I've left: Martha was able to make other people bear the blame for all her wickedness. I really have to admire Erick. What a horrible time he had at that point, and he has really done such wonderful things. The terrible thing about Erick's time in our company was that he was so terribly resented, whatever [the reason] was.

We knew Martha was in love with Erick, but I really think he loved her very, very much. Louis Horst was jealous of Erick's relationship with Martha, too. Martha couldn't love anyone, really. As a matter of fact, Craig Barton [a Graham Company board member] said that to Umaña [Ms. McGehee's husband]. We were in Zurich, waiting for the train to go to Vienna. This was the first time we had taken a European train that was an open car, not compartments, and Martha was this beast glaring at us. We had had a meeting with Gertrude Macy [the producer] about a little bit of money we felt we needed, or were due. Martha was furious. Before we got on the train, Umaña came up and said good morning to Martha. She barely answered, but she managed to say good morning back. . . . He went over to Craig and said, "What is the matter with Martha? Why is she so upset?" Craig said, "Martha's trouble is that she can't love.""But why? Everybody loves her so much, and she knows it is true." But she can't love anybody. Erick certainly felt that. He was perfect for Martha. As Umaña once said at dinner, "Perhaps you did not love him enough." Martha said, "Perhaps." Then we dropped it.

The turning point at Graham had come at the time of that review of John Martin's, which was very telling. He had written praising Martha's achievement of having created a company in her own image—individuals of great range and passion. I remember Geordie [Martha Graham's sister] came and said, "You are so wonderful —all you women are so gorgeous. And the review was just heaven." Uh-oh. Martha definitely became jealous of her own creation. As Martha could move less and less, she just couldn't stand it. She wasn't thinking straight.

After that Ethel and I did not want to go on a tour. It was a strange season in Mexico. They figured they had to have perhaps one of us go. I said I would go if I could have *Cave* or *Dancing—Ground* (1967) to perform. They decided they would do *Dancing—Ground. Dancing—Ground* was nice, and it was performed to live music. Bob Powell was with Takako [Asakawa], I ended up with Dudley Williams and there was all this dancing in between. All of Martha's works are like rituals. It was a wonderful title, *Dancing—Ground.* This was when Martha had done *A Time of Snow* (1968), which was a terrible piece, for herself, and the company was being torn apart—the company that had been working together for so long to create itself—and the work had begun to change. It was probably about seven years after the John Martin review and in the meantime a lot of people had gone.

There was a party before we left for Mexico. By then, I was back in the company and was going to go to Mexico, so I had to go to the party. I was back for a few years. Some people felt I was being difficult by demanding to perform *Dancing—Ground* because it had live music and in that case, Martha would have to dance to taped music. Well, I was in one room, and the people who didn't approve of my behavior went into the other room. You could see who hadn't become involved in the "plot." One by one, they would come out and talk to me. That was finally the end for me.

Ethel had been out at that party—she really used a lot of language with Martha! After I had left, Ethel came back. She did, I think, some performances of *Spring*. I don't know, really, because I just cut myself off from all of it. I had gotten tired of what was going on in dance, so I didn't really go that much. I saw some things. After I left the company in 1971, I didn't look at any of Graham's things.

I had a really strange interview with Martha before I resigned. I didn't know I was going to have it; I had gone to 63rd Street to teach. They said to me, "Somebody will teach your class. Go and see Martha. She wants to see you." We had this long discussion about my going on tour. She said, "There is no reason why you should go on the tour. All the reviews are in, and you have wonderful reviews." I said, "I'm not interested in the reviews. I want to dance. I want to dance the performance." This happened only a few months after she had stopped dancing, and she was being difficult with me. I think Martha had forgotten that she ever felt that way herself. It was then that I made up my mind to leave, but I didn't tell her.

At any rate, it was horribly nasty of Martha Graham. There was a very strange thing which I have never fathomed. At one point she said, "Is the machine working?" I said, "What machine?" She said, "Is the recorder working?" I said, "I don't know. I don't know where it is. I have no idea. You would have to tell me." I didn't see anything. She just asked, "Is it working?" Whether she wanted to frighten me or what, I don't know. After that, I went back to the studio. Norma [the registrar] had put up the teaching schedule. I said, "Norma, this won't do. You'll have to take me out. I'm not teaching." That was the end [of that]. The next day or so, I got a letter. I sat down and I wrote a response and I have never been back to the Martha Graham School.

Not everyone knew Martha couldn't love. . . . I think Bert was terribly disillusioned. I think he realizes now that that is what it was. He was really devastated when he had to leave, but circumstances were bad for everybody. It just depended upon whether you could take it or not. I have tenacity, but only in terms of myself, not manipulating, not maneuvering, other people.

Martha couldn't realize that because she had become so successful, it had become even more difficult for us to go out and do anything on our own. She wanted it to be difficult for all of us because it had been so difficult for her.

ROBERT COHAN

Carl Van Vechten.

Robert Cohan as "For Wind" in Canticle for Innocent Comedians, *1952.*

Robert Cohan was born in New York City in 1925. He studied with Martha Graham and joined her company in 1946, dancing a large repertoire that included creations in Canticle for Innocent Comedians, Diversion of Angels, The Witch of Endor, Cortege of Eagles *and* A Time of Snow. *He had leading roles in the Broadway musicals* Shangri-La *and* Can-Can, *and worked with Jack Cole in Havana.*

Cohan formed his own group and choreographed many dances, often performing with Matt Turney as his partner. He left the Graham Company in the early Seventies to direct the London Contemporary Dance Theatre, from which he retired in 1989.

Robert Cohan lives in London and the South of France.

I went to the Martha Graham Studio because of this fabulous accident. A friend from the Army days had a friend named Diane Meredith who was coming from Los Angeles to study with Martha Graham. She was the one who actually introduced me to Martha's name. It turned out I could only do two classes a week, and the minimum was three. But I had a job and I couldn't make it to the studio in time. The studio said they would waive the three times a week for me and I took the first class. . . . Right at the beginning of that class I had that electric revelation that one is supposed to have when they know this is what one is going to do for one's life. It was a fantastic, spiritual marriage for me: This was real motivation with real meaning, this is what I was going to spend my life doing.

I could only cope with my own odyssey because I was having such an experience myself. I don't really remember the other people . . . Donnie McKayle was around, Erick Hawkins was teaching—Bert Ross was a bit later—Stuart [Hodes] was around—Cunningham must have still been there when I first started. The company were performing. That was in May or April, and I took about six or eight classes and quit my job. I started to take class every night. Then there was a June course and I went into that in the advanced class. By then my parents thought there was something seriously wrong. They couldn't understand how I gave up this very good job that I had. Soon after, I left home. By the end of the June course Martha came by me and slapped me on the back, saying, "Work hard all summer, boy, because I want you in the company in the fall." That was it. I killed myself all summer.

I learned very, very fast. There was no shortcut. I was 21 when I came to Martha and I didn't do anything else. I was in the studio all day. I couldn't even walk home, but by the end of three months I was dancing. I remember saying to Martha, "I can't go on the stage. I don't know how to dance." She said, "Darling, there is only one place you learn how to dance and that is on the stage."

Martha was a magic teacher. When Martha taught, everything was right. The other classes were really trying to analyze what Martha had done in her class. We were codifying what she had done previously. We would make it work. We would practice to make it better when we took her class. It wasn't like now, where everybody [teaches] their own thing. Erick taught his own thing, to a certain extent; Erick had his own principles about soft tushes, Zen, relaxation and things like that. Martha was just the opposite. Everything was hard, like steel. We really practiced Martha's technique in the other classes, and then did it for her in her classes.

In that first year we never went into standing fifth or fourth position. We were only working in first or second position. Mostly we would work in parallel position. Martha was very upset that some of the kids were studying ballet. Martha had really fought against that because she felt it was unnatural to the language that she was trying to develop at that time. She would say, "I'm not going to teach those things because I don't have time for that. If you want them, then study somewhere else." But it bothered her that people were going someplace else to study ballet. I even had to study ballet because I had to support myself, and the only way was on the GI Bill. Martha Graham's school was not approved, but ballet was. I signed up at a ballet school and that allowed me to get my $65.00 a month on which I lived. For me, there was no comparison. I didn't want to study the ballet. I found the people teaching a ballet style totally false and artificial. I had a terrible fight about it with myself, but Martha, soon after, would bring in fourth position and fifth position to her technique. I remember when we first did fourth-position pliés and fifth-position pliés with Martha. It was actually very exciting because it was a [rediscovery]: She had a whole different way of approaching it—with the spiral of the body—and the bodies emerging from this bas-relief of one and two dimensions into three, four and five dimensions. It was the body emerging into walking out of its archaic past. It was incredibly exciting. I mean, one never got excited doing fourth position in ballet class. Martha rediscovered that in those early years, 1946-47, when I was first there.

I don't know how I got through that first tour with Martha, dancing and partnering Pearl Lang, May O'Donnell and Martha—walking with Martha, and having her slap me on the back because I was off the beat in *Deaths and Entrances.* I was carrying the precious body of Martha Graham around the stage.

Martha was able to be everything for you: man, woman, director. She could initiate any movement she gave you as a man. For instance, the men's movements in *Letter [to the World]*: She used to do them and she looked more male than any of us—stronger, more masculine, the whole carriage of her body and the way she attacked the movement, the speed and completeness of her movement. The statement was utterly clear—so you would try to imitate Martha always. Erick had a beautiful technique, and was very clear and good, and one did try to be as clear as him. Mark Ryder had a very good jump and jumped higher than everyone else. So everyone tried to jump as high as him. Martha was very good in those days in bringing out your own personality and making you feel committed personally to her work. That brought out the best in you. One wanted to please Martha and this image. But one couldn't please Martha, ever. If you ever got what she was doing, Martha would move on to the next thing.

Martha was a very strong lady. If you went into a relationship with her like Erick did there were no holds barred. I think Erick wanted to have his own life aside from his life with Martha. . . . Of course Martha didn't want that. She wanted it to be total as well. That is the way Martha wanted everything.

Martha's "Jocasta," in *Night Journey* (1947), where she is the mother, lover and Queen—that came about more out of Martha's relationship with Erick than it did out of her relationship to men. I think that was very specific. It was also a very good vehicle for her. Martha was looking for women heroines to hang her dances on and that was a very apt one at the time. She also did "Medea"

Arnold Eagle.

Robert Cohan and Martha Graham in Letter to the World,
c. late-forties.

at that point, and she is not a mother at all. *Errand [into the Maze]* (1947) was choreographed the year I came into the company. The technique was Martha's, so of course she knew what she was doing, but at the same time she was discovering the technique. So, in a way, she didn't know what she was doing.

Diversion of Angels (1948) was the best thing that happened for all of us at Graham that year. It was created at New London, Connecticut. Each of the dancers performed something special: Pearl Lang, Helen McGehee, Mark Ryder, Stuart Hodes and myself.

Eye of Anguish (1950) was tailor-made for Erick. Unfortunately, Martha should have done it herself, because when she showed Erick what to do she was an extraordinary "Lear." Incredible! I was very upset at one point that she didn't keep it in the rep and do it herself. You had to have someone like Martha or Erick. When Erick left there was no way you could repeat the piece. It had fascinating elements in it which Martha used later, especially the dance in the stretched fabric around the throne. It was something Martha would turn to later, using three women. There were other episodes that she used much, much later in other places. Some of the material she found for "Lear" himself, the character, she used herself in other pieces. [But] it wasn't the kind of dance that could last.

Canticle [For Innocent Comedians] (1952) had the problem of the set, which was enormous to carry around. It also had the problem of not having a satisfactory score. The dance, I thought, was very good, but it was done to an inept score and then they tried to redo the score many times and it just never jelled. *Canticle* was also a very good dance for the company when she choreographed it. It gave everybody a solo—everybody had something special to do. . . . Everybody needed that special attention at that time. It wasn't memorable as a full work but there were memorable solos in it: Bert's solo for the sun, Yuriko's solo for the moon—they were fantastic, by any terms.

After Erick had left, Martha had to work out her life and her life in dance with Bert, Stuart and myself. We were the three men who stuck by her and stayed with her. Martha was living her life out through us. We were three different aspects of men for her. Martha decided to build *Voyage* (1953) on this idea, actually. We spent a lot of time working in the studio on this dance. It was not what actually came out of the dance in the end. It was working out the drama for Martha. It was a strange piece. Every rehearsal was fascinating—what you would discover and how the three of us—Bert, Stuart and me—re-

Arnold Eagle.

Robert Cohan as "The Seer" and Martha Graham as "Jocasta" in Night
Journey, *c. early 1950s.*

lated as men with each other. We were very, very close, Bert, Stuart and I. We were together more than we were with our own personal friends. We were together all the time, and with Martha. We had to play it all very carefully. There were carefully set rules. We each had our own territory and we had to respect that with each other and we still had to compete with each other. The experience was incredible. It went on for almost two years.

We all finished *Ardent Song* (1954) for Martha, but Martha would think she finished choreographing it [herself]. Martha choreographed sometimes by giving you the setting—she has given you all the movement language—she gives you the music, she gives you the idea and then goes away. What is the difference if she goes away or sits in the room?

With *Ardent Song* Martha just ran out of time. She worked really hard on it. The piece was too massive for the time she gave herself to choreograph it. We were exhausted. We were going to London and had been rehearsing for months, or at least it seemed for months. We were so tired we couldn't stand up. [A] vote [was put] to the company: [Did] we want to go to London by boat or by plane? We thought if we [went] by plane, we [would] rehearse up to the day we [left], and we would get there and start rehearsing again, so we said, "Let's go by boat and we will have five days on the sea with nothing to do." We all voted for the boat, which we knew Martha wanted anyway. The moment we left New York Harbor on the *Queen Elizabeth,* Martha turned green, and she lay in a deck chair for five days. We were running all over the boat having a ball, drinking and partying nonstop. We got off at Southampton and Martha walked straight off and into rehearsal. The rest of us were so sick we could hardly move. For the next five days she killed us. We were lining up for injections of antibiotics and vitamins because we had all got the flu. We were all dizzy and throwing up. Martha was in great shape from her deck chair—she [had] had a rest. Anyway, she tried to finish the piece, but we had so much repertory to show London that we were coming to rehearsal at 10 o'clock at night, after the show had finished. We would rehearse the next program after we had changed out of our costumes.

What happened was that [the dance] wasn't that formed. She had most of it done, but there were huge holes in it. We did this run-through; we all agreed we would not stop dancing—we would fill up the holes. The music played and we did the dance all the way through. Martha came back afterwards and she said, "Well, darlings, that was wonderful. Whatever you did tonight, do it again

Cris Alex

Robert Cohan as "Mad Tom" and Pearl Lang as "Cordelia" in Eye of Anguish, *1950.*

tomorrow night." And it went on and just stayed that way.

Martha did get even with me once for having left her during the Fifties. In 1961, Paul Taylor, who had taken several of the parts I had done, was in some kind of argument with Martha's management, and he was going to leave on short notice. I got a phone call at my studio in Boston: Would I come down and replace Paul at once, tonight, in *Phaedra* (1962) as "Theseus"? I said, "Sure, why not?" And Martha tortured the both of us. The whole company was sitting on the side, watching this excruciating experience where Paul had to teach me his part in front of everybody, with Martha directing the rehearsal for three or four hours. Paul and I knew it wasn't going to happen, but I had to learn the whole dance anyway. Martha was getting her own back on both of us. We went through it and I went back up to Boston and that was the end of it. But then Paul did leave and I came back a year later.

Martha always said she choreographed the dances so she would have something to dance. Older women lusting after young men is true to life, like Graham performed in *Phaedra*. People don't like to see that but it is very true to life. Martha wasn't interested in doing dances for other people. . . . On the other hand, she would say, "I love to create work for the new young dancers." But she didn't, really. She wanted to do dances for herself. It was very hard for her to give up dancing or for her to relinquish her roles to other women.

I was in *Legend of Judith* (1962) and then Bert and I became co-artistic directors of the company. Both *The Lady of the House of Sleep* (1968) and *The Archaic Hours* (1969) were more or less Martha carrying on. There was one other dance Martha choreographed, *A Time of Snow* (1968), for me, Bert and herself. That was a fabulous role. That was Flaubert.

Martha wasn't a matriarch. Nobody knew how old she was. I figure now she must have been in her 50s when I first joined the company, but I thought she was in her 30s. She looked magnificent. She was still jumping. She could do a 180-degree split leap. Her body was amazing. She was an extraordinary woman. One had to submit to Martha's idea entirely. If you submit to that idea—not [to] her—and use that as the model, then that is the way you live your life. You either find it satisfying or not. It is true you have to work out your involvement with Martha. But it was easier as a man than it was for the women. The women were in competition with Martha—we weren't.

Martha challenged you to be her equal. I don't think there is any other way to say it. If you did it, fine, and if you didn't do it, you failed. If you failed then she really couldn't be involved. I think that is where a lot of people got hurt. There was no sympathy. Martha couldn't afford that failure or that sympathy. If you fail, go away. That is why when you were in the company Martha would die for you. She would lay down her life for you and support you in every way. The moment you left the company you were gone. You were no longer a part of her active life. You might stay friends, and see her from time to time and have nice chats, and all that. [But] it was not important to her. It couldn't be, because she lived her life on her sleeve. Her life was visual. It was the people she was involved with, and you have to accept that. You can't expect from Martha—and it sounds very unselfish—involvement with your life other than a casual one. Yes, if you were successful, I am sure she enjoyed it briefly. I am sure she thought about us all personally. She did give advice once in a while. But that had nothing to do with her life, which was an artistic life. She had to live her drama out with the people who were offering themselves as parts of her drama.

Martha certainly could lose her temper, and when Martha lost her temper it was really violent. Really violent. You would imagine afterwards that you saw sheet lightning go through the room. You actually saw this blue-white light thing shooting across the room. I've never known anyone [able] to do that except Martha. When she got angry, she got angry. And she always knew exactly the right word to say. It [could be] something as simple as "idiot"—you were "an absolute idiot." How could you disappoint her so?

It was hard for the women with Martha. She was still trying to out-dance them even when she was older. Most of the time she was able to create an illusion that worked. The good performances were so good that they were worth the half-bad. Unfortunately, when you were with her all the time, dancing all the time, you had half-good and half-bad performances. But if somebody came to see the show and saw the bad one and didn't see the good one, how do you rationalize that? The only way was to tell her to stop [dancing]. But at that point if Martha stopped, the company would stop—that would be the end. We felt we had to keep going in order to keep the company going and gradually she would stop, which eventually did happen. It just took an agonizingly long time.

There are two different aspects . . . one is in the very beginning, the other is what she became later. When I joined, the company was still relatively unknown. Martha was known as a great artist by a small group of people. We could barely play one week in New York. We only did one-night stands everywhere else. Over the next 10 or 15 or 20 years, she became accepted as the great dance artist that she was. As she got more successful, she was getting older and she became more matriarchal. I don't . . . think that what Martha did was uncalled-for at all. Martha was never tyrannical for the sake of power. I don't think Martha did anything that she didn't normally do; Martha was being herself and one had to accept that. . . . I remember once that somebody, a dancer who Bert Ross and I wanted to join the company, was available and there was an opening for a man. Martha wasn't sure. We convinced Martha finally and he came in the company. We thought it was right for him, for about two or three weeks. [Then] one day we were in rehearsals and he said, "I can't take it anymore." We said, "Of course it is hard because she is making great demands on you. Stick with it and try." We kept encouraging him. Finally, he went to Martha and talked to her. Martha came to us and said, "He has decided to leave." We said, "It is too bad because he was doing so well." Bert said, "What did he say?" Martha responded, "He couldn't get that personally involved in my choreography." In absolute disbelief she said, "What other way is there?" She couldn't understand how someone couldn't get personally involved in their art form. That is all there was for Martha.

For Martha it was very clear. She didn't go home and take care of the children at 6 o'clock. She didn't go home and cook and have dinners. She didn't have what we call a personal life, as opposed to an artistic life. For her, it was one life. How else does one live?

Martha wasn't a mother. Martha wanted to be a lover. You always had the feeling Martha was extremely feminine, and yet very strong. I know she became the matriarch later, but she was never one to me. I know there is a confusion between mother and lover, but I never felt that.

I felt I was cheating when I took over the position in London as director of the London Contemporary Dance Theatre. We were all together in trying to keep the Graham Company going. To come here [to London] and start something else and abandon that was in a sense cheating. On the other hand, there were all those people there—Bert, Mary, Ethel, Helen and Matt—who could keep it going, whereas here, there was nobody. I felt it was important to start proselytizing the Graham technique in Europe. Martha did too. I actually said to Martha—away from Robin [Howard], who wanted me very much to come [to London] and . . . was pushing Martha—"If there [is] the slightest doubt in your mind then I [won't] go. I was very happy dancing with you. I would only go if you thought that I should go, from your point of view." Not to worry about me because I could do either. "I really would like to stay and keep dancing with the company." Martha said she thought it was very important that her technique be taught in London, that her technique was going to be taught anyway, and she would rather that I be there teaching the technique properly. So I said yes.

I think Martha was disappointed when I left her for the first time in the Fifties. It was a shock to me that I had left, actually, because I hadn't planned to leave. I was furious. I was very angry by the way the company was being treated by her managers. I didn't think she knew that they were actually keeping us from performing. We ended up rehearsing for one and a half years [and giving] no performances. Somebody overheard a conversation saying we weren't going to open in New York that year, that we weren't going to open until the first of the next year. The excuse was [that] Stuart Hodes was not going to be there, he was going to be on the West Coast. Meanwhile we were rehearsing for what we thought was going to be our opening very soon. . . . We had already replaced Stuart so we could move this opening to September. We had a company meeting immediately, and we decided this had to be brought up to Martha. Martha defended the management, which she had to do. I was furious. She and I yelled at each other for one hour. The management wasn't treating us badly; they just weren't telling the truth. I don't know why they did what they did. Martha and I shouted at each other and then kissed and made up at the end of it. She said, "I'm a tiger and I love to use my claws." And I said, "I know. But I have claws, too. It is hard when we get together like that." She said not to worry, and we kissed, and I left her house. I went home and I suddenly thought, "I don't have to go back there. I'm really finished. I have no ill will about it [but I] just don't want to be involved with those people who are running my dancing life." I had no anger for Martha. It was quite the opposite. I wanted to be with her, but I was really angry with the management. So I sent her a letter.

And I never thought of it as a revolt against Martha. When I left Martha the second time, in the Seventies after I had come back to dance with her in the Sixties, I came here to London with her blessing. Martha was our artistic adviser for the first five years. To make the rule that all the dancers have to come from the school was fine as long as we were doing her dances because you could teach the Graham technique, develop the dancers to a high pitch and the school could be responsible for producing people who are capable [of] going into the company for years. What changed everything here [was] that we wanted to develop choreographers of our own. . . . We decided we would not have works brought in from repertoires in the States. There was no point in having a British company if you were doing the works of American choreographers. The moment we decided to develop British choreographers it meant that the technique would have to change—and it meant that the company's house style would have to change; all of these people would have different ideas on which way the technique of the company should grow and go. And that is what affected me a lot. That is what caused the big changes in the technique and style of the London Contemporary Dance Theatre.

I [first] went on tour [in] October 1946, and I stopped July 10, 1989. I think that is enough touring. Besides creating work, I became interested in teaching methods and how you can shorten the teaching time—how you can create an artist and how you can save time. My teaching has reduced so much of the Graham technique that it is almost classical. But if you know modern technique it is Graham. I've taken only the functional aspects of the Graham technique, not the emotional aspects or spiritual theory of Martha.

Martha was a fantastic, articulate mover. She had absolute total direction. So clear. So vivid. Everything she did was alive. You never felt you were learning with her—you were being with her. It was totally different. It wasn't getting a good workout—it was a magic, spectacular artistic experience.

THE
1950's

Arnold Eagle.

Martha Graham as "Jocasta" and Bertram Ross as "Oedipus"
in Night Journey, *c. early 1950s.*

BERTRAM ROSS

Arnold Eagle.

Bertram Ross dancing "For Sun" in Canticle for Innocent
Comedians, *1952.*

Bertram Ross was born in Brooklyn, New York, on November 14, 1920. During the late Forties, Ross danced with the Dudley, Maslow, Bales Trio and choreographed his own concerts at the Humphrey-Weidman Studio and at Manhattan's 92nd Street Y.

Ross was a member of the Martha Graham Company from 1950 to 1973. He became its leading male dancer and danced almost all of the principal male roles, usually as Martha Graham's partner. He taught at the Graham School, the Neighborhood Playhouse, the Alvin Ailey School, the Juilliard School and Ballet Hispanico. In the late Sixties, while Martha Graham was ill, Ross and Bob Cohan served as co-artistic directors of the Martha Graham Company. Upon Cohan's departure for London to become the director of the London Contemporary Dance Theatre, Ross served as co-artistic director with Mary Hinkson. He resigned in 1973.

Ross teaches modern dance at the Mary Anthony Studio in New York and performs a cabaret act worldwide with his companion John Wallowitch.

Bertram Ross lives in New York City.

I was so moved by Martha Graham I couldn't believe it. I thought I was the only one who saw that the feelings I had inside—feelings of loneliness or feelings of anything that you could never put into words—Martha was making it all by what her body was doing. I could feel those things. I never saw dance like that, so I ran all the way home. But I was all alone. I couldn't tell anybody. That was the most exciting revelation . . . the first time I saw Martha Graham. *Letter to the World* was on that program. I went two nights. They got the performance so that Elizabeth Sprague Coolidge could come and see what Martha was doing choreographically. It was Martha's audition for her [and she] ended up producing the Graham-Noguchi trilogy of 1944: *Appalachian Spring, Imagined*

Wing and *Hérodiade*. That was the best I've ever seen of *Letter to the World* because it was done in a park overlooking a lagoon, and all the trees were full, and the summer house was up there on a hill. There was a gazebo and a bench. It was unbelievable. I even remember the stars that particular evening.

When I was a child, Martha was part of a series at the Brooklyn Academy of Music, and my father wouldn't let me go to see her because I had a cold. My mother, when she came home, said, "Well it was a good thing you didn't go, you being a sensitive boy, because the audience laughed at her. You would have been sick." Then, years later (before I joined Martha's company), I saw Martha and I wrote to my mother, "No wonder they laughed at her. She is very funny." I mean, she did *Every Soul Is a Circus, Punch and the Judy*—that was hysterical. Erick and Merce were still with her then. Merce did "Pegasus" in *Punch and the Judy*. He would be Martha's flights of fancy. I still remember the movement. Martha would sit on his back leg and they would ride and ride. And jumping— they flew. *Every Soul Is a Circus* and *Deaths and Entrances* are very similar. One happens to be serious. I mean a tragedy, or heavy and dark. The other is very light. But it is still that battle that is going on between the "Poetic Beloved" and the "Dark Beloved." I guess sexuality and spirituality.

When I went to study at the Graham studio I didn't know that they were looking for a male dancer for the company. In fact, I was insulted that they would think that I came there because I wanted to be in the company. That was not pure thought. That was pushing myself. I was going to work on my own. I wanted to study dancing [in order] to make up my dances with my own costume designs and my own set designs. I wanted it all to come out of one mind—mine. I thought that would be wonderful. I got an interviewer for the Army that was very sensitive and wise. He understood the connection between modern dancing and modern painting and modern sculpture. He said yes, I could study both on the GI Bill of Rights, and I got my classes for nothing. I had the Art Students League in the morning and Martha in the afternoon. Then the summer course came, and Doug Watson, the actor, who had originally been with Martha, came from the Neighborhood Playhouse and he said, "Are you in the company?" I thought, "How dare you? I didn't come to do that. How impure." He said, "Well, you're perfect for Martha. You're tall, dark and handsome."

When I came to Martha, Merce had gone. Erick was still there. In fact, Erick was my first teacher. Erick told us to keep our buttocks soft. I was too terrified, for some reason, to see Martha. Somebody said, "Why don't you go and talk to them and see if you should study dancing." I just thought they came from some rarefied atmosphere—they wouldn't live in New York City. But they danced on Bennington lawns. And I brought a lot of friends with me when I came to study. Ten people who I got from the Art Students League must have come to study. Martha said, "What are you doing, standing on street corners soliciting people?" Proselytizing was the word she used. I still remember Erick from the photo of *American Document*—"I am one man—boom-boom-boom. I am ten-thousand men"—you saw the pictures in the Barbara Morgan book— Erick was gorgeous. Merce is a little bizarre. He is not conventionally beautiful. I still enjoy seeing Merce when I see him though. I always thought Erick was 10 years younger than Martha was.

You see, at the time I hated my body—hated it. I went to see Erick and he said, "If you're stiff, don't worry about it. I'll give you special exercises. But we'll watch you." I didn't know anything about dancing at that time. I saw pictures of people with their foot up on the barre. I was living with a woman who had one of those great big roll-up type desks where you sit on a stool, like in Dickens' time. So I rolled up the desk, stuck my foot up on that thing, turned around, and hit the floor with the palms of my hands, while my foot was still up on the desk. I didn't know what I ripped or tore. I couldn't move the next day. I knew nothing about how you had to be turned out properly. I just wanted to say to them, "I can get my foot around my head. I don't think I'm too stiff." I was so panicky I went to the doctor and he told me to take an Epsom salt bath and rest. I did. I took an Epsom salt bath every hour thinking that if one was good, 20 would be fantastic. I didn't realize that they were very enervating. I kept on getting weaker and weaker and weaker. Here I thought I had finally found the one thing in life I really wanted to do, and I destroyed the instrument I was supposed to use to express myself—I'll never be able to dance. So I cried myself to sleep.

Eventually I spoke with Martha, later, after my second class with her, [and] she scratched me down there, you know, at the groin. . . . She ran her finger-nail down to my knee, asking "Where is that turnout muscle?" She wanted me to work my inner thigh for my plié. We only wore bathing trunks and T-shirts. Tights didn't come into modern dance for Martha until she hurt her knee, but people aren't aware of that. She hurt her knee doing something. She smashed herself into the floor. I think it is because she didn't want to go to Europe with a company that was not the best one possible to show off her choreography. I have many memories about that in London: "You'll all hate me. You only like me when I'm strong. Now that I'm weak and injured, you all hate me." . . . I was already in the company after that English fiasco, where Erick left Martha. That I didn't understand. Here was Martha crippled and he left her. But God knows what she did to him. She laughed all the time she told the story of when she went to see the doctor after the accident in which she hurt her knee. . . . Erick was terribly concerned. The doctor started to fool around with her knee and Erick fainted. Martha thought that was very funny. That was her brain—Martha had a very sadistic humor.

During the second American tour I went on, Martha Graham and Erick were married but not living together, and they weren't speaking to each other. They sat together on the bus, but they were sleeping in separate rooms. They say that happens after many years of living together—you make it legal and the marriage falls apart.

The first dance of Martha's I performed was the "Christ Figure" in *El Penitente* at a concert Erick gave at the Museum of Natural History. Pearl Lang danced Martha's role. Bob Cohan taught me Merce's role, but I wasn't in the company yet. My first role with the company [was when] Martha had me perform the part of "Mad Tom" in *Eye of Anguish,* her dance for Erick, after only a year of study at her school. Martha thought I was enchanting. It was an interesting vehicle to show off Erick. There were stunning and sinister movements. Martha said she wanted the two evil sisters in the dance to "use . . . the breast as a weapon and [that] the mouth should be devouring in a predatory way," so that they would be able to intimidate the men. Martha felt foreign actresses use the mouth in a way that American actresses don't.

Martha wanted you to be her equal onstage. When I first began, all I had to do was meet her at a party sequence in *Deaths and Entrances,* where each man would walk up and grab her, then each man would fight for her and then they would leave. She would throw them off. Erick would be the last one, so I thought, naturally, because they were so passionate with each other. I was a little scared of Martha. I grabbed her and spun her around to face me and then she went and . . . looked right over my head. I almost lost my balance. She wouldn't look at me. I thought, "Oh my God, is that what she does all the time?" In the party [sequence], we would meet and she would be like that. One day on tour, during performance, she looked me straight in the face and said, "We've made it." So then Bob Cohan told me [that] until Martha knows who you are, she wouldn't risk losing her concentration by seeing that I may be so unconcentrated, if she ever caught my eyes.

Martha Graham didn't see my performance in Nina Fonaroff's *Lazarus* in 1952, but Helen Lanfer saw it, and she told Martha she couldn't believe it, that my concentration was so clear. I had a beard. I grew a moustache. My hair was long. Martha started choreographing *Canticle for Innocent Comedians* (1952) on me. I was very thin, and Martha had this vision of me being burned out in the desert. Martha called me the "wild prophet" because of the beard and because I was so thin. Then I shaved. The whole dance had to be redone. *Canticle* was [for] Martha's company. Each person had a section —I was "For Sun." It didn't dawn on me that I was doing the lead male. The nucleus of Martha's dancers were all my teachers— Bob [Cohan], Ethel [Winter], Helen [McGehee], Yuriko, Martha and Erick. Everybody thinks it is the other way around—that I must have taught them.

Voyage (1953) was my favorite piece of Martha's. It was the first dance she choreographed after Erick left. I was "The Beloved." Martha kept running away from me, her true love. At one point Martha was mysteriously part of my body. She was hooked onto me. Bob Cohan used Martha as an instrument, a lyre, to express himself. Stuart [Hodes] was shadowboxing in the dark. He was the opposing side. We wore evening clothes—the latest in fashion—made of silk, or polished cotton. I wore blue, Bob wore green, Stuart wore red and Martha wore an off-the-shoulder evening dress. They were form-fitting, like for riding. You undressed as you moved. These evening clothes, the height of sophistication, were stripped off, and you came to the barbaric, down to the skin, with savage hieroglyphics on our bodies. With *Voyage,* Martha was working out the fact that her dance partner and husband, Erick, had left her. She was experimenting and made me move in a way I had never moved before. Martha said, "I want you to move in a way that has never been seen in performance." I was new, and she was fascinated with me. She felt I was the most "dramatic" of the men. She was always prodding me for movement sequences, and I know she liked having me around. I remember in *Voyage* Martha developed this seemingly unmotivated turn which was like an explosion.

Martha took an interest in me. She molded me—she was my guru. She really did see me through a lot. She had a long talk about homosexuality with me: ". . . Most homosexuals dislike themselves," or something like that, and she said, "But who is to say in the long run . . ."—when I think of some of the things they sound so mixed-up— "[i]n God's eye what is moral and what is immoral?" She

said, "There is nothing immoral about being homosexual. The only thing I resent is it denies me as a woman." Then later she said, "Most women are interested in gay men because they are much more imaginative in their lovemaking
than their straight counterpart."

It was after *Voyage* that Martha took me to a drugstore with a soda fountain for
her favorite drink, an "Ambrosia," for energy. It was a raw egg mixed with a glass
of orange juice and a ball of vanilla ice cream all beat up like a milkshake. Anyway, she said that she wanted to work with me on *Night Journey*—the very first
dance I had a starring role in with Martha. . . . Even though we had danced together before, I imagine our partnership began then. Martha didn't want to dance
with a partner who was too young because she thought that was in bad taste and
it would look like she was seducing a young man. She didn't want to look like an
old mother either. She wanted the dance to have dignity. She wanted to redesign
my part as "Oedipus" because she felt she had choreographed it wrong with Erick.
Erick, apparently, was too cruel and violent. In any case, we finished the duet and
decided to let Yuriko watch a run-through. Yuriko cried, and said, "To think that
Bertram was my student." She thought the relationship between Martha, as
"Jocasta," and me, as "Oedipus," was beautiful. Martha told me she learned a lot
about me when I fell on her in *Night Journey.* She also told me if she ever had sex
again it would probably be very painful because "it" had been unused for so long.
I know Craig Barton (Martha's personal manager), Paul Taylor and Bob Cohan all
thought I was having sex with Martha and that I was her new young lover. I
wasn't. Martha [hadn't] wanted to give me too much too soon, and she didn't
want to be embarrassed by people thinking she had taken a young lover, either. So
at the same time she danced *Appalachian Spring* with Stuart [Hodes], *Dark Meadow*
with Bob [Cohan] and *Deaths and Entrances* with John Butler. In that sense she had
me split the roles up with various men in her company.

I only danced *Letter to the World,* which many people thought was my best role
with Martha, partnering Martha, in Europe. Later, in America, I danced *Letter* with
Pearl Lang. I didn't do Erick's choreography. Martha totally rechoreographed with
me. Pearl Lang objected. This is a very interesting point: Pearl Lang objected to
Martha's letting me rechoreograph my role because it made me, the character, so
introspective. So Pearl said, "That is a figure of her imagination. It should be
strong," and this and that and the other thing. I said, "Why wouldn't an introspective and introverted personality in her fantasy-life think that there is a man—a
mate—that would be just as understanding, not some brutal lover?" Why wouldn't

she envision somebody who was as sensitive as she was, who would understand her and also suffer, and understand what her suffering was? Martha, of course, had the sex act completely reversed: She thought the male was the one who had to be let down gently after having sex; for a woman, it's over right then and there—you get up and wash and go back to sleep, whereas the man was the sentimental one and had to be loved.

I knew a lot of the kids, and when the company went through Washington, D.C., [they] took classes with Ethel Butler. They were murderous classes because that whole technique . . . nobody knew it at the time. . . . Mary Hinkson saw movies that were taken at Bennington which I never saw. They found the films at the school. They were doing falls where they would just stand up and keel over on their sides—bang! Mary said, "Never." In fact, when they revived *Primitive Mysteries* Helen McGehee said, "I'll never do that. I'll pay somebody to do my part," because it was so damaging and taxing on the knees. Martha's attitude toward men was that they perform a service like everything else—women, props or men. Martha very rarely demonstrated the technical movements for the men. She would give you images of how she wanted the men to be onstage. When we went up to Jacob's Pillow, where I danced *Errand into the Maze* with Helen McGehee, Ted Shawn took my hand—and I never got it back during this long conversation he had with me and Martha—and said [to Martha], "I do love the way you choreograph for men." Martha said, "I love men." And Ted said, "Well, so do I." Then they giggled.

In *Clytemnestra* Martha cast me as two different people. I first appeared as "Agamemnon," and at the end of the first act, Martha, as "Clytemnestra," killed me. In the second act I returned as "Orestes," and killed Clytemnestra. When we were experimenting with the style of this dance-drama, Martha was intrigued with the concept of what you kill in life eventually kills you. Martha was frightened by the scope of *Clytemnestra*. It was very demanding.

The company was uneasy about *Clytemnestra* because we had to finish choreographing the dance for Martha. Martha started out very much on top of things, choreographically, in regards to *Clytemnestra*. She had a very clear vision. I spent hours listening to the score with Martha, plotting the action of this dance-drama. But in the middle of this process she had to drop everything to go to Berlin to perform her solo *Judith*. Her creative rhythm was broken. Martha depended a great deal on me—I did lots of improvisations for her. Martha said the company didn't see how all this movement material was all going to come together. Martha also said she wanted to list me in the program as co-choreographer, but she knew I would refuse that credit. I didn't think anything at all. I just did. I had choreographed. I gave concerts before I got in Martha's company. I did a lot of pieces for Louis Horst. When I said to Martha, "What difference does it make whose name is there in terms of choreography? The thing is the dance, that the work will get out to the world," Martha said, "Not everybody feels that way." I was not listed as co-choreographer.

After we had filmed Martha's *A Dancer's World* in 1957, Martha wanted me to partner Yuriko. Yuriko and I danced *Embattled Garden* the same year we did *Clytemnestra*. It started in rehearsal with sweet and gentle little primitive images of Adam and Eve. We did illuminations, little pictures. Then a huge transition happened. Martha asked Yuriko to pull the pins out of her hair and let her hair down, and then Martha told her to beat my chest with her hair. It was shocking and violent. Martha said, "wouldn't a psychiatrist just love to be in on some of these rehearsals?" That was the end of little illuminations . . . they disappeared. When Bob Cohan left Martha never looked at *Embattled Garden*—she wasn't in it and it reminded her of Bob. Glen Tetley replaced Bob and partnered Matt [Turney].

When Balanchine invited Martha to collaborate on *Episodes* in 1959, Martha agreed—on the condition that I was her partner. She didn't want to work with one of the New York City Ballet dancers. Martha danced "Mary, Queen of Scots" and I danced "Bothwell." From that time on, I was consistently Martha's principal partner until the end.

The next year, Martha danced *Acrobats of God* and *Alcestis*. This was a bad period for Martha because she was drunk all the time. She was panic-stricken. I choreographed entire sequences of *Acrobats*. [I had] the idea of performing a plié upside down on Noguchi's spectacular set. Martha sat on the sidelines costumed in a dress in which she couldn't move, except [to move] her feet apart maybe six inches. At the time, she couldn't move herself anymore. In a sense she was paralyzed. I tried to help her out by choreographing movements and then she would turn around and say, "Look at all the work I've done." In *Alcestis,* Martha wanted me, as "Thanatos," the figure of death, to be drop-dead seductive so that when one looked at me they would realize that to be dead would be attractive. They therefore would sleep with me and understand the reason behind suicide. At this time, Martha understood death as the end of sexuality.

It was during a trip to Greece that Martha thought of her dance *Visionary Recital* (1961), and she wanted it to star me. After one of our tours to Europe,

Martha wanted to stay on and see Greece, but she would only stay if I remained to travel with her. Martha could be impossible in traveling situations. She would always overtip. Sometimes she would give a tip bigger than the bill itself and then say it was because the Americans have such a bad reputation for not tipping at all—Martha was going to be an American ambassadress. In Athens, she stayed at the Plaza Athénée and I stayed in a rooming house. At one point she said, "Why don't you move into the Plaza Athénée too, and I'll pay the difference?" I was furious with Martha's managers, Craig Barton and Lee Leatherman, because I thought they should accompany Martha. I felt inadequate; I was not equipped to travel in Martha's style. I loved Martha, and I always sent her letters and postcards from wherever I went, but I never wanted to be Martha's "walker." But Martha said she would feel better if I stayed in the same hotel. . . . When we traveled around Greece she requested separate quarters, but they always gave us a room with a king-size bed, as though we were married. Eventually Martha requested a suite, and she would always ask if I had to go through her bedroom to get to the bathroom. As it turned out, we had a great time. Glen Tetley told me it was such a wonderful gift to Martha that I traveled with her.

Visionary Recital was going to be a spiritual dance with no romantic attachments whatsoever. Of course, later Martha decided she would be in the piece, but it wouldn't take anything away from [my] being the star. She wanted to appear as my soul. She would be inside my cape but the audience wouldn't see her. In that sense, she would still be able to witness the actions that took place on the stage. In the dance I lose my soul and find it.

When we were rehearsing *Visionary Recital,* Martha left the room and said to me, "Find an ending." Meanwhile, Paul Taylor had found out that I made more money than he did. Paul was furious. Martha found out about Paul. She said, "I need him. But when I don't need him . . ."—she angrily slapped her hands as if she would make him vanish—"he'll be gone." She came back, but not to do the ending. She said to me, "You can go to hell. I'm going to the theater. I fought for you. You've put me on an island all by myself." Martha went to the theater and said to the people there that she had "[her] usual blowup before opening night with, of all people, Bertram." Then I came to the theater and got into position for a run-through. Martha and I faced each other with the palms of our hands touching. I bent over and kissed her on the forehead. Martha said, with her eyelids going up and down, "I still mean everything I said." Then she said to me, "I'm so nervous. I don't know my part." I wanted to punch her in the face!

Anthony Crickn.

Bertram Ross as "Hippolytus" and Martha Graham as "Phaedra" in
Phaedra, *1962.*

The same year that Martha choreographed *Visionary* she also choreographed *One More Gaudy Night.* I wasn't in that dance, and later Mary Hinkson said to me, "Isn't it funny that Martha's only choreographic failure you didn't dance?" The next year Martha gave her role from *Visionary* to Mary Hinkson and changed the title to *Samson Agonistes.* That dance didn't last in the repertory.

By 1962, Martha was the "high priestess" of modern dance, and she choreographed for herself the role of "Phaedra." I was cast as "Hippolytus," and through me Martha wanted to show the glorification of the male body. Because of my dedication to the laws of chastity, represented by Artemis (Helen McGehee), the goddess of the hunt, I spurned Aphrodite (Ethel Winter), the goddess of love. In revenge, Aphrodite inflames Phaedra, my stepmother, with lust for me, Hippolytus. I appeared in Noguchi's capsule-like set which revealed different aspects of my anatomy. Originally Martha wanted a shoji screen with sliding panels, but what she got was Noguchi's phallic structure with six doors. She said she wanted to reveal the "beauty of face, beauty of limbs and beauty of genitals." Since most of the men were homosexual, Martha was very frustrated. Nothing can come of it. Here she was, the head of a dance school with many gorgeous men, and none of them would give her a tumble. Martha's situation with *Phaedra* was very similar. The dance of the men was the glorification of the male anatomy and chastity. Life without women. In that sense, the dance of the men became a decorative bull dance instead. Martha became more interested in the intensity of seduction and rape that she wove for herself as "Phaedra."

I thought *A Look at Lightning* (1962), which I danced with Matt Turney, Dick Kuch and Bob Powell, was Martha's best choreographic piece. It was abstract, with Matt playing this mysterious goddess figure highlighted by three very distinct and different male personalities. Each of us related to the goddess figure in a different way. Dick was the prizefighter, Bob was the singer of songs and I was the poet and dreamer. Each man was transformed by his relationship with Matt. Matt was the perfect unattainable goddess figure. Matt was this "Circe" figure a year before Martha created *Circe* for Mary Hinkson. The music by Halim El-Dabh was wonderful. Of course, he had done the music for Martha's *Clytemnestra* and *One More Gaudy Night.*

Also in 1962, I danced *Legend of Judith,* with Martha as "Judith" and Linda Hodes as "Young Judith." I played "Holofernes." Martha's premise was that an act of lovemaking was an act of murder. She felt it was illustrated as soon as a man entered a woman with his erect penis forcefully and vigorously and the

Courtesy of Bertra

Bertram Ross and Mary Hinkson in Diversion of Angels, *c. 1950s.*

woman kills the penis, making it limp after she has been satisfied.

I loved partnering Mary [Hinkson]. I had partnered her in *Diversion of Angels*, which many people felt was Mary's dance as the serene woman in white. I also loved partnering her in *Seraphic Dialogue* where she danced three roles: the total "Joan," the "Maid" and the "Warrior." In *Seraphic* I thought Mary captured Martha's spirituality. When she danced the "Warrior" one couldn't see what I saw as "St. Michael" because her back was to the audience, but after I inspire her to overcome her fears her face was so ecstatic. Then she did a back-fall and she never lost the impact or physicality of that moving moment.

I danced *Circe* (1963) with Mary Hinkson, and it was a very successful dance. Martha said [that] "the piece had to go through" me as "Ulysses." The statement of the dance was made clear by the violent movements [by] which all the men were transformed metaphorically into beasts. Once Martha almost broke my neck during a choreographic rehearsal of *Circe*. Bob Powell was trying to show the movement she wanted. He was too gentle. Martha was taking his part, saying, "I am the snake and that's what I want to be," and she took me and threw me down. She went back to her chair and started laughing. She said, "No man would ever be that cruel to another man. Only a woman can do that." She had pulled the top of my hair. Since I was lying on my stomach on the Noguchi boat, my back was already arched. Then she snapped my head back, so my face was to the ceiling—I saw stars. It was another one of Martha's violent moods to me.

In 1965, Martha was "The Witch" in *The Witch of Endor.* I was "King Saul." She said with such relish in rehearsal, "I beat him and beat him," but then onstage she forgot what to do. I was saying, "Beat me," and Bob Cohan, as "King David," was yelling across the stage, "Beat him, beat him." *Part Real—Part Dream* premiered at the same time as *The Witch of Endor,* but Martha wasn't in that dance. Mary, Matt and Bob Cohan were in [it]. Martha was so drunk [that] she never showed up for rehearsals. So once again, like with *Clytemnestra,* I finished most of the movement sequences. I always felt *Part Real—Part Dream* was the other section of *Embattled Garden*.

I would say that *Cortege of Eagles* in 1967 was Martha's great comeback, choreographically. She was very firm in what she wanted us to do in a twisted Egyptian style of movement. Martha wouldn't allow any contributions from the dancers. [This] was also when Martha fought with Noguchi, and after that year he never again designed a set for her. I danced the roles of "Achilles" and "Polymestor." Martha was "Hecuba, Queen of Troy." *Cortege of Eagles* was a good part for her—

Anthony Crickmay.

Bertram Ross as "Ulysses" and Robert Powell in Circe, 1963.

she sat a great deal. Noguchi designed two stools, one stage right, one stage left. Martha had a place to sit when she wasn't dancing. Her movements were high kicks and step draws, high kicks and step draws, and falls.

I also thought "The Abbess" in *A Time of Snow* in 1968 was a very good part for Martha. I was "Abelard." It was a dream of Martha's to play this Flaubert character in a film, but that never happened. Once again, the dance was violent: I, in a cape, was castrated and beaten. In *The Lady of the House of Sleep* (1968), the last dance Martha and I premiered together, I was all tied up, and eventually beaten and killed. It was another one of Martha's sadomasochistic dances.

In 1969 Martha and I choreographed *The Archaic Hours* for Helen McGehee and Bob Cohan. Bob Powell was also in that dance. Bob Cohan, Bob Powell and I had a kabuki section. Martha's idea was to show a beautiful woman, played by me, seduce a young man (Powell) and then reveal herself (me) as an evil demon. I was to get the young man to come to me in this disguise and then attack him. I danced the kabuki section with both Bobs. Takako Asakawa taught us how to do a kabuki walk. I had a 10-foot-long tongue which I manipulated by two poles. As usual, Martha had been absent during the choreographic sessions. When she asked to see the dance in rehearsal, she said to me, "What are you doing? You look like a woman." I said, "Don't you remember your idea?" Martha said, "Oh, no, we can't have cross-dressing in my theater." She completely denied having told this story. But this was immediately before Martha got sick.

I can't believe Martha was still functioning [in the end] because I know how she was functioning when I was around. In fact, I thought she would dance "Jocasta" forever—even though she was old enough to be my mother. The more she danced, the younger she got in her body. Her [*Appalachian*] *Spring* got better as she got older. Her sister, Geordie, had said it was obscene that Martha looked so young as "The Bride." But [after Martha stopped dancing], she became ill and developed cirrhosis of the liver. She was a drunkard. She drank herself into mad stupors and would go back and forth between the studio and the apartment. Before, she could drink and then burn it up dancing. But as she could move less and less, she became sick. I kept her drinking a secret. When she was in the hospital I had to carry her to the bathroom, and she hated me to see her that way. But at the time she was drinking so heavily. She should have been locked up so she wouldn't be able to destroy what she had created. But Martha was strong-willed enough to stop drinking. Still, Martha was too old and vain. She was still hobbling around.

When Martha did return to choreograph in 1973, we premiered *Mendicants of Evening* with Matt and me. This was another transition period for Martha because it was the first time she worked since she retired from performing. It was also the first dance she choreographed after her illness. Martha used a modern painting by Fangor as the set. Martha wanted me to show off my male torso and had me costumed in a long train of a cape [that went] over one shoulder, so it would reveal my one side of my torso. I wasn't completely nude. Unfortunately, this was when Ron Protas [current artistic director of the Graham Company who is not, and never was, a dancer or a choreographer] was following Martha around constantly with a notebook and a pencil, writing down what each movement of Martha's meant. He even lamely tried to learn how to do Martha's knee-crawls. Can you imagine a pedestrian, a neophyte, crashing to the floor, trying to execute those movements? And Martha, in her perverse way, would encourage him, "Oh, that's very good, Ron."

During the rehearsals for *Mendicants* Ron would sit with Martha and start explaining about the "truths of drama." I thought this is all I need—to have to listen to his psychobabble. At this time, Mary and I were co-artistic directors of the company. We had kept the company going during Martha's illness. When Ron first started hanging around backstage Martha said, "Get that creep out of here." Later, though, Ron convinced Martha that we betrayed her and were trying to steal the company away from her. When Ethel Winter told Martha she had to meet with her co-directors, Martha said, "There are no co-artistic directors. I am the only director."

I remember Mary talking about Martha—a great dancer, a great performer, a great creative person, a great choreographer, but lovable?—a singularly unlovable woman! At any rate, Mary Hinkson was the one who spotted the difficulty at Graham long before I did. She said that in order for Ron Protas to be successful, he had to get rid of the two of us. Ron turned Martha against her disciples. He poisoned her against us. And now, even though he is not an artist, he is making artistic decisions. Of course that only breeds mediocrity, and ultimately, the death of the art of dance.

The reason her dances weren't any good anymore . . . was because she didn't have the people around her that she had trained; she had all superficially trained dancers. I thought Martha was concerned with the inner life of a dancer and what motivates the movement, which is essentially what a good teacher of the Graham technique professes. Martha didn't have faith in what she had once preached. So each generation gets weaker. You want to train the body to know its physical sensations so that you can call on and remember them when you need to perform. It is an experience you want to be able to draw on. I remember . . . when Martha and I danced *Cave of the Heart*, she told me that she saw my eyes roll back in my head as though I was demented [when I danced "Jason"] and that sent her off into Medea's dance of vengeance. Martha said I fed her. Eventually Martha said to me that she saw me in all of the male roles she created.

Martha's whole technique was based on breath. I speak about breath a lot as a teacher. One breathes differently with the different human emotions—anger, sadness, tiredness, ecstasy. Men have to breathe the same as women do. The contraction was based on breath, the letting out and the taking in of live energy. Martha said, "You must drain yourself to take something in." You cannot build a technique on rage and anger. Look at Martha's *Letter to the World*. It is very soft and lyric. When Martha did *Appalachian Spring*, every solo was completely different. I never saw Martha do *El Penitente*, but Helen Lanfer told me the three Marys—Mary the Mother, Mary the Magdalene and Mary the Virgin— were three completely different characters for Martha to dance because Martha was a great actress.

It was very creative when I was with Martha, but I didn't have all the responsibility to finish all that work when I left. Martha told Yuriko [that] I was the most selfless person she ever worked with in her life. I was Martha's partner for 25 years, and now everyone tries to cover that up, too. Paul Taylor, who wrote me a wonderful, honest letter about how he and all the other men in Martha's company looked up to me, in terms of dedication and loyalty, as the prototype for Martha's man, said about my working with Martha, "It bordered on the insane."

I loved being insane and playing epileptic; I loved being blinded, beheaded, beaten, castrated and murdered. And I never missed a performance with Martha. But in the Seventies I was eager to get out of there. I had to leave finally in 1973. Mary didn't even bother to resign. She walked out. I sent Martha a telegram. It said, "You must know this is the saddest day of my life. But in the circumstances there is nothing for me to do but resign."

LINDA HODES

Arnold

Linda Hodes dancing the central Joan role with (from left to right) Matt Turney ("Joan as Martyr"), Helen McGehee ("Joan as Warrior") and Mary Hinkson ("Joan as Maid") in Seraphic Dialogue, *1955.*

Linda Hodes was born in New York City, in 1933. At the age of 9, she began her dance training with Martha Graham. Hodes joined the Graham Company in 1952, when Graham choreographed her into a trio in Canticle for Innocent Comedians. *By 1955 Graham had cast Hodes as the central Joan character in* Seraphic Dialogue. *It would become one of her signature roles. In addition, Hodes created roles in* Acrobats of God, Phaedra *and* Legend of Judith. *She danced with the Graham Company as a member and as a guest artist for close to 20 years.*

In 1955, Hodes married fellow Graham Company member Stuart Hodes, with whom she had 2 daughters. Their marriage ended in divorce. In 1963, Hodes moved to Israel where she taught Graham technique to the newly formed Batsheva Dance Company. From 1968 to 1970 she was co-artistic director of the company. In 1968, she married Batsheva's rising star, Ehud Ben-David, with whom she later had a daughter. After Ben-David's death in 1977, Hodes returned to work with the Martha Graham Dance Company at Graham's request. She was Associate Artistic Director of the company from 1977 to 1991.

In 1992, Hodes became Director of the Paul Taylor School and of Taylor 2, the second company of the Paul Taylor Dance Foundation. She has been associated with Taylor for over 30 years, from the time they danced together with Graham.

Linda Hodes lives in New York City.

I went to Martha's school because I lived around the corner, on 11th Street. I was 9 years old. Martha's studio was on Fifth Avenue, between 12th and 13th streets, so my mother didn't have to take me on the subway. There were five children in my first class with Martha Graham. At that time it was very usual for Martha Graham to teach the children's classes—Martha taught all the classes at that time. Actually, I think Martha had a couple of children's classes before that year. Maybe I could have had a totally different life if I had lived around the corner from someone else, like Balanchine.

I took classes with Martha Graham all during my school years. I was dying to be in Martha Graham's company. I was still a teenager. I had to get out of some of my high school classes so I could work with Martha Graham. My friends thought that was really cool. Bob [Cohan], Bert [Ross] and Stuart [Hodes] were all new in the company then; Pearl [Lang], Yuriko and Helen [McGehee] certainly were around. Of course, I was intrigued by these artists. They were role models for me, especially the women.

The first time I danced with Martha was at a lecture-demonstration for Walter Terry's dance series at the "Y" in 1951. This lecture-demonstration was the first performance Martha did with her new company. It was shortly after Erick [Hawkins] and Martha split and her whole company had broken up. We danced the "Sarabande" from *Dark Meadow* (1946). Mary [Hinkson], Matt [Turney], Patsy Birch and I were the four girls, and Bob, Bert and Stuart did the men's roles. That is when I dated Stuart, and we got married within a few months.

In those days, marrying within the Graham Company was definitely "all in the family." Before the ceremony Martha called me into her dressing room for a little talk. "Always wear a little makeup to bed," she said. I didn't take this advice. Our first child was born in 1956, our second in 1958. Poor Stuart had to practically give up the Graham Company because we couldn't afford to feed our kids. Martha was a bit upset that we didn't name our first child after her. But we did name our second child, Martha, after her. When I told her we were naming the baby Martha, she said to me, "That's a very difficult name." I said, "Well, we'll take our chances." I think she was pleased. When my daughter Martha was a baby, she got very sick and ended up in the hospital. Martha Graham did something which I think is so typical of her. I had called Martha to tell her I wouldn't be able to work that day, and a few hours later there arrived by messenger, at my house, a check for $100 and a bottle of bourbon. It was Martha Graham arising to the crisis. To a certain extent, she was interested in my daughter Martha's life—when she was being chatty. When she was interested in her other thing—Martha Graham—she could close that very easily out of her mind.

Martha didn't seem to mind when I got pregnant. If it had been right in the middle of Martha's season and I had said, "Sorry, I can't dance," she would have been furious. In those days, we had plenty of time: Modern dance was not the big thing that it is now. We didn't tour a lot—not like today, where companies tour over 30 weeks a year. I wasn't in *Clytemnestra* (1958) because I was pregnant. "Cassandra" in *Clytemnestra* was choreographed on Matt Turney, but when she became pregnant I danced her role. Between us all and all of our babies, we actually had a great deal: We got to dance each other's roles by replacing each other. It was much more interesting than dancing the same roles all the time.

The first dance Martha choreographed on me was the trio with Patsy, Mary and me in *Canticle for Innocent Comedians* (1952). The trio was a prelude to the "fire section" that Stuart danced. We were onstage during his little dance, then we danced some movements with him. The next dance I was in was *Ardent Song* (1954).

That [dance] had one of Martha's huge "holes" because she hadn't finished choreographing it. Martha was in one of her "bad" moods and said, "I don't care what you do. Just get out there and do something," which is literally what we did—"something." Mary, Matt and I did this horrible trio that we had to improvise every night. I don't even know what we did. We were running around, "triplet-ing" and falling and running around, and "triplet-ing" and falling. She did have a lot of trust in us to let us do that. The men had a section, which was all choreographed, which followed ours when the music changed. The men would stand in the wings of the stage and try to make us laugh during our improvised trio.

Martha worried less about the women and more about the men. Maybe that is why she choreographed their sections. She always said that men never could be together, and the girls were better at that. She liked the men, though. She played more to the men. She flirted with the men. When I came to the company she did not have the Erick figure anymore, she didn't have the Merce figure—she didn't have a male to rely on to do the men's movement. She was just beginning to trust Bert, Bob and Stuart to create their own movement.

We were very steeped in Martha's technique, so I think she trusted us with her movement vocabulary, in terms of improvising in her dances. A lot of those movements had come into Martha's technique through the process of her choreographing the dance. The technique incorporated the "shoulder-fall," the

Arno

Linda Hodes dancing "For Moon" with Bertram Ross dancing "For Sun" in Canticle for Innocent Comedians, *1952.*

"front-fall," the "back-fall" and whatever. We didn't call it codified then, but it was, and we learned it, and then we all could produce it for Martha. We were taking class with Martha, we were all very loyal and involved with Martha. So except for those few times when she was having a hard time—there were periods when she was very down and depressed, and couldn't think of movement phrases, didn't want to—Martha most definitely did the choreography. Sometimes she didn't get up and jump around, but she would tell you what to do.

It is a very difficult question, this business of who does what choreographically. A lot of times dancers think they are choreographing, but they are not: They are being led and directed. You see, Martha changed from dance to dance. Sometimes she was very specific about what she wanted. When you dance the "Chorus" in *Night Journey* (1947), you realize that there is not a fingernail that isn't accounted for. There were other sections where she was more free: She only knew that she wanted something jumpy, or something low. In Martha's case, the dancers were choreographing within a certain prescribed scenario and syllabus that Martha herself had created. It's her movement. Many people said that Martha would say, "Start here and do this," and then walk out of the rehearsal studio. I never had that experience with her. In *Legend of Judith* (1962), she certainly did not walk out of the studio. Maybe it was me. Perhaps Martha didn't trust me. Martha would say, "Do a turn. Do a fall. Do this. Do that." When you had a ton of movement, she would give you a chance to shape it and make some transitions, and then she would look at it again—and if she liked it, fine, and if she didn't she would change it.

I think all dancers participate in the process of choreographing, to a certain extent, [but] I am not an advocate [for] dancers saying they choreographed their own movement material with Martha. In reality, they didn't. Of course if you are up there with your leg in the air, you are doing it—to a certain extent. There were times that you, inadvertently, as the dancer, would do something else, something that Martha didn't ask for; then she would say, "Oh, I like that," or "Save that, and we can use that next." I can distinctly remember Martha choreographing *Phaedra* (1962). In *Phaedra*, of course, I had my great role as "Pasiphaë." We used to call one section the "Fire Island Five"—because it was me and all of Martha's men dancers. My costume involved this huge cape which covered practically the entire stage. She might have said, "Let's see what happens if you turn that way," and the cape would do a certain thing simultaneously, [but] she really choreographed *Phaedra* from start to finish.

When we premiered *Canticle* at Juilliard in 1952, Martha also performed a solo, *The Triumph of St. Joan,* on the same program. She danced the whole bloody thing: "Joan as Maid," "Joan as Martyr," and "Joan as Warrior." It was a good half-hour-long solo—that is a long solo. She eventually realized that it was something that she couldn't do in repertory—because it was impossible. I don't know whether it was because she was too old. It was one of those things where we never knew how old Martha was. We never thought of those things. When I was very young and I saw Martha Graham, I thought she was very old. She was probably only in her 30s or 40s. But then, as I got older, Martha seemed to get younger. In any case, Martha decided she couldn't do this solo, so she said, "I'm going to do it for the company." I don't think Martha Graham ever had a person in mind to take over her roles. We women dancers were all adjuncts to her choreographic process. In her later years, when many dancers were doing her roles, she told me she no longer thought of them as "hers," but [that] they belonged for the moment to whomever was performing them. And in a less benign moment, she told me she no longer recognized her role at all, but she was resigned to that.

After Martha broke her Joan solo up into pieces for the company dancers—*Seraphic Dialogue* (1955)—Noguchi did the cathedral-like set. I have no idea why she selected me to dance the central Joan role in *Seraphic Dialogue*. In fact, what happened was that I was originally cast as "the Martyr," and I don't think Martha had gotten around to choreographing my part yet. Then Martha realized that she needed a figure that tied the three Joans (Martyr, Maid and Warrior) together, and that is how the central Joan role was created. She took me out of "Joan as Martyr" and put me in the central Joan role. Bert was "St. Michael." . . . I danced the role of "Joan as Martyr" later, and I did it wrong. I learned it quickly, to cover an injured dancer. They are still doing it wrong at the Graham Company. I can confess this now. We did a videotape of *Seraphic Dialogue* the day after I had learned the part of "Joan as Martyr," and I did it wrong in the videotape—I switched two phrases. To this day, they are still doing it wrong because they are learning the dance from that videotape. *Seraphic Dialogue* went through various changes. It evolved over a period of time. When we were in Asia, Martha completely changed the "Warrior" section.

For me, it was all exciting in different ways. With Martha Graham, when you are a dancer, whatever you are doing then is what you want to be doing. *Seraphic Dialogue* was a spectacular dance. It was a wonderful piece and beautiful. . . . *Judith* was with Bert and Martha, who were working very closely together. There was this whole wonderful section that was very exciting for me as a "Young Judith" to Martha Graham's "Judith" and Bert Ross as "Holofernes." There was this constant interchange of Martha with Bert, then me with him, then Martha with him and me with him. Because Martha and I were the same person, there wasn't any confrontation between us. Being the same person as Martha was very interesting for me. I kept expecting to feel differently, or maybe dance differently. Perhaps I should have worn makeup to bed.

Martha said to us, "Look, I have to do this thing. . . . " It was this collaboration (*Episodes* [1959]) with Balanchine that Lincoln Kirstein had talked her into and she really didn't want to do. Well, she probably did want to do it, but she always pretended she didn't, because it was ballet. That was her defense. Martha said, "I told them I couldn't work with those ballet dancers, I have to choreograph on my own company first." We didn't expect to perform it, ever. Balanchine and Lincoln came to Martha's studio to see what she had choreographed. They sat, uncomfortably, on those low Noguchi benches. They freaked out because we were on our knees or rolling around most of the time. I am sure they said there's no way our dancers are doing that movement. Then we were told we could perform it, so we were very happy. We had a great time.

Martha was beginning to feel she didn't have the freedom of movement anymore. She was in her late 60s. She was having trouble with her memory. The men who partnered Martha always had to know her choreography; they helped her out when she needed it. *Acrobats of God* and *Alcestis* were in 1960. *Acrobats* was fun, but not challenging. I didn't have a "role" in *Alcestis*. I was dressed in pink and fluttered around the stage. I personally didn't like what I was doing. Martha, Bert and Paul [Taylor] had roles, as usual. Paul was always cast as a bad, or evil, character. He was so "bad," he was good.

It was a hard time for all of us. Martha was still dancing, but she was also drinking a lot. We would come to rehearsal and we would sit around. We didn't even have a schedule. We didn't know what we were doing. Poor David Wood was trying to keep things together as rehearsal director, and Bert was so busy, pulling Martha through all her traumas. Martha lived vividly and vicariously in her characters. Since her dances involved stabbings, poisoning, hangings, beheadings and other assorted bad behavior, we often had to put up with Martha's corresponding moods. She would come late. She very often wasn't in very good shape to work at night, which is when she liked to work. It was a difficult rehearsal period.

In 1961, I was "Gaudy" in *One More Gaudy Night*; Ethel and Paul were "Cleopatra" and "Antony." I did triplets around the stage forever, with a mirror. I only did three steps in the entire dance. There were some wonderful moments in the dance for Ethel and Paul, but it never got itself together. We were all scattered around the stage. I don't know what that meant.

Martha had, at that time, already established herself. She had already proven that she could work on the floor, or illuminate the flexed foot, as opposed to the pointed foot. Martha would often change dances when she wasn't dancing anymore because she saw things differently then. I think that change really started with Mary Hinkson. Mary was a beautiful dancer. Even though she wasn't a ballet dancer, there was something classical about her. She had beautiful feet and beautiful legs. And Glen [Tetley], too. Paul was spectacular in his own way. He had a very high jump and a sinuous way of moving. I think Paul had a strong influence on the Graham technique at that time. Many dancers have tried, and few have succeeded, to emulate his particular brand of Graham technique.

The company was not dancing a lot, so I went to Israel, in 1963. Stuart and I [had] split [by] then. Bethsabee de Rothschild had asked me to come to Israel to teach. I said no way. Martha called me and said, "Oh, please go and teach in Israel." At first they were only asking me to go for four weeks. Finally, I said I'd go and I asked for what I thought was a large amount of money—probably $500—and Bethsabee said yes. I got to Israel and I loved it there. I fell in love. I was ready for a big change in my life.

When I went to Israel, the Batsheva Dance Company was just beginning—actually, they had their premiere when I was there. Martha gave her dances—*Diversion of Angels, Embattled Garden, Hérodiade* and *Errand into the Maze*—to them, which no other company in the world has ever had in repertory at the same time, because she felt she owed it to Bethsabee. I was there to oversee the rehearsals and teach class.

I decided to stay in Israel for personal reasons. When I told Martha I wasn't coming back, she was fine about it because her company wasn't working much. I was teaching the Graham technique to all of Israel—in Jerusalem, in Tel Aviv, everywhere. I got married again five years later to Ehud Ben-David, but we were together all that time. I couldn't get married in Israel because I was divorced in Mexico; we eventually married in London. In 1970, two years after we were married, my third daughter was born. Those were wonderful years. Batsheva attracted some major talent to Israel: Jerome Robbins, [John] Cranko, [Glen] Tetley, [Anna] Sokolow, Tally Beatty, Don McKayle and many others, including Martha Graham, all worked with the company.

I became co-artistic director of the Batsheva company in 1968, very grudgingly. I never wanted to be an artistic director. I didn't believe in myself as an artistic director for that company. I felt they should have an Israeli director, which fortunately they now have. I did some choreography. To be very honest, I choreographed *The Act* and it was a success. I later gave it to Norman Morris for Ballet Rambert. But I never thought of myself as a choreographer.

I kept in touch with Martha through my whole Israeli experience. Martha would come periodically to see Bethsabee, and to look at the company. But Martha had her own worries in the United States. In 1968, I came back to guest with Martha at the Brooklyn Academy of Music. I danced *Seraphic Dialogue, Dark Meadow* and *Hérodiade.* I think there were two more times [when] I came back to dance a season.

I missed the whole period when Martha was sick. I missed the period when Bert and Mary left Martha. Also when Helen, Yuriko and Ethel had their specific problems with Martha. I missed all the hullabaloo. I was lucky, in a way, because it allowed me later on to come back to Martha Graham and work with her company without the baggage of those times. The other dancers couldn't do that. They had been too involved. I stopped dancing in 1970. At first I just came back to help them rehearse, and I danced *Hérodiade* during one season. When I came back in 1975 to rehearse the company, I walked into the studio and didn't know anybody. The company had changed so completely. I was stung. It's like walking into your house and not knowing anybody who is living there.

Martha was always fine with me coming and going. She never made me feel bad about it. Then I came back to Martha for good. My husband died in 1977 in an army-related border circumstance . . . he was much too young to die. Martha asked me if I wanted to come back . . . I didn't know what I wanted to do at that point; I had a 3-year-old child to take care of—the other two girls were older, and more established. Martha was wonderful. Martha sent me a plane ticket to New York City and I am still here today.

Nobody from my generation was at Graham, so that is why they probably needed me to come back. . . . I stayed for 17 more years. It was difficult and hard on my friendships with Mary and Bert, who had departed from Martha with so much hostility. There was a definite split in our friendship at that point. It wasn't a spoken thing. We just didn't see each other. It was hard for them to see me . . . and it was hard for me to see them because I didn't want to hear the negative consequences of their careers with Martha. I had to separate myself from all that. Mary and I are back being friends again. I'm grateful for that. Anyway, then, I needed a job. I had a child to raise, and I didn't have any money. Practical things must come first. I was lucky to have a job that I liked. Basically, I loved Martha's work. Pearl [Lang] was still teaching—Pearl still teaches there. Martha probably identified with Pearl much more than she identified with me, but it was easier for her to work with me—I was able to give Martha the support she needed without pressure.

Martha and I never had any problems. I think there was enough distance in age between us. I saw a lot of different aspects of Martha Graham, from my childhood to the middle of my adulthood. Martha and I ended up being very close friends. We had a very "girl" relationship: In addition to the work, we shopped, dined and spent hours on the phone gossiping. When I was a dancer in Martha's company we had a different relationship. We didn't talk about dance when we were outside of the studio. We talked about clothes, make-up. Martha didn't have a lot of friends. I filled the role of "girlfriend" to Martha. I was someone Martha could let her hair down with.

Martha never considered herself a choreographer when she was a dancer. In the later years, she became a choreographer because she had to figure these things out. It wasn't physical instinct anymore. By the time I returned in the late Seventies, Martha's technique had developed—it was much more set than when I was there as a dancer. There were long streams of movement to call on. When I was a dancer in the company, Martha would often get up and whip off a series of movements and you had to follow her. She didn't talk about it, she didn't explain it. She didn't give you any helpful hints. Once she had stopped dancing and she couldn't really move anymore, and she was sitting in her chair, she became much more verbal. In my time, the role's characterization came through the actual movement. Later on, she talked more about intention and the "why" of things. Ritual was important to Martha—she maintained it gave one a code of behavior.

I loved *Sacre* [*du Printemps*] [*The Rite of Spring*, (1984)]. I thought it worked. It was very Martha, totally Martha. She wasn't moving then. *Sacre* is a good example of what Martha choreographed toward the end of her life. I don't know how old she was, but she was chair-bound at the time. She wanted that certain twisted movement, and she drove the dancers crazy to get it. Martha was discontented through that whole rehearsal period. Martha wanted movement that this particular company, at this particular time, was not used to doing at Graham. It was very distorted for them. They kept softening and refining the movement. Martha didn't want that softness or prettiness in her dance.

It was a process between Martha and the dancers, but it finally happened. They learned to think as she did when she was trying to construct dances, and to reproduce the moment she was trying to design. They learned the process of producing what Martha was thinking. The dancers were very tuned into that process of working with Martha. I would love to say it was through me—that I translated Martha's idea for the dancers—but in all honesty, it didn't have to be me. It could have been anybody else. There would have always been someone to complete that transference from Martha to the dancers. I didn't feel it had to be me, [but] I'm glad it was me for a while.

Ron [Protas], of course, was on the scene. I had heard from everybody horrible things about Ron. The first time I met him I was surprised because he was very nice. Once I decided to work with Martha, I made up my mind I had to deal with everybody's personality—Martha's and Ron's and all the dancers. With Martha around, I didn't have to deal with Ron in many ways—I dealt with Martha. I didn't deal with Ron. If it was a question of what are the programs or what was the casting, I did it with Martha.

I certainly feel Martha trusted me to maintain her dances and her vision. That is one of the reasons I finally had to leave, because I felt this particular vision was being tampered with by Ron Protas, to say the least. I knew Martha wanted her stage to look a certain way—in all fairness to Ron, I think it came down to economics. But it also came down to who had the power. He was starting to eliminate things that I didn't really feel could be eliminated, in terms of music, sets, lighting [and] costumes.

I don't know if Martha ever thought that it would be a catastrophe [for] Ron [to take] over as artistic director. Martha said in the end, "I've made a mistake"—in terms of Ron not being an artist, or a dancer, or a choreographer—but she didn't change anything. Martha choreographed half of a dance which she never quite finished, called *Eyes of the Goddess*. Martha couldn't finish it because it was too traumatic for her. It was about death. So she left it and choreographed *Maple Leaf Rag* (1990) instead. Ron and Yuriko finished *Eyes of the Goddess* after Martha died. Even though Ron never danced, he would say "do this" and "do that"; and I suppose he felt it was as [Martha] wanted it.

The truth of the matter is that Ron filled a great need for Martha. He was there for her. None of us wanted that job. None of us wanted to stay up all night with her, or be there on weekends, or constantly be in attendance. I had a family of my own. Martha needed that person like Ron, who was vicariously living Martha's life. She needed that person to fight against. I wasn't that person; Martha and I didn't have that kind of relationship. I was usually sympathetic with Martha. I tried to understand her from her point of view, even if I didn't always agree with it. I was trying to meet her needs in the studio.

Listen, we all have had our fantasies about being Martha Graham. Now Ron is living his fantasy of being Martha Graham. When I told Ron I was leaving he said, "You can't do this to Martha"—and this was after she was dead. What he was really saying was, "You can't do this to me." He's lucky—he's happy we've all left, because now he can do whatever he wants and no one will know. Peggy [Lyman] left before me. Yuriko took over as co-artistic director when I left, but then she left. Ethel left [in 1993]. He is the only one in control there. As for me, I'm lucky because I'm working with Paul Taylor once again.

We hate to think that someone could be so destructive—not to care about all that work she had choreographed—but it's her work. Other people have said it, and I think maybe it's true, that Martha did it on purpose and that she herself wanted to remain the legend: Legends carry no blame—legends are admired and venerated. In any event, it is what Martha chose to do.

MARY HINKSON

Anthony Crickmay.

Mary Hinkson dancing "Circe" in Circe, *1963.*

*Mary Hinkson was born in Philadelphia, Pennsylvania, in 1925. She gradu-
ated from the University of Wisconsin where she majored in dance. Thereafter
she studied dance primarily with Martha Graham. She later undertook extensive studies in classical ballet.*

*Hinkson became a member of the Martha Graham Company in 1951. Martha
Graham created the title role in* Circe *for her in its London and New York premieres in 1963. She was a principal dancer with the New York City Opera Ballet under the direction of its primary choreographer, John Butler. She also was
a guest artist with Balanchine's New York City Ballet and the American Ballet
Theater, dancing in a specially-commissioned ballet created for her by Glen Tetley.
Mary Hinkson retired from performing in 1973 and focused on guest teaching
around the world. In addition to teaching, she is president of her family's bakery, the D&G Bakery, in Manhattan's Little Italy.*

Mary Hinkson lives in New York City.

I decided that I had to come to New York City after a wondrous and glorious
introduction to dance at the University of Wisconsin. Matt Turney, my roommate, and I were both excited about the prospect of performing, even though
we had no specific plans. Actually, I have Martha Hill to thank for making it so
clear to me that to study with Martha Graham was a "must." When I came to
New York I was taking these courses at N.Y.U. and both Martha Graham and
Hanya Holm were there for eight weeks each of guest teaching. I took both of
these courses. I remember when I did Martha's class . . . [the steps were] triplet, triplet, step back, back—I turned the wrong way. Martha said, "That's all
right, that's all right. You made it look all right."

In retrospect, I realize what a significant time it was. Erick Hawkins was just
about to leave forever. Whatever I know about Martha and Erick's separation is

hearsay. I am not an authority on that. What I heard was from Louis Horst. He simply said Martha was absolutely hung up on Erick. It became an obsession with her. Erick was less and less to be controlled by Martha. Martha became more and more obsessed with the idea of Erick and when she was losing him she became very self-destructive. I was told that in that particular section of *Appalachian Spring* where she plunges to the knee—the back leg is in arabesque, you plunge to the knee, get up and do a fan-kick, and plunge to the knee again and it is repeated—Martha did this again, again, again, again, again, again, again, again, again and just destroyed her knee. So Martha was just recovering from this devastating knee injury. Many of her longtime dancers had scattered. It was truly a major transition period. In fact, it was the beginning of a whole new era.

I was thrilled to be one of the advanced students chosen to rehearse for a lecture-demonstration with Walter Terry, the dance critic, in which excerpts from *Dark Meadow* and *Diversion of Angels* were to be performed. It was during that demonstration (in 1951) that I first heard Martha speak about "Jocasta," her character in *Night Journey*. She said she wanted to know "what this woman ate for breakfast." It really fired my imagination to realize she wanted to know this character inside out.

In the beginning I was the understudy for the "Sarabande" from *Dark Meadow*. One of the performers didn't measure up to Martha's standard so I was the replacement. This was my first experience with any kind of Graham repertory, and it was an experience never to be forgotten. In fact, it was one of the most wonderful and memorable experiences of my life. The feeling was almost that of a religious ceremony. *Dark Meadow* is an incredible dance. That was my beginning with the company. After that lecture-demonstration, little by little, other dancers began to reappear and were on the scene again.

The following year, Martha was commissioned to choreograph *Canticle for Innocent Comedians,* and a new company was formed. The dancers who had been with Martha previously (Pearl Lang, Yuriko, Helen McGehee, Bob Cohan, Bertram Ross and Stuart Hodes) all returned and were now the soloists. Bert, Bob and Stuart were Erick's replacement as Martha's partner. Then there were the new dancers: Linda Hodes, Patsy Birch, Mimi Cole, Matt Turney and myself. Martha choreographed around our qualities and began moving the technique in a new direction. I think we were much less grave and more free, and sometimes [we] even had an almost zany quality which would often make Martha

Arnold Eagle.

Mary Hinkson as "For Earth" in Canticle for Innocent
Comedians, *1952.*

titter. It was amazing to see Martha sit on those Noguchi benches listening to the music. Sometimes her eyes would roll back in her head, and then, as if possessed, she would suddenly get up and demonstrate a phenomenally intricate passage of movement. We would try to capture what she had just danced, often only approximating her elusive and complex timing. *Canticle for Innocent Comedians* was such a beautiful piece. It was magically lit by Jean Rosenthal, and [the dance was] based on St. Thomas Aquinas' worship of the elements in nature. This was only the second so-called "company piece." *Diversion of Angels* (1948) was the first. Prior to that time, all the works were built around Martha. Incidentally, during this period Martha was dancing superbly, and she was teaching brilliantly. She had just choreographed and performed two marathon solos, *Judith* and *The Triumph of St. Joan*, in 1950 and 1951, [respectively]. Just think, Martha had been told she might never dance again after her knee injury!

The making of *Canticle* was for us such an amazing time. Martha called us, the new group, her "coryphees." The dance was woven together by movement interludes in which we the group pushed the beautiful, blue wooden sculptures about, like dancing stagehands. By blending our bodies into the concave curve of the pieces, we were able to make them glide in and out of light, and on and off the stage as if by magic. Each interlude set the stage for a solo. The first one was "In Praise of Sun," by Bertram Ross.

"In Praise of Earth" was to be performed by Natanya Neuman, but because of a conflict Martha chose me for the role. The solo was choreographed in quite a short time. Martha would smile during rehearsals and say that I had to learn how to gain stamina. It was particularly true because I was still needed in the dancing interludes. I would dress to be a coryphee, then run into the wings to change for the "Earth" solo, and then change again to be a coryphee. Originally *Canticle* closed with Pearl Lang's "In Praise of Death," which was gorgeous. Typically, Martha was uncomfortable having her work end with "Death," or "Night," as it was later called. She decided the dance had to end with the concept of rebirth, or spring. We all felt this was due to Martha's fear of death. So, once again, I changed my clothes and reappeared as "Earth," or "Spring," a symbol of life continuing.

After the season at the Juilliard Theatre, Martha, as always, continued to experiment with movement in class. She added some startlingly different elements to the technique, such as formalized breathing with the legs crossed. The movement was becoming more elongated and extended. It was much less percussive but no less powerful.

Arnold Eagle.

Mary Hinkson dancing "For Earth" in Canticle for Innocent
Comedians, *1952.*

Many of these movements were incorporated into a new company work, *Ardent Song* (1954). The night before the scheduled premiere in London, because of so many pressures, the dance [still] had no ending. In her frustration Martha said the piece was canceled, and we were all sent home, exhausted, at about 2:00 a.m. At 8:00 a.m. we were summoned back to the theater. Pieces of fabric were hurried over to a shoemaker to be sewn together because, as usual, the costumes were not ready. The unfinished parts of the work had to be talked through and that happened onstage. There were six couples on stage, and we had to breathe together and move as one. There was absolutely no count to the Alan Hovhaness score. The concentration was so intense it probably made it one of the greatest performances ever.

It was also in London that I first danced "The Girl in White" in *Diversion of Angels.* Pearl Lang was "The Girl in Red." In the beginning these roles were clearly defined and distinctly different. When Pearl dashed onto the stage and plunged into that famous body tilt her hair literally touched my ankle. It was so daring. Unfortunately, through the years this wonderful body plunge has been watered down to a leg extension.

In the same dance there was a "conversation" between "The Girl in Red" and "The Girl in White." In the original choreography—this, too, had been Natanya's role —the opening sequence involved melting to the floor from the same standing leg to the knee. My knee could never, ever, do that. Consequently, in each run-through when we got to that point, I just stood there. Finally in a dress rehearsal, when it was clear that Martha was not going to choreograph those few measures, I felt the tears coming. Martha said, with annoyance, "Go ahead and cry." I ran off the stage in a deluge of tears. Bob Cohan said to me, "Now listen. Everybody who has ever danced that role has been psychologically defeated in some way. Now get yourself together and work out something." Yuriko (Kikuchi) coached me through that trauma in a very significant way, and helped me iron out the creases in what I had come up with to dance in the space of those four measures. That is the way it was performed from then on.

During that London season, in 1954, the audience was totally unprepared for the theater of Martha Graham. For the most part, they found the movement very athletic, unbeautiful and incomprehensible. It never occurred to us that audiences could possibly see Martha as a woman past her prime. In our eyes she was dancing ecstatically. Every night Matt and I used to watch Martha's "mad dance"—as it was called—in *Deaths and Entrances*. We were mesmerized again and again. It was inconceivable then that I would be performing that same role in about 15 years.

Often with Martha, creating a new work was an unpredictable process. This was certainly true when she decided to make her solo, *The Triumph of Saint Joan* (1951), into a company piece, *Seraphic Dialogue*. Noguchi did that stupendous set. Originally Martha was to be the central Joan, but Linda Hodes was the first to dance that part. Helen McGehee was to be the "Warrior," but she and Martha ran into problems so I actually danced the role in the New York premiere in May 1955.

Typically there was a lot of hysteria as opening night approached. Almost always Martha postponed finalizing costumes until the very last minute. For her, it seemed to be a way of calming her nerves. For us, it was devastating. I can remember standing in the wings opening night, with Jessica, a sewing helper, removing pins from my tunic just seconds before my entrance. Believe me, I went onstage looking as though I had been shot from a cannon. It is . . . interesting that John Martin described the work as "stillborn." Martha did not take that lightly.

There were usually big gaps between Graham performances, no doubt because of a shortage of funds, particularly since we performed always in a Broadway theater. This gave Martha the luxury of working without time pressures. It also meant, for me, cravings to be on stage. During one of these long lulls, John Butler had invited Glen Tetley and me to be his principal dancers with the New York City Opera. I told Martha that I very much wanted to accept this offer and I yearned to perform as much as possible. When provoked, Martha often used her clothing to dramatize the situation. She smoothed her elegantly fitted dress over her hips and said, "You will have to make a place for yourself." I said, "That is exactly what I am trying to do." Then she began with her gloves, carefully working on each finger, and said, "Very well, then. But you won't be in the new piece." As it turned out, that was *Seraphic Dialogue*.

I chose not to go on the first Asian tour in 1955-56 because I was soon to be married. Martha was not pleased, but I think she respected my reason. It seems my replacement in the role of "Warrior" in *Seraphic Dialogue* did not fair well in Indonesia [even] though it happened to be her native land. Apparently, however, this was the impetus Martha needed to resolve this ongoing challenge. Her new concept of the role, I was told, was born late at night in the ballroom of a hotel. Once more she summoned Helen to dance the "Warrior," but this time with Bert Ross as "St. Michael." Now "Joan the Warrior" was "Joan the victim"—vulnerable, frightened, reluctant, but pressed to fulfill her commitment by the benevolent urging of St. Michael. Finally everything fell into place. This version worked beautifully.

When the company returned to New York after nearly six months, Martha asked me to come to her apartment. She explained what had happened, and that she knew this version of the dance was right, and that I would no longer be cast as the "Warrior." Clearly it now called for a person much smaller than I. That Martha felt I deserved an explanation as to why I had lost the role was in itself remarkable. That she invited me to her apartment so that I would hear it directly from her was even more extraordinary. Eventually I was asked to dance "Joan the Maid." I loved dancing the "Maid." That is the most beautiful role in terms of sheer dancing, dancing, dancing. And of course, later I inherited the central Joan role and I loved performing that part, too.

During this period, Martha began choreographing more works on the company. It was a time of great stability, despite long lapses between seasons. More and more individual dancers were receiving recognition. In some ways the mid-Fifties through the mid-Sixties were a kind of "golden era" for the Graham Company.

When we filmed Martha's *A Dancer's World* (1957) I was in my early stages of pregnancy. Martha liked the results of that film, but at the same time, she was also very frustrated that she had to speak directly into the camera. She didn't mind recording the voice-over when she was introducing the Graham dancers, but she was put off when she actually had to be filmed. It was a traumatic time for Martha, and she had temper tantrum after temper tantrum during the process of making this film. I am sure it was her vanity, and of course she was very conscious of her age. I think the film captures Martha's choreographic elements of her technique and how well it lends itself to a flow of movement. Today people still like to see that film.

Over the next year Martha worked on her libretto for *Clytemnestra*, which premiered in 1958, the same year my daughter Jennifer was born. I sat in the audience on opening night to see *Clytemnestra* and I was overwhelmed by its beauty, in terms of the choreographic magic of different scenes in the dance-theater. I was flabbergasted, but I hadn't done my homework to grasp the scope of the *Oresteia*. Never in a million years would I have thought that in

1973 Martha would be coaching me in her title role.[1]

When Balanchine invited Martha to collaborate with him in the making of a new work, *Episodes* (1959), I was really disappointed not to be included in the casting. Also, at the time I was not inclined to spend much time at the Graham studio. It was during this period that I became more and more enchanted with taking ballet classes. That, of course, did not sit well with Martha.

However in 1960, in the midst of a rehearsal period for Graham's next Broadway season, due to the urging of Arthur Mitchell, I unexpectedly was invited to privately audition for Balanchine. Even more unexpectedly, I was invited to dance with Arthur in Balanchine's *Figure in the Carpet*. What a dilemma! On one hand, I was thrilled by the prospect. On the other, I was terrified at the thought of presenting this to Martha. I would have to miss a lot of rehearsals, and she was choreographing a new work at the time, *Alcestis*.

I used to have "psychodramas" with myself if I had something to say to Martha. I used to have to practice at home. This called for another big psychodrama at home. Martha was very frightening to go up against. Finally when I faced the moment I was stunned by Martha's response, which was, "I think this is very important, and I think you should do it." Martha had that strange, defensive attitude, combined with admiration, about anything having to do with ballet. In the beginning when I first went to Martha's studio, if you did anything that looked like you had been near a ballet barre you were slapped down verbally, "Don't do that in my studio." Martha could be so unpredictable.

Martha went to see me perform in *Figure in the Carpet* and called me at 2 in the morning. She said, "I'm amazed you were so able to capture the style in Balanchine's work. It was wonderful." It was a thrill that Martha called me, and I was also pleased that she went to see the performance.

I almost wasn't in some sections of Martha's *Acrobats of God* (1960). My favorite section in *Acrobats* is the bolero. I adored doing that. In my next life I'm going to be a Spanish dancer, anyway. At the time, I was still teaching at Juilliard. When Martha was choreographing if you had a conflict, if I said, "I'm sorry, Martha, I have to teach today at Juilliard"—even though I was teaching

---

[1] Martha Graham gave Mary Hinkson an archer's ring as a gift after performing *Clytemnestra* in 1973. In her note Graham wrote, "To Clytemnestra, From Clytemnestra. May you always hit the mark as you have done this season. May 13, 1973."

for Martha Graham at Juilliard —Martha would say, "All right, go," and you would be gone. Then Martha would choreograph a new section, and if you weren't there, then you were not in it. Tough luck. So I was disappointed Martha choreographed the bolero for *Acrobats* the day I was teaching. I don't know how I got to be in it. Somebody was out. That is the way it always was with me. It was so frustrating. We would always be hanging around, hanging around, hanging around, hoping, hoping, hoping that Martha was going to choreograph some wonderful new juicy section of a dance and we would all get to dance. All of our husbands were horrified that we were there on a platter to say, "I'm yours."

One More Gaudy Night in 1961 really turned out to be a bust. But it did work for me. I remember Bob Joffrey saying after he saw it that he was embarrassed by the whole dance except for my one little dead-pan, humorous segment. My part drew big laughs. Martha is divine with humor, and that was well-established long ago with *Every Soul Is a Circus* back in 1939. Martha can be so dry, so funny, so satirical.

As I look back, I realize how often I inherited roles. When Martha chose me to dance her role "Delilah, The Awakener" in *Visionary Recital,* she retitled the work *Samson Agonistes.* In those days, when Martha relinquished a role it was almost always totally rechoreographed, and in this case it had a totally new look. Can you imagine this biblical character dressed in a leotard and tights? The only thing that was carried over from the first version was a voluminous cape which I found very difficult to maneuver. I made the mistake of asking Ursula Reed, our marvelous costume-maker, to shorten it. Martha was livid, but it was too late to do anything else. As it turned out, the dance didn't last long in the repertory.

Later that year (1962), the company was scheduled to tour 12 to 16 weeks in Eastern Europe. I could not possibly leave my daughter, Jennifer, for that length of time. Matt couldn't go either. Martha was very angry and accused both of us of trying to sabotage the company.

The following year the company was invited to the Edinburgh Festival and to London. Even though I was once again out of favor, Martha decided she needed me to go on that tour. However, she made it clear that I would have little to dance. After much soul-searching, and still another psychodrama at home—my husband, Julien, was my strength in these sessions—I called Martha and said, "It sounds as though you don't really need me, but instead a coryphee." For me that took a lot of rehearsal. Martha used to count on each one of us individually—the women in her company—at different times. Women were essential for her company. In some instances, women were a threat to Martha. Martha was interested in men—Martha in relation to men. Martha used to control everybody by promising you, promising you, promising you, and it got to be a joke among all of us. You would be called in: "Darling, I have this new role in mind, and I see you as a goddess." Martha would say that. And everybody was going to be a goddess, it didn't matter what it was. It got to be very predictable. Anyway, in our next conversation Martha said she was choreographing a new work, *Circe* (1963). She said [that although] she wasn't sure she could "pull it off with me," she could see me in the title role. That, of course, was my reprimand for being so bold.

It turned out to be a fabulous experience. After inheriting so many roles, it was divine to have a piece created on me and, better still, with seven men! It was also the first time I knew what it meant to be really directed by Martha. I think too often we were left to our own devices in approaching a role. She was very clear and specific and said, "You must never take your eyes off of Ulysses." Then she added that of course it is not your eyes, but rather what you sense. It is as though you have tentacles at the base of your skull, and like an animal, the gaze must always be oblique. She gave image upon image, each one geared toward understanding how an enchantress casts a spell.

Say you had just learned the choreography, or Martha had just choreographed such and such on you. Then she would leave you with it. You would be with a musician in a room, and you were to become more comfortable with the phrasing and try to remember it the way that she had recommended. You would work by yourself, and [then] Martha would come back in. And inevitably, after working by yourself, we would nail it, so to speak, and get it down. We had to make sure this was exactly right, or that this turn was very sharp. Then Martha would come back in and tear you to pieces. She would frequently say, "It is moving very well, but it doesn't mean a damn thing." This is a standard that Martha set.

When Martha began to think about *Circe* she had intended to dance the great Greek heroine herself. I don't know that what Martha choreographed for me was so different than what she would have done for herself. She identified me with certain things, and she put all these things she identified me with in that dance, *Circe*. I found out what Circe ate for breakfast to an extent.

Noguchi's set worked very well for *Circe* even though it was made for *Voyage* (1953). One time when Martha was choreographing *Circe* there was this very dangerous drop. There were some very dangerous things in *Circe*. First, I had to stand on Bob Powell's shoulders and fall, which was 11 or 12 feet. Dick Gain, who was one of the greatest partners in the dance world, was the receiver. It had to be done so that he took the weight. He picked me up, turned me around and I had to get into his cape. In any case, while working on this, Martha said, "Get me down, get me down." Martha was identifying with me up there on his shoulders. Now that I think about it, Martha would never have made the dance the way she made it if it was for herself. Not in a million years. For me, *Circe* was definitely one of the biggest things that ever happened in my career.

The premiere of *Circe* in London was a great success. The same British critics who had been so harsh to the Graham Company nine years before were wild with enthusiasm this time. Martha was quite pleased.

A year went by, and we were trying to get *Circe* together to perform again with a video. We did all the movements that were in the video. Then we did it with music—live piano music. Somehow, we did all we had to do and there were yards and yards of music left over. We couldn't figure out whatever it was. We had done all the choreography and the music was going on and on. I got so upset, and I said to Martha, "This is a disaster. We can't put this on." Martha . . . was always so busy with herself it was very hard to get her to pay attention come theater time to what you had to do. Jean Rosenthal, the lighting designer, watched it and she said, "It's all there. You just have to find it in your performance." Martha also said, "You'll find it in performance." You see, everything had taken much longer to do. It was truly an example of how you had to make the movement speak. There wasn't that much choreography. It was what you did with it that mattered.

Martha used to say to me, "*Circe* is your piece and yours alone." After we had our big "hoopla," the first thing she wanted to do was revive the piece for another dancer.

Another part that was my very own was the mysterious figure in *Part Real— Part Dream* (1965). I love that title. Matt and I had a wonderful time fantasizing about who we were in the piece, and playing with all kinds of possible meanings. It all started when Martha went into the costume room, which was literally stuffed with everything imaginable, pulled out some wind chimes hanging from a wooden bar and said, "Try dangling these over your head, like a genie." That was the beginning of my role, the figure who enters the dark side of a dream. Martha had this kind of murmuring chuckle if she was pleased. It was not a big laugh, it was a very inner thing. So she was pleased with that. That was the opening of the dance, in silence.

That was the period when Martha was very much out of it. She would come to rehearsal in her street clothes and she wouldn't change. She got me wrapped up in this material with a train that was 12 to 16 feet behind me. Martha, in her inimitable fashion, wrapped the fabric around and through and around my legs and it was caught to the other side. She was very specific about what my opening move should be. She was so particular about how my body should be executing a slow développé and fall. Beyond that, she would say, or guide, or direct me with, "Try something. Try this. Try that. Try going into the air." When she saw something she liked she would say, "Keep that. Keep that walk." At one point, we would get to a non-productive few minutes, which would stretch out, and Martha would say, "Mary, you're in that cloth, I'm not." It was really very funny, when you think about it.

I did Louis Horst's courses in Pre-Classic Forms and Modern Forms. In Modern Forms our assignment was to choreograph an earth primitive and an air primitive. Louis Horst liked my air primitive so much that he took me with him when he would do lectures . . . to illustrate my air primitive. What I used choreographically in *Part Real—Part Dream* were elements of my air primitive.

Matt and I loved who we were in that dance. I'm not sure who we were— we were certainly contrasting figures caught in a spell. It was very magical. It is not magical enough to talk about good and evil. It was very otherworldly. I don't think the dance was supposed to come into focus in very concrete terms. It was supposed to cast a spell and it did, and you were left with whatever you were left with.

It is interesting, and disturbing, to look back on what a dark period this was for Martha. She sank further and further into periods of despondency and self-destruction. Many of her performances during this time were disastrous. She could not face the passage of time.

Amazingly enough, however, *Clytemnestra* was so well received in Lisbon in 1967 the applause continued on and on, even after the asbestos curtain came down. It had to be raised for more bows. Martha pounded her fists against her breast and said, "Oh ye of little faith."

This was the one tour I felt might be workable to have my daughter, Jennifer, travel with us. We shared a room with Helen McGehee and had a great time. Jen's response to *Clytemnestra* was, "Why haven't I seen this before?" I had always chosen for her the lighter programs. This really made Martha chuckle with pleasure. On Jennifer's next birthday, the doorbell rang and there was a special messenger from Tiffany's. Martha had sent her beautiful pearl earrings.

Those performances in Lisbon probably represented Martha's last real triumph on stage, though she continued to perform through our season at the Brooklyn Academy of Music in 1969. During that season I danced Martha's role in *Deaths and Entrances* for the first time in New York City.

What an ordeal it was to recover that choreography! It meant looking at very old, poor quality films without sound, and with absolutely no help from Martha. For five months Gene Lester, our rehearsal pianist, Sally Graupner, Martha's kind of "girl Friday," and I struggled with this film that raced along like a Charlie Chaplin movie. When we finally dared to try a run-through Martha begrudgingly came in to see what we had done. Her response was "it is moving well, perhaps better than ever before, but it doesn't mean a goddamn thing." That was a real blow, but we were already contracted to appear at the Blossom Festival with the Cleveland Symphony Orchestra [and] *Deaths* was on the program. After the performance Martha said very little to me, but to Pat Birch she said, "Now I know how to go to work on her."

And she *really did*, before the next performance at the New London Festival in Connecticut. In a certain way I had the worst of it and the best of it. She unleashed her fury on me, but at the same time she used every device imaginable to make me go beyond what I had done in Cleveland. I was deeply touched when she put her hands on my shoulders, after crucifying me, and said, "You know, I want to do this so much I can taste it." Then she added, "Maybe I didn't do all these things myself, but I meant to." That was surely the most intimate and meaningful exchange we ever had. Later, in a handwritten note to me, Martha said, "I am especially grateful for and moved by Medea and *Deaths*—your mad scene is a bewilderment of pain and deep beauty." For me that was the culmination of everything.

There were no surprises anymore, except downhill surprises, the way everything went at Graham. We all knew not to count on anything. When Martha became ill it was Bert Ross, Lee Leatherman (the general manager) and myself who kept the Graham Company running so she would have a company to work with when she returned. When Martha did return, Ron Protas assumed more authority. I used to call Ron the "Iago" character because he was continuously whispering in Martha's ear.

At one point I finally had it, and left. I went to the corner of Third Avenue and called my husband, Julien. I said, "I just walked out." He said, "Great. I'll open a bottle of champagne." I have never once regretted leaving. And it does not diminish for one moment my 23-year commitment to Martha Graham.

Martha Graham was provocative. Sure she was. What she made you realize was to try to find a way to make your body speak, not just dance. The thing Martha hated was facility. She didn't want to see facility. She didn't want to see you flipping this off as though you could do it in your sleep. She wanted you to participate and be a part of it. She wanted you to experience it, to make your body speak. Martha wanted to emphasize not only a physical expression, but to go beyond that, so the psychological implications could come through your body—not through mugging or facial expressions, not through being fake [but] through being real. This was always, always, always the challenge. We were often reduced to tears in the effort. Often, we would go onstage in a role for the first time a total failure. Total failure, really. Martha would say, "You have to find it through performance."

Like most everyone, I was totally in awe of Martha, but unlike many, I fell in love with dance before I knew anything about Martha Graham. I think this was the key to survival.

To be exposed to Martha Graham was a singular, extraordinary experience— often very frightening, but certainly enriching. If you survive the experience— because I think you will either survive the experience or you won't—you will either come out stronger or defeated. I think the best thing that can happen to you is you come out whole.

MATT TURNEY

Jaacov Agor.

Matt Turney dancing "Ariadne" in Errand into the Maze,
c. 1960s.

Matt Turney was born in Americus, Georgia, in 1925. She graduated from the University of Wisconsin, where she majored in dance.

Matt Turney joined the Martha Graham Company in 1951. She performed major roles in New York and on European and Asian tours until the early 1970s. Among her creations for the Graham Company are one of the "Aspects of St. Joan" in Seraphic Dialogue, *"Lilith" in* Embattled Garden, *"Cassandra" in* Clytemnestra, *the "Betrayer" in* Visionary Recital *and* Samson Agonistes *(as it was called when it was revised the next year), and the only woman's role in* A Look at Lightning.

Turney also danced with the companies of Donald McKayle, Alvin Ailey, Paul Taylor, Pearl Lang and Bertram Ross. In addition, she performed many joint programs with Robert Cohan.

Matt Turney lives in New York City.

Author's Note: Matt Turney is the one artist in this collection who preferred not to participate in an oral interview. Rather, she poetically wrote her answers to my questions.

I met Nancy Hauser, my first dance teacher, in junior high school. She taught in an afterschool program of the Milwaukee Recreation Department. It was her guidance that took me to University of Wisconsin, where I majored in dance. Right after high school I went to Chicago to see a performance by Katherine Dunham. Nancy encouraged me to see all the visiting dance companies that came our way. I was excited by the evening, and went backstage in hopes of meeting K.D. I was told I could not see her but she would be holding auditions the next afternoon, and I could come if I wished. Next day I told her

I was a dancer, and had enjoyed the performance the evening before. She asked if I had something to show her. I said, "If one of your musicians will play something, I will improvise." Someone played piano, others joined in, and I did "whatever." She asked me to call my parents and tell them I would be joining the company and going with them the next day. My parents would not hear of such a thing. I was ordered home immediately and shipped off to summer school post-haste!

When I arrived in New York, I first studied at the New Dance Group. I met and performed with Mary Anthony,[1] Donald McKayle,[2] and Pearl Primus.[3] While doing a session of classes with Jean Erdman, someone suggested study-ing at the Graham studio. So my good friend from Wisconsin, Mary [Hinkson], and I did just that. We had classes with Erick Hawkins, Yuriko, Helen McGehee and, of course, Martha. We worked concentratedly at Martha's, and performed whenever we got an opportunity. [I] occasionally did a TV show when John Butler needed to augment his company or needed additional dancers for his City Center Opera productions.

[I] earned [very] little during this time of classes and sporadic performances. My father financed the New York venture. He was certain I would get the "dancing bug" out of my system in short order and go on to more reasonable and reputable pursuits. Accustomed to summer breaks, I took an extended va-cation. [It was during] this interim [that] I saw the Graham Company in perfor-mance in the Midwest. I was astonished to see many of the dancers I'd been taking class with a few months before in the current company . . . looking good! Still "dance-infected" and homesick for the more adventurous New York scene, I made the logical move and returned. This time I studied consistently at the Graham studio and added a ballet class taught by [my] next-door loft neighbor, Karl Shook (mentor of Arthur Mitchell, artistic director of the Dance Theatre of Harlem).

Like all young people with a little exposure in a specific subject, I arrived in New York thinking I knew a lot about dance and thinking I had something to

[1] Mary Anthony, (1920-). American dancer and choreographer.

[2] Donald McKayle, (1930-). American modern dancer, television and theatrical performer, and choreog-rapher. See pages 228-235.

[3] Pearl Primus, (1919-1994). American pioneer of the anthropological modern dance movement.

offer as a performer. Well, I had much to learn, and I learned it at the Graham studio. With the assurance of the innocent and the naïveté of the inexperienced, I began the dancer's saga with many other "nearly arrived would-bes." My identity was "dancer" from junior high school on; two years with Martha, my identity was forever after "Graham dancer." She was my greatest teacher. That is, everything preceding had been a preparation for her. I was not thinking in career terms nor was I starstruck and seeking bright lights, but rather I was pursuing the dance experience itself, the physical exhilaration, the satisfaction of total involvement and the promise of endless adventure.

Martha was adamant about the technique. She had to be. She was making a difference in dance. She was breaking old molds and creating new forms. Her dancers had to be taught and trained in these new forms in order for her singular vision to be realized. Taking class with Martha was vital. Her presence and energy pervaded the room. We learned as much through osmosis as by instruction. Her major emphasis was on the dances, her own performance and her stage. Teaching was necessary, but incidental to her choreographic goals and iconoclastic stage.

The technique was challenging and difficult. I became completely absorbed in it, living for class . . . the daily ritual. I would leave the studio exhausted, but keenly alive, ready for "life"—no anxiety about the future, content to live from "dancing day" to "dancing day." The gypsy character began to take shape in me, but I remained on call to Martha and loyal for the next 20-plus years.

Mary [Hinkson] tells me I first danced with the company in *Canticle for Innocent Comedians* and my first actual "role" was "The Ancestress" in *Letter to the World*. She knows. She is good with dates and figures and who did what and when. It is true one tends to remember the good and pleasant and not the negative and unpleasant. My "Ancestress" role never worked. We were on our way to Europe and she had no one else to put in the part. Martha was very dissatisfied from the first rehearsal and she gave me a really hard time at every successive rehearsal. She tried everything, even tried being encouraging and nice, but mostly she used the old director tactic: destroy [the performer] emotionally in order to break through to another level to what [the director] wants. Company member David Wood, who lived next door, used to console me. I would say, "I just can't take another rehearsal like that, but I want to go to Europe." The next day David would say, "You still want to go to Europe?" Me: "Yeah, yeah." David: "Well, hang in there! Don't break! Don't crack!"

Throughout the European tour Martha would take each principal in *Letter* by the hand to the center of the stage for a curtain call, but never me. I felt this as a repeated insult. Her attitude of loathing and disdain might have been a conscious strategy to evoke a different or more convincing performance. Real or feigned, the result was a terrorized dancer. Martha could as well have been holding a knife at my throat. I had no recourse but to go into the spotlight completely undermined and do my terrified best. Rage may have been what she was after but what she got was stoicism. Isn't that another kind of rage? After the last performance of the tour Martha sent word for me to come to her dressing room. When I arrived she apologized for not ever giving me a curtain call. Now I felt nothing. I had not responded for six months, I could not respond now—no sense of forgiveness, just nothing. She may have been sincere, maybe not; it didn't matter. I learned I could not project the matriarch . . . and puritanism was not in my genes or muscle fibers. Authenticity requires more than cerebral understanding and flexibility. Pearl said, as she fiddled with my hair and costume one night before the curtain went up, "God, you're like the other woman in *Letter,* not the autocratic figure of gloom and doom." I want to explain and justify my performance in this role, but I won't. Today, at this particular point in time, I still may not be able to play Martha's "Ancestress," but I could play the hag.

Martha did not trust me from early on. She expected, by virtue of my physical type, a certain dancing quality. I did not meet her expectations, i.e., the "Ancestress" in *Letter.* By the end of the European tour, though, she knew that I was strong and not defiant, reliable and committed to dance. . . . My role in *Appalachian Spring* was working, and [the chorus in] *Diversion of Angels* was working. After our return, she tried me in other roles. The European and Far East tours were fantastic experiences not only from a dance point of view but I was seeing the world for the first time. My perspective was changing, and I was learning.

Had I had my choice, I would have been in the couple's dance of *Dark Meadow.* It is one of the most exalted, beautiful dances ever, but as was often the case, I was too tall or too something to fit into a homogeneous group. Lyricism and fleetness were the qualities that were usually asked of me. [But] these qualities were not appropriate for "She of the Earth," [the role I was given]. I grew to love most every role I ever danced, but this one came with many challenges. The style and quality of the role was markedly determined by the costume, an elongated to the ankle, body-tight, knitted sheath, completely revealing and frustratingly limiting. A step could not exceed six inches without putting extreme stress on the hem. So much for fleetness! At first I stumbled and fell with every attempt to bring a sense of dance to the role. I had to race across the stage to change a set piece or manipulate a prop on cue in a definite, specific way, another dancer dependent on split-second timing. How could I make these utilitarian moves dance? So I worked with images and qualities inherent in the sheath dress: strong, straight tree trunk . . . rooted, long stem, lithe, reed flexible. Means of locomotion: sitting on heels, straight back scuttling faster than a rattlesnake; wind-tossed, uneven lunge; rolling tumbleweed-like over the floor, never leaving the ground, literally "down to earth." At the same time I had to fiercely hang onto my abdominals and lengthen my spine to get away with that costume. Once the choreography, facilitated by the images, was mastered, this role was still difficult, even treacherous, but wonderful to dance.

In the performance of *Dark Meadow,* the setting was magic, real magic. The music, the lighting, the costumes, the props, beaded, feathered fetish wands, water ceremonies using ancient bowls, [a] flowering branch of rebirth and spring, all brought ritual transforming to the moment. So to dance in this magic atmosphere was to be natural. My shy, self-conscious self was no longer present . . . the spirit of the Earth priestess inhabited the body and lived again, I hope.

I learned the role in *Dark Meadow* from a film. As was the way with new casting, whenever possible there was at least one rehearsal with the original dancer. Left to my own devices, I handled the choreography (which I found inseparable from the images) to the best of my ability, consistent with my technique, life experience and understanding to date. This is all that one can ever do: bring the total self and "then something" to the situation. The "then something" usually happens in performance, in the magic setting. All of us were nervous and anxious at the first complete run-through with the totally new cast. Martha had not been present at any of my rehearsals. She sat cross-legged, back to the mirror, on a low bench at the front of the studio, probably as much in anticipation as we were. My earthiness was a Fifties rendering, rather than the original Forties. It was a younger, devotional, fervent image—a lighter touch. I'm sure she was surprised by the differences, but she must have felt [that my] "She of the Earth" was valid or I would have been replaced.

Most often dancing was hard work, but it was also always exhilarating, providing the necessary energy and desire required. These were also the unusual, effortless times in performance when there was no thought of sequence or anything technical; it seemed [like] I did not even initiate the movement. The dance poured through me as though something ancient were recurring. Afterwards I would ask myself was I dancing or watching or dreaming?

Errand into the Maze was the most challenging dance I performed. I had to reach for an increased technical strength and characterization beyond anything I had done before. I had to hold the stage alone much of the time. I loved the powerful Menotti score; there was a demonic walk to a boogie beat along a treacherous path to a secret lair that I still do in dreams. The challenge was to not be pushed by the music to the nth degree, full-out energy level, but to vary the dramatic intensity for the sake of physical endurance as well as audience receptivity. This was hard to do in the face of the insistent score. After Martha evoked the ancestors within you, the rest was technical direction: "Don't move until you hear the tympani,"she would say, synchronizing musical and movement accents. "Don't anticipate . . . don't even out the dynamics." On occasion, with the adrenaline of performance, timings change. So a syncopation was set up with the orchestra—a delayed lightening-fast attack after the sound that seemed simultaneous. Sometimes waiting for the tympani seemed half a lifetime, and I would think the conductor must be waiting for me to move. Unable to sustain another moment, I would fly into action and the sound would be there! All the antennae operative, the ancient hunter instincts return. Every nerve ending grasping for the slightest change in the atmosphere, the terrain. . . . You feel the heat of light on your cheekbones, the draft from a wing as you rush past, a shadow space changes to bright, a false note in the orchestra, the rhythm of your heart—it's racing. You exhale and stabilize. Each moment so attenuated there is time enough to notice everything: the cough in the front row, the stagehand in the wings, and time enough to calculate and take a chance, defy gravity, precede the beat into the air, delay the landing. Time is not inevitable. It can stop long enough to lose yourself and find yourself again between two beats of a conductor's baton. I often did not know whether I took the cue or gave the cue—it happened!

Canticle [for Innocent Comedians] and *Ardent Song,* these dances were very similar company works—*Ardent Song,* no set; *Canticle,* with set. The mobile scenery in *Canticle* was rearranged in surprising and adroit ways. The group work in *Canticle* was particularly outstanding for its fleetness, lightness and even playfulness. We, the Chorus, fairly flew from wing to wing, resetting the stage for each solo or duet. We chased each other across stage. Then suddenly in unison, hips swaying, [an] abrupt tumble to the floor, a roll over and up and off again. Martha used the unique qualities of her solo dancers, and the effect was lyric, new. Her audience wondered was the "Greek period" over? But *Clytemnestra* was still to come. The Chorus had worked together so long and so often [that] we had developed unexpected rhythms of our own—a style within a style—breathing together, we were daring and free. Our solo obligato flights moved on a common breath and always returned to an unfaltering beat. A dancer leans against a standing ponderous wave, like a surfer caught in the curl. Seemingly effortlessly she slithers to a new place. . . . Body resting in the curve, she slides in slow motion to the floor, a sculptured figure in an upstage frieze.

Three dances of Martha's—the "Martyr" in *Seraphic Dialogue*, "Lilith" in *Embattled Garden*, and "Cassandra" in *Clytemnestra*—were choreographed, learned and performed at very different points in time. Martha was absolutely deliberate and definite in the choreography of each.

Seraphic Dialogue was originally a solo for Martha that she decided to put on the company. How could Martha have done this entire dance—we could hardly get through our single sections! In the transfer to the company I'm sure the choreography was altered just enough to push each dancer to the extremity of their technique—one more jump than was possible, timing that demanded faster or slower than possible—but we did it: [We] danced on the edge physically [and] emotionally. The "Martyr" was first learned by Linda [Hodes]. [Then] she went into the central "Joan" role and I went into the "Martyr." The challenge of this role started before the dancing began, sitting suspended on a slim rod, less than an inch in diameter, [a part] of the Noguchi set. Three of us perched there in a sustained "lift": The delicate rod could not support our weight . . . so the feet braced and pushed from the floor, and the body was held as if jumping. The rod could have slid from under us and we would have remained as placed. The bourrée across the stage preceding the solos may have had a floating quality, but it was done energetically to wake the feet that had fallen asleep. This was also a time for releasing and relaxing the abdominals. Thank God for those voluminous cloaks!

The first costume was white, but [it was] later changed to black with red appliqués at [the] abdomen and groin. Because [of the] fast knee-turns on a groundcloth or irregular stage . . . I often wound up with a bloodstreaked skirt. I suppose I could have spared the costume by dancing in some altered, lesser fashion, but in those days I preferred—obviously Martha did too—dancing to the limit, rather than [having] a pristine dress.

Opening night of *Embattled Garden:* the lighting on stage is tropical; "Lilith" (my role) will be contradictionally languorous and fiery; Surinach's score, urgent and propelling; the set, intriguing and supportive; and Martha—Martha who was never sentimental—could be as caring as a doting mother. Opening nights were always scary, with much uncertainty. Martha would hold you by the wrist, tightly, just before the curtain. She would add an invisible amulet to your costume, or make some small adjustment to your headdress, then stand quietly in the wings, sensing the atmosphere of her own stage, the energy and intensity of her dancers, and emitting some shamanistic power of herself to the event. If there is such a thing as transmission—the direct conveyance of know-how from master to apprentice—this is the moment when it took place. Not in the rehearsal studio of effort, failed attempts and frustrated feelings in collision, but now, in this vulnerable moment of intent and focus. The next time you glanced into the wings, she was not there . . . but you knew she had been assured and . . . so were you. I liked everything about *Embattled,* but mostly my partners. It started with Bob Cohan, [who was] replaced by Glen Tetley, then Paul Taylor. What an illustrious lineup!

It was obvious that Martha loved this character, "Cassandra," in *Clytemnestra.* She enjoyed choreographing it and I enjoyed dancing it, except [for] that long wait onstage before dancing, and that interminably far back-fall at the beginning. So scary! I had to allow one foot to leave the floor, which left the other in relevé digging into the floor for dear life . . . to sustain the angled thrust of the torso in contraction high above the shoulders for just a frozen moment. Then spiraling up to stand and again struck, shoulders to the ground and again. Did this happen one, two or three times? All the other elements of the choreography appealed to me. Back-falls were a part of classroom work, but the reason these were so different is that they were done on a slanting platform, so that my shoulders landed lower than [I] ever practiced, and the recovery was uphill, rather than ground level. The beginning of Cassandra's dance might have had a dramatic quality of panic, but I was in a real panic dealing with the technical problems. The wonderful, driven sequences—half-mad stare through fingers, hips gyrating; desperate knee-crawls with staff; frenetic sudden dashes about the stage—and all with a distraught and zany timing. I did the Helen of Troy role once, but "Paris" having danced originally with Ethel Winter as "Helen" never adjusted to me (taller, heavier) as his partner—nor I to him. The first act of *Clytemnestra* is the most riveting, beautiful and enthralling scene that has ever been on a stage. The spell of this dreamscape endlessly shifting from one exquisite dance into another more exquisite dance intensifies to a transmuting point: Tragedy is nullified by beauty! Or is Beauty intensified by Tragedy?

To dance *Phaedra* and *Errand* was the greatest of terrifying honors. I was never psychologically at ease in these roles. Who could fill Martha's shoes or, more explicitly, step into her footprints? Truthfully, I must admit, I would love to dance these two dances once a week, at least, forever. With *Phaedra*, there were two fantastic sections that I especially liked: the opening solo bed scene and a duo, with the stepson (Bob Powell) crossing downstage; the power was inherent in the demanding movement phrases. Since "Phaedra" was onstage throughout the piece, with intermittent dancing, much was required in the way of acting as well.

One of my favorite dancers to watch was Bob Powell. His technique was breathtaking, his performance always on an "out of this world," soaring plane; he took every movement to a daring point, held nothing back, gave everything. To dance on the same stage with him was to catch fire. His portrayal of the stepson [in *Phaedra*] was insidious and taunting, demanding one to reciprocate in kind. His performance surpassed his rehearsal to such a degree I was always shocked.

With *A Look At Lightning* (1962), *The World of the Kalahari,* by L. Vanderpost, provided images for me in this role. Perhaps Martha used Vanderpost's ideas as a point of departure, too. She never discussed his writings with me. I knew she read him and she probably knew I read him too. These nomad people of the desert followed the lightening for practical reasons of survival. What a dramatic image—thunderstruck legends to live by! My character represented for me the muse, inspiration, prodding conscience, mirage. The obvious metaphors as image—stroke of lightning as:

inspired idea	flash of lighting
breakthrough solution	streak of lightning
sudden insight	bolt of lightning
water in desert	storm in desert

I had three fantastic, totally-different-in-quality partners (Bert, Richard Kuch and Bob Powell). Of course, I loved that.

Martha's stage was ritual, completely literal ritual for me . . . the first and purest vehicle of meaning. The curtain parted and time cracked open . . . like a firecracker, showering insight and sudden illuminations. This attenuated "nontime" seemed to stretch back to the beginning and extend into the future. The action was powerful and magic; the telling, ominously clear. The curtain closed and time seemed again with "now." Try as I might I could not sustain the miraculous sensations and deep revelations, but I was always permanently affected, as though a truth-tipped arrow had found its mark . . . that place where mystery, beauty and intelligence are inseparable. *Visionary Recital* (1961) was a showcase of legendary essences, with a surreal quality of eternal recurrence. [One] solo for, Akiko [Kanda], was the epitome of silence, delicate as a jade carving, or an almost-transparent Lalique crystal. *Visionary* and *Mendicants* [*of Evening*] (1973) were primarily visual and meditative . . . a quiet encounter with "self" rather than [an] opponent. These works did not contain the usual and expected dramatic excitement of Martha Graham's previous works, but they did lead back through history, abstracting to timeless essence and the pinpoint ad infinitum. Or perhaps it was the audience's cue and responsibility—like the Cassandra character or the Scheckly science fiction hero to jaunt (a verb meaning to jump and fly) from reality to infinity.

In *Part Real—Part Dream* (1965) I felt quite glamorous . . . really dressed up, very glittery. I took the title very literally—as a puzzle, as a description of a personality trait, as well as a situation, meshing what is so with what is not, the demarcation [between them] unclear. The female characters portrayed opposite aspects and so did the male . . . one real, one dream, but which, and when? I always danced straightforwardly, so any innuendo was unintended—and real.

The last two dances I performed were *Mendicants of Evening,* where the format was a traveling ritual theater—timeless—an actor with a dancer counterpart and a dancer with an actor counterpart, and *Myth of a Voyage.* I do not remember the dance, but I love the title. The story (Myth) about the story (Voyage) that is the same journey for everyone, yet unique.

I want to say much more about everything: all of those wonderful dancers in the company at that time, other dances I was in like *Spring, Cave, Circus.* . . . At the moment I am saturated with the "unending past" . . . it can go on forever.

Working, dancing with Martha was so completely involving—all the preparation, the discipline, daily class, long rehearsals and costume fittings, emotional wear and tear—I never had time to think about questions of philosophy. I was

Milton Oleaga.

Matt Turney as "The Betrayer" with Bertram Ross and Martha Graham
in Visionary Recital, *1961.*

not analytic. It is only in retrospect I realize [that] during that period I fulfilled a dream I had never dared to dream. My young adult life was a tale fraught with all the terrors and triumphs of the legends I was dancing.

All of the other choreographers and dancers were marvelous and fulfilling. When Alvin Ailey asked me to dance with him as a guest [artist] I was extremely flattered. The music was "Creation of the World" by Darius Milhaud. Alvin was the strongest partner I ever had. Impossible lifts were no problem for him in spite of my gangly height. It was a joy to dance in his very musical, smooth and rippling style. But working with Martha was the most fulfilling and exciting. The scale was different—genius scale—greater in every way. The challenges were greater, the dances, the trauma, the accolades—greater! The completely professional production and presentation on the grand scale gave me the greatest sense of accomplishment.

These special persons like Martha Graham are not motivated by altruism, but rather a deep sense of self that demands to know by its own experience. Depth-probing, resultant from fascination with a subject, exploration and exploitation of a talent inevitably leads to who, what and why are we? Martha's quest was as old as time, and the same as that of the mystic, the scientist and all artists: To find answers to basic questions of what is "human," and to convey their truth through their chosen form of expression, be that a philosophical system or practice, theorem or artwork. Martha's choice—*DANCE*—was the most affecting for me [and] made it the easiest to side-step my mind and confusion into her clear terrain of the inexplicable.

She believed in Jung's "collective unconscious," believed in subterranean reservoirs within us and that was all tappable. We were her raw material willingly, having been seduced like she by awe and curiosity. Her every work defined "human" for me, so I was automatically caught up in her processes. She never imposed or championed a single philosophical idea. In rehearsal she didn't talk much. It was dance she was after.

Martha said enough in her poetic way to evoke the subtle, the primal within you, to direct you to a primordial source. The reason for and the quality of a back-fall: "Your heart leaps up, but caught in a vise of contradiction you plummet to the ground." Setting the stage for an opening curtain: "It is steamy hot! A tropical sun so enervating you cannot move. Then the storm that breaks and the drama that accompanies 'nature in extremis.'" The closing curtain: "All is over as suddenly as it began, but it will happen again and again. . . ."

DAVID WOOD

Arnold Eagle.

DavidWood in Acrobats of God, *1960.*

David Wood was born in Fresno, California, on February 24, 1925. He began his professional career in dance in 1949 as a teacher for the Hanya Holm School of Dance. Before joining the Martha Graham Company in 1953, he performed with José Limón, Charles Weidman, Alwin Nikolais, Doris Humphrey and Helen Tamiris. He also danced in numerous Broadway musicals and operas. As a soloist with the Graham Company he created many roles in leading works, such as Acrobats of God, Clytemnestra, The Legend of Judith, Cortege of Eagles and Secular Games. He was with the Graham Company for 15 years (1953-1968), and served as its rehearsal director from 1960 to 1968.

In 1968, David Wood and his wife, Marni Thomas, who was also a dancer with the Graham Company, moved to California to join the faculty of the University of California at Berkeley. In addition to creating a dance program within the university's Department of Dramatic Art, in 1970 Wood founded BARD (Bay Area Repertory Dance), its resident dance company. In 1989 Wood, working in collaboration with the eminent Berkeley physicist, Marvin L. Cohen, created an original work that was shown on a program on superconductivity from the Emmy Award-winning PBS series, NOVA. David Wood retired from the university in 1993. He since has written his autobiography and is currently at work on another book.

Wood has received numerous awards and honors, including the Distinguished Teacher Award from UC-Berkeley (1987), and he has been the recipient of two National Endowment for the Arts fellowships for choreography (1970 and 1978). He also has been a guest teacher in Sweden, Mexico, Israel, England and Japan.

David Wood divides his time between Berkeley and New York City.

I came to New York to be an actor in the fall of 1947, [when] Martha Graham was teaching movement for actors at the Neighborhood Playhouse. And she was really difficult at that time because she was "Miss Hush,"[1] and hated it. She hated playing "Miss Hush" week after week, and she took it out on the students. At that point she was much wilder then when I danced for her later. Martha would hit and scratch the students who didn't follow her instructions. She was a very violent woman.

In her movement for actors course she would do strange things, like make us recite Shakespeare while hanging from the barre. Once in a while Martha would teach us a regular technique class because she couldn't dream up anything else to do. And that is when she would be the most violent. She felt we violated what was very sacred to her—the human body. It didn't make any difference to her that we weren't trained dancers. . . . She felt that if you knew intellectually what to do then there was no reason why you couldn't produce her technique. That also translated to a lot of Martha's teachers as well. They didn't understand that there is a great deal of difference between understanding intellectually and understanding kinetically.

Martha was stimulating. She was inspiring. Everybody was in complete awe of her, even more than [of] Sanford Meisner, the acting teacher. But she was difficult. She was very, very difficult. She didn't like teaching there at the Neighborhood Playhouse, but she was indebted to Mrs. Morgenthau,[2] who ran it. Martha was very good about paying off her debts in terms of loyalty. Mrs. Morgenthau had done a lot for Martha's career. In the early days of the Neighborhood Playhouse it was a performing organization, and Martha and Charles Weidman danced there. It gave Martha a very strong start—a place where she could experiment, which she wouldn't have been able to do otherwise.

Louis Horst was also at the Neighborhood Playhouse. He taught composition. I had both Martha and Louis, and that was my first introduction to dance. In fact, I had a class with Louis Horst where I had to make up a dance before I ever had a dance technique class.

[1] "Miss Hush" was the name given to an unidentified voice who would broadcast clues to her identity over the radio every week. Listeners who had sent in 10 cents to participate in this March of Dimes contest were given the opportunity to guess her identity. Those who correctly identified "Miss Hush" were awarded prizes.

[2] The Neighborhood Playhouse was founded in 1915 by Irene and Alice Lewisohn. Rita Morgenthau, a social worker and the sister-in-law of Henry Morgenthau, was the administrator of the school.

Once we had to have class at Martha's studio at 66 Fifth Avenue. And Martha was livid with us. She was just furious that day. Finally Martha said, "All of you go to the corner." We all went to the corner. Martha took a chair and put it out in the middle of the room and she said, "All right. I want you to walk up to the chair one at a time, turn around, sit down in it and get up and walk off." We all laughed. Then she said, "By the time you have left, I will know everything about your sex lives." Everybody totally panicked. It was really marvelous to see because everybody changed their personality. It was then I realized that Martha Graham had a tremendous power over people. There were these huge guys who had been in the war and who were on the GI Bill, and they were petrified of just what Martha said—knowing everything about their sex lives. And the women didn't know what to do. Martha could totally gain power over people. She was an amazing woman.

I really didn't care for Martha too much at that time. As much as I realized she was a genius—because I had gone to her performances and all—I thought [her style] wasn't for me. Another mitigating factor was that I was told that Martha only liked tall men as dancers—I was 5' 9." So I went elsewhere when I decided to dance. I went, finally, to Hanya Holm, saw a class and got so excited I went there to study. Hanya was just getting work in musicals then. Hanya's technique suited me much better than Martha's. My sister was a dancer, a ballet dancer, so I was more aligned towards that anyway. And somehow, although I didn't like ballet, Holm blended with what my knowledge of dance was at that time. It was also easier to understand for me.

Both Hanya and Martha were such strong women. Oh God, I had such a time with them! I [had been] with Hanya a very short time [when] she offered me the chance to go to her summer school in Colorado with her because she needed men. I wouldn't earn money, but I would get my transportation and . . . living [expenses] all paid for. It was a chance to get out of New York. In Colorado I had a fantastic experience. Hanya liked young men. She promised me [I'd be in her musical *Out of This World* the next year. I had only just started to dance—a little bit at the Neighborhood Playhouse and two months with Hanya. I thought it was ridiculous. I mean, [of] all the dancers Hanya could choose in New York, why pick me? I didn't have any training. But who am I to turn Hanya down? As it turned out, *Out of This World* was postponed one year. [In the meantime], I . . . still [took] dance class at Hanya's and [went] down to the Henry Street Settlement to take class with Nik [Alwin Nikolais], who was Hanya's main disciple.

I started dancing with Nik, who was then forming his own company, and Hanya objected to that. I thought Hanya was much too restrictive. I liked her, but she caused me all types of trouble. Hanya could be very upsetting and difficult. It would be hard for me to compare Hanya and Martha because when I knew Hanya she was on Broadway, choreographing musicals. Hanya was in show business—which is very different from Martha's concert dance. Both Hanya and Martha had to struggle from poverty to plenty and they both did it—survived—in a totally different way. Hanya did it on her own and Martha did it with backing.

Then I danced with the Dudley, Maslow, Bales Trio, José Limón and Pearl Lang. And I always went up to the American Dance Festival at Connecticut College in New London. Martha gave a lecture on the first Monday of the opening of the summer school and it was the first time I really heard Martha speak. I was overwhelmed and I thought it was the greatest thing I ever heard. Bob Cohan dared me to come take class with Martha the week she was teaching in Connecticut. I did, and by then I was totally caught up with Martha Graham—the way she spoke when she taught, her images, everything. I decided when the summer school was over I would go study with Martha in New York City. I had had a little more Graham training from dancing with Jane Dudley and Sophie Maslow. I started in the beginning class at Graham's and it was after only about four months Martha called and. . . . She is a very crafty lady besides all of her genius. She was very sly. She said, "I don't know what your commitments are, but I need a boy to dance in *Letter to the World*," for Bethsabee de Rothschild's first American Dance Festival. She knew of course I was scheduled to dance with Doris Humphrey.

Being shorter than most of the men dancers, and [not] being . . . the type of man Martha liked particularly, I knew that [this] was my one chance to dance with Graham. I also knew I could not dance with Doris Humphrey and Martha Graham at the same time. I had to call up Doris and tell her I was going to dance Martha's *Letter to the World*. She was understandably very angry and said, "If you don't dance in one thing, you shouldn't dance in another." I said, "I've already made up my mind." Doris hung up on me. I spent a lot of years after that getting Doris her lunch at the Connecticut College summer school, bringing it to her, and all kinds of other things, just trying to make it up to her. We never spoke again about my dancing with Martha, but we finally got over our difficulties.

Then I went into Martha's season dancing *Diversion of Angels, Deaths and Entrances* [and] *Dark Meadow*. I danced other pieces. We went to Europe and I danced in *Ardent Song* (1954). It was the first dance I was in while Martha was choreographing it. It was a strange dance. I thought it was a beautiful work, though the excitement and confusion of going to Europe deterred Martha from finishing the choreography. It didn't go over successfully. Martha's work at that time only had a secondary effect on the British. *Ardent Song* wasn't thought of as a primary Graham dance at all. The interludes between the sections that were choreographed for Yuriko, Helen and Pearl—the connecting sections—weren't finished. The sections with the four couples were completed, so we decided to follow Bob Cohan and whoever he was dancing with because we could all see Bob. We ran through the unfinished *Ardent Song* the day of the scheduled premiere improvising the undone parts, and it was exciting. I have never known a Graham Company to work so cohesively as with the run-through of that dance. It was the best performance *Ardent Song* ever got. *Ardent Song* was a very strong example of the technique . . . coming out of the dances Martha choreographed: the whole breathing exercise and the use of the spiral and the back Martha used as the opening of *Ardent Song*. When Donnie McKayle came on the Asian tour with Graham, she changed *Ardent Song* again. And that is also when Paul Taylor first worked with her, in 1954. The Asian tour ended in Iran and then we were to go on to dance in Israel. Martha announced that Paul would be going home instead of to Israel. Matt Turney went to Martha and spoke to her about Paul and about how unfair it was he couldn't continue the tour to Israel. Matt put herself on the line, and Martha changed her mind about Paul. Paul said, "I'm sorry, I have other plans," and flew back to New York.

I went to Connecticut College with Martha one summer and [continued to go] for the next 10 or 11 summers, always for that week [when] Martha [taught]. I was never comfortable with Martha, but at Connecticut College we were always very close. Martha would work out a lot of her technique on me. The changes she made in plié—both demi and deep—she worked out up there on me because she was bored to death in the country.

Clytemnestra (1958) was, again, a difficult process. I was supposed to perform the watchman's solo in *Clytemnestra*. We had rehearsed it, and Martha had almost finished it. One day I came into the studio and heard the music for the watchman's solo. I looked through the crack in the door and there was Gene

McDonald rehearsing the watchman's solo with Martha. I waited, and went into the back room, which was Martha's office. Martha came in when they finished working. I said, Martha, "I heard the music for the watchman's solo being played. That's what I was doing. I was wondering what's going on." And she just blew up because she didn't want to be confronted. Quite logically she said, "I have too many characters in *Clytemnestra*. They are all at loose ends. I am trying to bring all the people who created death, destruction, [that] kind of thing, into one character." Which she did do—the prologue, the death figure; Paris, the death figure; the ghost of Agamemnon, the death figure—she brought these all together. And she felt the watchman, who was the omen of death, was a part of that, too. Martha said to me, "Maybe I'll find something for you later on."

Martha had a hard time with my image; I wasn't the size that she liked. I would say Martha finally found a niche for me in her choreography with *Acrobats [of God]* (1960), *Secular Games* (1962) and *Legend of Judith* (1963). She said I was one of the best character dancers in the United States, so she always thought of me as a character dancer. This is how Martha worked. But I think by being different than most of the men there I challenged her in a way. People very seldom spoke up to Martha. She was hypnotic and charismatic, and she held a control over people. If something went wrong and she was obviously angry with me for something, I would go up and say, "What is the matter, Martha? What is bothering you?" Nobody else would do that. And Martha hated that in a way. But in another way, I think it intrigued her and challenged her.

I knew she was having a horrible time with *Clytemnestra*. Twice I gambled with Martha and won. I told her, "If I can't dance anything in *Clytemnestra*, then I don't want to perform anything at all this season." She didn't even get mad. . . . At that point she didn't even say a word. Then she said, "I don't know. I don't know." Then I came down with the mumps. Martha called and said, "David, David. I hear you have the mumps. Oh, how terrible. How are your genitals?" She comes right to the point. Then she said, "Is there anything you want? Do you need food?" There were a lot of esoteric books that Martha had in her study at the studio. I said, "If I can get some of those books in some way I would like that." She said, "I'll see what I can do." That evening I heard, "David, David." I didn't believe it. It was Martha carrying a load of books. She hadn't gotten Bethsabee [de Rothschild] to drive her down to 23rd Street, and

[she] brought this load of books herself three flights up to my loft so I would have them.

While I had the mumps she called up and said, "I think I have an idea for you in *Clytemnestra*." We scheduled rehearsals for over one month, and she tried everything—now this is the woman's genius—[just] to find what I would look like. We would come in [and] not do anything but try to create an image of how I would appear. Martha had to have an image before she could do anything choreographically. She wanted to find some way to give me a sense of height. Finally one day she came in with this skull cap. Then she said, "Take your tights off." So I did, and she made my costume, pinning it to my dance belt. I was bare from skull to crotch, with a purple skirt trailing beyond my feet. Martha had done the impossible: She had made me taller. She found a big pole and gave it to me. Then she sent me upstairs with her ideas to work something out to dance. I came downstairs a week later. She said, "Let me see what you have done." This is why I object to dancers saying they choreographed their own roles with Martha. I mean, they did in a certain sense. On the one hand that was a beginning. Martha would then say, "Change that. Do this. Do that. Add this. Take away that." What I ended up with to dance after working with Martha was nothing of what I came downstairs with in terms of my own choreography. What I [came] downstairs with . . . was a stimulus for Martha to create or edit. It was the same choreographic process for *Acrobats of God, Alcestis* (1960) and *One More Gaudy Night* (1961). Even when Martha was out of it she still didn't have other people choreograph her works.

It was a pretty wild time. Martha was drinking all the time but she still choreographed. She was "there" enough to be able to do it. With the role of the "Messenger of Death" in *Clytemnestra*, I felt I had won my gamble. My role started the whole dance-drama. I thought it was a great piece. Unbelievable! I remember distinctly standing in the wings before the dance began, thinking, Goddamn it, I won. Here the whole thing was starting with me as the first person, the first image the audience would have.

Martha and I had these kinds of fights through the 15 years I worked with her. It was the way I worked with her. Nobody at Martha's ever gave up anything in terms of roles. One danced in every dance, and fought for the role and never gave it up. I remember doing the "yellow section" of *Diversion of Angels* in 1960, and suddenly I thought, I'm close to 40. This is a dance of young love. I'm too old, and so are these other people, but they don't seem to know it. I shouldn't dance it anymore. By then there was Dan Wagoner, Dick Kuch, Richard Gain and Bob Powell, who were younger and could dance it very easily—[and] they didn't have anything to dance. I decided to speak to Martha, and [I] told her exactly how I felt. She didn't get angry, which I thought she would because her premise was always you keep everything you can. She went into her office and came out about an hour later. She said, "David, come here." We sat on these little benches, and that is when she suggested I become the rehearsal director. She [had] thought it through, but I think she still had qualms about such a big change in her way of working. She went through the whole thing and said, "Now think about it. You go home and think about it. Then you let me know." I knew once we separated the question of me taking on the rehearsal director's role would never come up again. It was such chaos rehearsing at Graham's. You never knew what you were going to do or when you were going to do it. Some order was needed. So I decided right then I would do it. I said, "Martha, I don't have to go home. I'll do it." I think Martha was so shocked she didn't know what to do. Martha said, "All right, we will go tell the rest of the dancers." We walked into the big studio and Martha made this announcement, and the look on their faces was wild. Martha said, "You are answerable to David. Only beyond him you are answerable to me." Then she walked out and left me to oversee a rehearsal for *Diversion of Angels*. I was rehearsal director for Martha for about seven or eight years. . . . That didn't mean I wasn't dancing though. Part of the arrangement was that I was in charge of every dance except the dances that Martha was just choreographing. Those she was in charge of, and I could dance in them.

Along with this job, she made me the role of the taskmaster in *Acrobats of God,* which she was choreographing at that time. That is when she was really out of it: She was drinking all the time; she would come late; she wouldn't know which dance she was rehearsing. On the other hand, she hated to have us rehearsing when she would come into the studio late. I gave orders to put somebody by the front door so we would know when she came and then we would stop. And I also gave orders that when Martha came in nobody could sit down, because if somebody sat down they were a captive audience, and Martha would go directly to them to talk. Martha hated to rehearse! With *Alcestis,* which was done the same year as *Acrobats of God,* Martha said she was experiencing the "Alcestis syndrome" and that she was "going to hell." And I think Martha was experiencing hell at that time—loneliness, age and the end of her sexuality.

When we did *Alcestis* she had those big Noguchi sculptures, which worked well in the rehearsal studio but when we got them onstage they banged against each other. In the theater there were too many people in the dance. I had never seen so much chaos in my life. Plus [the transition] from the piano—which we practiced to—to the live orchestra [made] Vivian Fine's music unintelligible. We didn't know what was going on. Now this is one of the two times I saw Martha Graham cry. She was beside herself, and we had to premiere *Alcestis* the following night. We decided we would all meet onstage at 9 o'clock in the morning and work the dance out. The orchestra would come at 1 o'clock and we would do the opening performance that night. At 9 o'clock we were all there except Martha. We waited about 30 minutes. Finally I said, "Well, we have to do something." I made arrangements. I replaced people. I moved Noguchi's set pieces. We timed it. I took some of the girls out of the end section because there were too many people in the dance. By noon we were through and everyone went to lunch except Bert, Helen and myself because we wanted to finish working out the dance. Then at 1 o'clock the orchestra came. The dancers and the stagehands came back from lunch and Martha arrived. The stagehands asked me if I wanted to mark the new placement of Noguchi's set on the floor. I said to Martha, "I've made quite a few changes and the set pieces are in new places. I don't think it will affect you at all, but the stagehands want to know if they should mark them permanently." Martha turned on me and said, "How should I know until we dance the piece?" We ran through it. Everything worked smoothly. Martha did her role, nothing wrong. Everything was fine. The stagehands came up again: Do you want these places marked permanently? I went to Martha a second time. I said, "Martha, now we've done it. The stagehands want to know if this is all right." She screamed, "Of course it is all right. Why shouldn't it be all right?" I was really upset, having done all her work, and without any acknowledgment or even a thank you. Martha had walked in at 1 o'clock and expected it to be done. At that point I didn't understand Martha, and I was really depressed. Jean Rosenthal, the lighting designer, said to me, "Martha can't do everything. It is impossible for her to do everything in this world of her theater and to dance as well, so she tries to find the people who will do the job, no matter what, just like she would, to the best of their ability." Then she added, "You know something? Martha's right." That is the way Martha operated.

Martha's dances went downhill. *The Witch of Endor* (1965) was unsuccessful.

The only person who could dance "Phaedra" was Martha. There was so much personal movement of Martha's, not technical movement, that no one else could dance that role—because one can't imitate Martha's idiosyncrasies. *Cortege of Eagles* (1967) I felt was not successful. It wasn't a total disaster—there were certain sections that Martha choreographed well. But I felt that with *Cortege of Eagles* Martha had for the first time told a story instead of finding the essence of the story and using that synthesis like she did in *Night Journey, Dark Meadow* [or] *Cave of the Heart,* where the story wasn't the most important thing—it is what [was] told about women and women's relationship to men. In *Cortege of Eagles* she just told the story of Hecuba and the Trojan women and it didn't make too much sense. Her role as "Hecuba" was a way for her to still get onstage—which is fine—but as a piece I thought it was unsuccessful.

The other time I saw Martha cry was when Pearl Lang performed Martha's role in *Appalachian Spring.* It reminded her of herself, Erick and happiness. Martha danced usually the way she felt. Martha was very happy when she choreographed *Appalachian Spring;* she wasn't happy choreographing *Diversion of Angels.* She didn't dance in it. But she did choreograph *Diversion* before she and Erick got married, even though they had been together off and on for about ten years. Anyway, *Appalachian Spring* was a happy piece, and she identified very much with it. Martha, at the theater, had gone up and delayed the rehearsal by talking to Pearl. Finally Martha said, "All right, let's do it." I was sitting out in the dark, and Martha came out and sat just in front of me. The curtain came up and the Copland score began and I saw a tear coming down Martha's face as Pearl entered the stage. Martha had the same feelings that every other human does.

You see, Martha was a paradox. She was every aspect of the individual human odyssey. There is every extreme with Martha. Martha was extreme in the dances she choreographed, too. Martha was always sexually oriented, but in another way her sexual orientation was puritanical. That's part of her paradox. When I was rehearsal director, Martha was often in an alcoholic state and the loneliness . . . that is when she was so lonely. She would call me up when she was inebriated and go over things about the dance. We would talk for about one hour, then she would hang up and call back a little bit later, as if she [had] never spoke[n] to me. It was sheer hell for me. I have a hard time talking on the telephone now because of that experience. One time she was furious with me because I wouldn't teach the children's class. When I arrived home my roommate said, "Martha called and was livid with you. Better call her back." It was about midnight. Martha started in on me, screaming and shouting like she always did. Amongst the things she said was, "You have no concept how diffi-cult it is to be a woman in charge of a dance company. And you are the worst because you won't play the game. It is not that you have to sleep with me. It's not that you have to even think of me sexually. But you have to play that you do. All life is a game, and you don't play it." Then she went on about Erick, and how that was the difficulty with Erick. She loved Erick, but the problem was she was so [much] more talented than he was, which is absolutely true. Erick didn't think so, but Martha did, and most of the dance world did. Finally, she wore herself out and hung up.

My wife, Marni, and I moved out to Yonkers. One night after Martha discov-ered that Marni and I were leaving her company to teach in California she called, drunk, and was furious with me, accusing me of all sorts of things. Marni said, "You'd better do something about it." I drove into New York City to see her at her apartment on 63rd Street at about 11 o'clock at night. I knocked on her door and said, "Martha, it's David." About 10 minutes later she opened the door. She had to prepare herself. Immediately she said, "Do you want a drink?" We spoke until about 3 o'clock. Martha had an amazing memory and she reviewed our entire time together. When she finished we had each arrived at a point of completion.

My last day in the studio I was teaching my part in *Acrobats of God.* Martha said, "It must be so difficult for you to give up dancing *Acrobats of God.*" It wasn't—it was time to move on. But this time Martha finally won. I played her game and said, "Yes, it is," for that is what she wanted to hear. I taught a few more classes and left. There is life beyond Martha Graham, but I shall always treasure and value the time I worked for her. So seldom is one offered the opportunity to work with greatness.

DONALD MCKAYLE

Y. Hayata.

Donald McKayle and Ethel Winter in a studio rehearsal shot for Ardent Song, *c. 1954-55.*

Donald McKayle was born in New York City, in 1930. He attended City College of New York, and studied dance at the New Dance Group and with Martha Graham and Merce Cunningham.

McKayle danced as a guest artist with many leading modern dance companies, including those of Anna Sokolow, Charles Weidman, the Dudley, Maslow, Bales Trio, Merce Cunningham and Jean Erdman. He danced with the Graham Company during its tour of the Orient in 1955-56.

The winner of several dance awards, including the Capezio Award in 1963 and the 1992 Samuel H. Scripps/American Dance Festival Award for Lifetime Achievement in Modern Dance, McKayle choreographed and performed many dances for his own dance company, among whose members were Alvin Ailey, Eliot Feld, Lar Lubovitch and Arthur Mitchell. Several of his classic works, Games, Rainbow Round My Shoulder, District Storyville, and Songs of the Disinherited, are taught to dance companies around the United States as part of the American Dance Festival's program, "The Black Tradition in American Modern Dance."

As a choreographer and director for theater and television, McKayle received five Tony nominations for his work on Broadway, including Sophisticated Ladies and Raisin, and an Emmy nomination in 1975 for Minstrel Man, and he choreographed the Emmy Award-winning childrens special Free To Be You and Me. Among McKayle's film credits are The Jazz Singer, The Great White Hope and the Disney studio release, Bedknobs and Broomsticks.

He is a full professor of dance at the University of California at Irvine. In 1995, he was appointed artistic mentor and choreographer of the José Limón Dance Company, based in New York City.

Donald McKayle primarily lives and choreographs in Southern California and New York City.

I started [dancing] at the New Dance Group in 1947. My professional debut was one year later in the New Dance Group Festival held at the Mansfield Theatre on Broadway in the companies of Jean Erdman and the Dudley, Maslow, Bales Trio. Jane Dudley, Sophie Maslow and William Bales were the resident choreographers for the New Dance Group Company. At the invitation of a friend, I attended a concert given by Pearl Primus. From that moment, I wanted to dance; so I followed Pearl Primus to the New Dance Group where she was on the faculty. I knew nothing of dance, but growing up in a family that came from the West Indies, we always went to dances. We did all the jump-ups and calypsos.

At New Dance Group, I took all classes. Everything was offered there. I took modern technique—Graham, Humphrey-Weidman, Hanya Holm—and ballet, which was taught by Nina Golovina. I took African-based work with Pearl Primus, Haitian with Jean-Leon Destiné and tap-dancing with Paul Draper. I took dance of India with Hadassah. Both Sophie and Jane taught Graham technique. I started my studies with Sophie. Jane arrived later because she was pregnant when I first came to the New Dance Group and wasn't teaching. Sophie's choreographic aesthetic was quite different from Martha's, whereas Jane's was more similar.

I met Martha Graham in 1948 at New London, Connecticut, at the American Dance Festival. But, of course, my teachers, Sophie and Jane, had both been with Martha's company. Martha was scheduled to teach at Holmes Hall, which was a small studio across the highway from the main campus in a nice little house that she liked. But her class was so large that they transferred it to the gymnasium. Martha came to Holmes Hall, as scheduled, and Sophie said, "Donald, would you please take Martha up to the gymnasium?" So, we walked and had this little talk while I guided her there. That is how I got to meet Martha Graham. We became friends right away.

That summer at New London was very important for me. I had only been studying a year and wasn't proficient at much of anything, really, except I loved to dance and had a natural gift for it. As soon as Martha saw me, she gave me a scholarship. I went to study at her school and stayed a few years. But I didn't work with her professionally until 1955.

When Martha was teaching we would have a new forward and back extension every year. You see, she was choreographing and performing. The choreography went into the technique. It was after she stopped dancing that the technique became classified. It became a classic technique. One could say, "And . . . " and go through at least an hour of Graham's exercises without stopping.

I felt there were some problems with the Graham technique. I don't think the extensive floor technique accommodates the male pelvis, which, in most men, usually does not have the requisite opening for the complex and beautiful fluid manipulations built into the floorwork. Even when I taught at Martha's school, I never taught completely just Martha—I always had my own other things. I said to Martha, "I would like you to come and see what I'm doing." She watched class and afterwards said, "Thank yoouuu," and left, so I surmised it was fine. I just didn't do all that floorwork. I got the class off the floor and worked in other areas because I find it very hard on my knees to sit in those positions. What happened was you would make up ways of doing the floorwork that would look right but weren't technically correct. The problem was if you did it the right way, you would hurt your knees. I think you can work with the Graham technique choreographically, but when you spend time with that daily 20 minutes seated in the turned-out, open pelvis position on the floor—I found it is just not healthy.

I made my professional debut in one of Sophie's dances in 1948, one year after I had started to study dance. I had a great deal of talent but I didn't have the finished quality of dance. I knew because I could see that I wasn't doing things the way I wanted them to be done. When one has the eye they can say, "This is not as good as it should be. . . . " I had that eye! I was completely open as I started dancing, without a great deal of knowledge of what the process was. I was making up dances right from the very beginning. I thought that was what dancing was—making up dances and performing them. In fact, I had started making up dances as a choreographer before I knew anything about Martha Graham. You see, I had a very strong identity of my own already, but I appreciated Martha's work very much. If Martha suggested something, I would just do it. Martha would say, "Oh, Don, that is very nice!" It was up in Connecticut that Martha looked at me with those intense eyes, pointing at me with her dramatic fingers, showing all the lines of her hands, and said, "Don, you are very vulnerable," whatever that meant. Actually, I think she was saying that I was open to all styles of movement.

I took Louis Horst's class in dance composition, and he would allow me to do things he wouldn't let anyone else do. Louis Horst was a very strict teacher. He would say, "Why did you turn? There was no indication in the first measure that there would be any turn." I would be running across the floor in a cross-legged scurry and everyone would look at him. He would make excuses, demonstrating a *glissando* on the piano that would bridge the repetition of a phrase in a different register for textural contrast. I think when he saw someone that was really creative he would push them. When he saw someone who he felt was limited, talent-wise, he would make them stick to the rules so they would get a *craft*—because they couldn't depend upon the gift that he felt they didn't have. He was wonderful in terms of critiquing, a marvelous mentor for Martha.

The leading men with Martha's company at that time were Erick Hawkins and Mark Ryder. Bertram Ross, who became Martha's partner, had just started to dance in 1948 and rose up through the ranks. You can tell what Bertram added to Martha's choreography because it was so uniquely special to him. Martha allowed that. In *Ardent Song* (1954) there were times when something wasn't finished and the dancers would improvise, but one had to improvise in Martha's style. You knew when you saw the dancer performing execute a certain swooping turn, she was about to exit the stage and the next in line would enter. Even the shape of improvisation was structured by Martha.

When Martha was creating *Diversion of Angels* I would go up to the balcony and watch her develop her choreography. Martha was at the height of her creative powers, and it was a transitional period for her in the sense that she was always the main performer and a choreographer. *Diversion,* however, was Martha's first dance for her company where she wouldn't perform. Originally the dance was called *Wilderness Stair,* from a line of a poem by Ben Belitt, and it had a wonderful set by Noguchi that Martha dropped after the premiere. Pearl Lang contributed movement to her role in *Diversion.* Later, as a choreographer, she was accused by the critics of being derivative of Graham, when, in fact, she had contributed original movement to the palette that became exclusively identified with Martha Graham.

I remember Martha showing me a gift that Pearl had given her—a double-edged dagger—and saying, "Look what Pearl gave me. She says it's wonderful for sharpening eyebrow pencils. Isn't she sweet?" I always thought that Pearl and Martha, who had such a strong identification with each other, were going to self-destruct.

Louis left Martha after he conducted the premiere of *Diversion of Angels* (1948) in Connecticut. Louis couldn't stand Erick. Martha was creating this rapturous dance because she was so in love with and enamored of Erick. Perhaps she realized she would eventually lose Erick, which happened in two years time. I remember the caretaker coming to me in the dormitory saying, "I'm very worried about Mr. Hawkins." Erick was lying naked on the floor all tied up and banging a gong. He was choreographing his own Oedipus dance called *The Strangler.* The year before, Martha, of course, had choreographed *Night Journey,* her interpretation of the Oedipus legend from Jocasta's point of view, and Erick had danced the role of Oedipus. Louis called Erick "the Queen's Consort." When Erick performed Martha's *Eye of Anguish,* Louis referred to the dance as "The Egg of Eyewash."[1] Martha wanted to support Erick as a choreographer, but after their separation she could not get herself to attend his performances. John Butler told me that she called him and asked him to accompany her to one of Erick's early concerts at Hunter Playhouse. They circled the theater, walking around the block three times, and then she went home. She had made her appearance.

When I danced with Martha's company (in 1955-56), she was beginning to lose some of her physical prowess as a dancer, and as a result was very involved with herself and her own performance and would quite often leave us alone and to our own devices. Martha wanted to redo *Ardent Song* when I came into the company. She wanted to put in a new part for me but she exited the choreographic process. She would come into rehearsal when I was working with Ethel Winter and say, "Very nice." We would wait for some further comment and she would say, "It's wonderful, but it needs more 'sa-de-sa-da,'" and she would quietly disappear. So we would put 'sa-de-sa-da' together for the evening. Martha had an intuitive feel about people she worked with. She called me into her dressing room after the first performance of *Ardent Song* and said, "Thank you. . . . "

In another section of *Ardent Song* she put me in the middle of three women, Matt Turney, Ellen Seigle and Ellen Van Derhoeven, wrapped in a large cloth, and said, "Now, dance." She gave me the theatrical device and trusted me to sculpt my own movement sequences. I was working with the three solo women, Linda Hodes, Helen McGehee and Ethel Winter. I had a duet with each of them. I was the only male figure that was a soloist. The other men were used as a group.

---

[1] According to Agnes de Mille's *Martha: The Life and Works of Martha Graham,* the phrase is "The Angst of Eyewash," (New York: Random House, 1991. p. 285).

Y. Hayata.

*Donald McKayle and Ethel Winter in a studio rehearsal shot
for* Ardent Song, *c. 1954-55.*

Diversion of Angels and *Ardent Song* were the only dances I performed on the 1955-56 tour of the Orient. I also learned *Dark Meadow,* but we didn't perform it because we couldn't transport the Noguchi set. I have wonderful pictures from that tour, some studio shots taken of Ethel Winter, myself, Paul Taylor and Matt Turney.

In the Sixties, when I was working in London, I sat in the audience to watch Martha dance *Phaedra.* She had those brilliantly sculpted set pieces by Noguchi, who always created resting places for her to recline into some wonderful position. Then she would drape herself with some marvelous fabric. As "The Temptress"—she was already in her late 60s—she had on red tights underneath her dress, and all of a sudden her legs went up into the air. The two women next to me, being very English, said, "Oh, dear."

I wouldn't say I learned the craft of choreography from dancing with Martha. What you learn is to observe, participate and glean. Martha definitely was the proprietor of her own invention. We came out of Martha, but I don't think she pushed us into our careers. I remember rehearsing at the Graham studio . . . I was choreographing on Matt in the corner. Martha said, "don't do that. I'm a thief, and I steal whatever I can." The idea of choreographers not allowing input from the dancers is sort of a thing of the past. I, as a choreographer, would allow for improvisation if that is what I'm working on. Every work has its own reason for being and its own way it should be done.

When I teach choreography, I give the students assignments, but I also have them bring in independently focused work which is not a classroom assignment. I talk about aesthetics and ask, "What is your own aesthetic?" The students write this down for themselves and for me. I say, "This is an ongoing document and it is a contract with yourself." This is what Martha had with herself.

I don't think Martha encouraged the individual quest. I don't think she ever did that. She was always very interested when it happened, but she was very much about herself. She wasn't there to push or promote anybody else's work. I had so many things I wanted to do, so I didn't stay. I tried Broadway. It was very hard for a black person to get a job on Broadway in the Fifties, but I performed in a Broadway show, *Bless You All,* in 1951. Bertram Ross was also in that. In 1957, I was in *West Side Story.* Then I did a show with Anna Sokolow, *Copper and Brass,* also in '57. I was her assistant. I was in the original cast of Sokolow's *Rooms* and I was in her *Lyric Suite.* I felt Martha needed you to be very committed. Martha had a way of absorbing people and was an indomitable force in the dance and art world.

PAUL TAYLOR

Arno

Paul Taylor, Bertram Ross and Martha Graham in Alcestis, 1960.

Paul Taylor was born in Pittsburgh, in 1930, and raised in and around Washington, D.C. He received a painting scholarship to Syracuse University and later dance scholarships from Juilliard School of Music, Connecticut College School of Dance (summer school), the Martha Graham School and the Metropolitan Opera Ballet School.

From 1955 until 1962 Taylor was a leading soloist with the Martha Graham Company. He also danced in the companies of Merce Cunningham and Pearl Lang. He formed his own company in 1954 and began presenting his own work in concerts in both the United States and Europe.

Taylor is the recipient of many varied awards and honors. He was elected to the rank of Chevalier de l'Ordre des Arts et des Lettres by the French government in 1969. He has since been elevated to the ranks of Officier (1984) and Commandeur (1990). Taylor was elected one of ten Honorary American Members of the American Academy and Institute of Arts and Letters in 1989. He is the recipient of 3 Guggenheim Fellowships, a MacArthur Foundation Fellowship, the Samuel H. Scripps ADF Award, and six honorary Doctor of Fine Arts degrees. Other awards include the New York State Governor's Arts Award (1987) and the New York City Mayor's Award of Honor for Art and Culture (1989). He received the 1992 Emmy Award for outstanding individual achievement in choreography for Speaking in Tongues, produced by WNET / New York in 1991. Taylor was awarded a Certificate of Special Merit from the Association of the Graphic Arts for his poster "The Golden Gang." He was a recipient of the 1992 Kennedy Center Honors and in 1993 Taylor was awarded a National Medal of Arts by President Clinton in a ceremony at the White House. He received the Algur H. Meadows Award for Excellence in the Arts in 1995.

Taylor's autobiography, Private Domain (published by Knopf and in paperback by North Point Press), was nominated by the National Book Critics Circle as the most distinguished biography of 1987 and is in its third printing.

Paul Taylor lives in New York City and on Long Island's North Shore.

◆ ● ◆

It was in the Barbara Morgan book, *Martha Graham: Sixteen Dances in Photographs,* when I was in college, that I first saw Martha Graham. I preferred Graham from the very beginning, from the minute I opened those books.

Initially, I saw dancing in the movies, but I could never see myself doing it in the theater or wherever. When you are in grade school, some little girl does a ritual fire-dance, but dance didn't really click with me until I got a job sweeping the library steps in college at Syracuse. I remember going in the library and looking through the magazines. I ran across a dance section in the back of a magazine; I got some dance books as well. There was a curiosity and excitement that I didn't understand or try to figure out. I had to work, so then I got another job; I drove a car for a dance school up in Bar Harbor, Maine. There I saw dance classes. I didn't take anything. I don't remember any precise moment that suddenly I thought, Oh yeah, there is something called "dance."

I preferred Martha's work to José Limón's,[1] not because of what it meant or the content, but because of the movement itself. The Humphrey movement and Limón's—I don't know if there was any difference, I don't think there was—was stiffer, somehow. Martha's movement made sense physically, to my body, and I naturally gravitated towards it. I didn't care what it was about.

Martha said, "I want him." She didn't say it to me. She said it to someone else. "A good man was hard to find," and Merce and Erick had left Martha before I came. Of course I had a little prep for working for Martha by dancing with both Pearl Lang and Merce.

[Martha] started to choreograph special roles for me. I went into some other roles that were not choreographed on me, but they were nice things to dance of Martha's. Bertram [Ross] was Martha's main man and main partner. Bertram stalked around a lot. Martha couldn't jump. She could throw her foot up in the air, roll over—it was amazing what she could still do—and she had Noguchi's furniture to roll around on.

---

[1] José Limón (1908-72). Mexican modern dancer and choreographer who became the protégé of Doris Humphrey and Charles Weidman.

I just wanted to be a dancer. The first thing was to learn how to dance—to get out onstage and perform it. Martha didn't need me. They really didn't need me. I was an augmentation to the company. With Martha, the men were the equivalent of a male Barbie doll. The men never got to wear any clothes with Martha—it got even worse with Halston designing for her—at least we usually had our butts covered up. We were sticklike figures who were basically sex objects. We didn't dare say anything. In fact, I think we kind of liked it. With Martha's women, they were pretty much covered up. Very few of them had very good legs, to tell you the truth.

Ethel Butler explained to me the theory behind the Graham technique. I was already getting Graham movement, more or less, when I danced with Pearl and Merce. Pearl, of course, is Martha's disciple, and Merce was doing a lot of very Grahamesque movement at that time, and still does, but nobody seems to want to say it. It is treason to say that Merce is like Martha. Merce's moves are peripheral. Like ballet, it is peripheral: You move your arm and your leg. But sometimes it is Graham in its mannerisms. Linda, Mary, Matt, Ethel, Pearl, Helen [and] Bert were all very individualistic as performers, but not as choreographers. They all had a sense of Martha's theatricality. I don't think Anna's [Sokolow] work is Grahamesque; Pearl's work is very Graham. May O'Donnell—I am not familiar with her work, and if I had seen some of Martha's work when Sophie Maslow was in her company, I might see more similarity in their choreographies. Helen McGehee was a good choreographer, but very Grahamesque. Those people used Martha's vocabulary.

Martha was funny. There was a lot about Martha that was not egotistical. It was Martha's vision. There was something always very big about Martha. Our devotion as dancers went beyond devotion to an individual. We all saw Martha's faults and flaws every day. Martha was human, if not more human than most people. Martha's sense of theater and the dance was big—something big to participate in. We were acolytes, not so much to her, really—and she wouldn't like that so much—as to the theater of dance. But she loved people to fall at her feet. She couldn't walk into a room and not be the center of attention.

We performed big. We performed big with a lot of passion, performing passion. It was something that was passed on to us in that situation. It wasn't a matter of a technique you learned in a classroom exactly. There were innuendos in the classroom exercises [from which] you could learn a little bit about the theatricality of the performance. Certainly through the concentration that people brought with them, their devotion to dance verged on the fanatic.

Martha always let the older members [of her company] choreograph their own roles. I wasn't an older member, but I was sort of egged on. Martha would leave me in the room and say, "Do something." Martha was overseeing the general plan of the dance. She was like an editor. You would set something and Martha would glance at it. It was very free. I can't remember a single premiere that ever went on with the last part of the dance set.

I only worked [at the studio] when we [were getting] ready for a season or a tour. That was not very many weeks out of a year, except [for] that first long Oriental tour I went on. They didn't need me in that repertory; they sure didn't need me on that Oriental tour. I was sick one night and couldn't get out of bed, I had dysentery so bad. It really knocked me out. Donnie (McKayle), my roommate on that part of the Oriental tour, said, "Well, I'm going off to the theater." I said, "Hey wait. I've got to get there too. Wait, don't go. Help me up. I've got to make it." Donnie was gone. I got out of the bed. I got down the stairs. This was in Raffle's Hotel in Singapore. It was a big flight of stairs. I dragged myself down the stairs. I ran into Jessica, who was sort of a secretary on the tour. She always had a lot of pills. I asked her to give me some medicine because I was sick. She did, but it didn't help. Anyway, to make a long story short, I never made it to the theater. To this day, I don't think Martha or anybody knew I wasn't there. The dance went on minus one person.

Martha was very much into Greek mythology. For *Clytemnestra,* I think a book was recommended for me to read but I didn't read it. I just needed to know that he ["Aegisthus," my role] was the bad guy. Martha was the "Queen," and she and "Aegisthus" were plotting to take the throne from Bert, who was "Agamemnon." Anything I learned about mythology in the dance I learned through the dance itself. I didn't read about it. It wasn't explained to me. But the relationships of the characters [are] quite clear in the episodes of that dance. I knew their names. Everyone had a name. Martha told me, "'Aegisthus,' he's bad." That role was fun, creepy, and it was changed immediately when I left. It was drastically changed.

I don't like squabbling or friction in a working situation. I know some people thrive on friction. Martha thrived on stress . . . because it got her adrenaline going. I can understand that. She needed it. She was old. I have done that also, but I really prefer not to be anxious and hysterical.

Episodes was a nice break. It was very different: It was very organized and craftsmanlike. It was also a very calm atmosphere and seemed to work like clockwork. It was very different, but I really didn't work with Balanchine much. Five rehearsals with him by myself, and no rehearsals with the cast. I didn't even know, until I went to the theater for the performance, about the cast. After *Episodes,* Balanchine wanted me to dance *Apollo.* I did go back several years later to dance my solo in *Episodes.*

Episodes was the result of a lot of things that [had] happened before. . . . Edwin Denby and Lincoln Kirstein had wanted me to choreograph a dance for the New York City Ballet. They asked me who I wanted to design it and I said, "Bob Rauschenberg." He wasn't known yet, and Lincoln asked him over to talk with him. Lincoln took an immediate dislike to him and was untactful, and Bob walked out. The dance wasn't off, it was just stymied. The next thing I knew, Lincoln was saying, "George wants you to be in his new piece"—that was to be something else, not *Episodes.* That turned into this so-called "collaboration" between Martha and Balanchine, which wasn't a collaboration at all. Martha and Balanchine traded dancers. That is, Sallie Wilson went from the New York City Ballet to dance in Martha's "Mary, Queen of Scots" piece, and I was a guest with Balanchine's company.

I never saw the dances. I only was in them. There is quite a difference. *Visionary Recital* was abstract in Martha's sense—that you didn't know what the hell the story was supposed to be. It seemed to have one. It was one of those no-man's land pieces which can be wonderful. As a dancer, I remember nothing about *Visionary Recital,* except Bert strumming the set, which was made of all these wires like a harp across the back of the stage.

One More Gaudy Night (1961) was the Antony and Cleopatra story. I was terribly happy to get to dance with Ethel Winter in *One More Gaudy Night* because I thought she was a wonderful dancer. I was delighted to dance with her. Martha was in one of her vulgar or sex-crazed moods. Everything was phallic and "cloital," or whatever the female equivalent is. That was the beginning of a whole series of dances that were on a blatant side; *Phaedra* was the very next year. I loved that one because it starts with this big Noguchi vagina opening. On the other hand, Martha was very prim and puritanical—she was both. In those days, her pornography side was getting the better of her. Antony and Cleopatra—*One More Gaudy Night*—was not as pornographic as some of Martha's dances that followed, certainly. Martha wasn't in that dance.

Noguchi was creating sculptures for Martha. They were furniture that looked like sexual organs. They were three-dimensional. Martha was never content with where they were, so she always had us push them around the stage, flop them over, turn them upside down. Noguchi would never have a back and front to any of his design object[s]. They were always to be seen from every angle. He probably knew that Martha was going to turn [them] around—the wrong way, sometimes. He was prepared. It was a great idea, if for no other reason than for the dancer's sake. It is like a costume that has a detail that no one can see but you. It makes you feel like somebody. If you are working with a set piece that looks just as beautiful in back as it does in front, you perform better. You really do. It was nice . . . [and] a big difference from traditional theater design: The backs looked as good as the fronts, and you could turn them upside down if you wanted. All of that was perfectly obvious and certainly was an influence on me because I liked those things about Martha and Noguchi. I myself could never afford 3-D art objects on stage.

Martha was the big matriarch—she was the big "to-do." Martha and Doris Humphrey, both. A lot of the learning was done by observing Martha Graham participate in her own odyssey. I didn't really approve of all Martha's emotional stuff. I wonder how Mary [Hinkson] pulled that one off, being cast as "Circe"? *Circe* (1963) would have been perfect for Martha, as [were] all the other Greek heroines—Medea, Clytemnestra, Ariadne, Phaedra, Alcestis, Hecuba. Any of the pieces Martha wasn't in nobody really cared about.

All Martha's grandeur was a little too grand for me; it was of another era. It was Martha's era, it wasn't my era. Things had changed. All that grandeur seemed like pomposity. I wouldn't do it myself. I performed it for Martha because that is what the dances demanded and that is what the style was. I am not sure that I ever had a role with Martha that was *really* complex. Martha didn't use me that way. I was always a bad guy. I was slithery and evil. I hardly ever got to be pompous. "Hercules," in *Alcestis* (1960), was a bumpkin. He was just a muscle guy; he was a bodybuilder type. No brains. A man of brawn. *Acrobats of God* (1960) wasn't a role. It was me just dancing.

Martha said she wanted to give the company credit for choreographing *Acrobats of God,* but we all knew she didn't mean it. We were amazed during the premiere of *Acrobats of God*: Martha started doing things that she had never done in rehearsal. In fact, we were all led to believe that Martha's role was serious—she was this great, mystical magician-type who was pulling strings, ominously; we were her little dancer puppets. Martha started camping the role because the audience almost immediately began to titter. *Acrobats of God* wasn't meant to be funny. She just completely did an about-face and camped the whole role up. Everybody ate it up. Poor David [Wood], who had to do a duet with her, didn't know what was going on. He wasn't surprised because Martha was known for her spontaneity on stage. You never knew what she was going to do onstage. It was kind of fun, actually. One would have to play along with Martha and be ready. You didn't know what was going to happen. You had to either cover for Martha, or go along, or be her straight man.

Graham encouraged individualism, and she always knew I was going to leave. Martha knew before I did. We never talked seriously. I knew Martha liked me. I knew she liked that I was doing my own work. She would come and see it. Of course, she would then give me some criticism afterwards which I wouldn't listen to. It was done tongue in cheek. We had a great joking relationship.

Martha wasn't in the rehearsal [when] I had to teach Bob Cohan my role in *Phaedra*. I rehearsed Bob myself and it wasn't horrendous, [but] I was doing things that didn't set right on Bob's body. It was very difficult to transfer these movements of mine, which I had choreographed anyway for Martha's dance. They were not movements from the Graham vocabulary that Bob had learned. [They] didn't translate. It wasn't Bob's fault.

Martha played all kinds of games. I didn't need to go in to rehearse. I wasn't forced in—I was being responsible for my part. I naturally assumed that if you leave Martha Graham, then somebody has to teach [your] part to another dancer. Since Martha did not know my part, and nobody else knew it, naturally I should teach it. I didn't feel inconvenienced. I felt frustrated when we actually set down to work [because] I couldn't get these things into Bob's body. But it didn't matter. And Martha knew it didn't matter. Bob would do something else and it would be fine.

When I started it was very late, and I didn't have much time because the draft was chasing me. I couldn't stop to think about choreographing. When I did manage to avoid the draft—that is, I was classified 4-F because of a heart murmur—I was in New York on my own, not connected with any school. I found that to keep busy every day all year-round I would make up my own dances to do when I wasn't dancing someone else's choreography. That is how I got started choreographing, but I never thought of myself then as a choreographer. It seemed very unglamorous. Let somebody else do that; I'll get out, perform and get all the credit. The dances I choreographed were avant-garde. I didn't know it. That is not why I did it. I didn't do it to be avant-garde. Yet I didn't feel any obligation to go along with anybody else's work. I simply didn't like anybody else's work enough to want to emulate them.

I don't think you can learn much from anybody else about choreography. You can learn rules, regulations, theories and exercises of choreography. I don't think we learn much from that. My own participation in Graham's choreographies might have opened some doors. You learn whatever you do by doing. Most of what we learn is by experiencing it. Sometimes it is a painful experience. I don't think that just because a dancer works with a choreographer that they are going to have too much to go on to start a dance of their own. I mean, they can steal a few steps. It is how those steps are used or the invention of other movements or maybe just putting old movement together. Even that isn't the main thrust of the thing. The main thrust . . . Oh Lord, what is the main thrust? I think it is simply living. Twyla [Tharp], for instance, was with my company for three or four years. She never really got much to dance and I think that is mainly why she left me. It wasn't that I wasn't interested in her. She was the newest company member, and I would make dances for the older members, so that when I got to Twyla, there wouldn't be any music left. Twyla did much better on her own. I don't think there is, or could ever be, a teenager who is a good choreographer. I think to be a choreographer, in order to have some feelings to express, or an idea to express, or attitude to express, or a vague feeling of anything to express, you simply have to experience. Not through books. That could help, but in the end it is somebody else's view.

Even though I was with Martha only six years, I was still in my 20s, and you can pack in a lot into those years. It seemed like a long time, and a lot happened during those six years, but it wasn't that long of a time. It wasn't until I stopped dancing that I thought of myself as a choreographer. Let's face it, this choreography business is nothing but trying to get other people to do what you want. If you get 30 percent of what you want, then you're getting a very good average. It is a terrible situation to be in, trying to get people to do what you want. I mean, they want to do what they want.

DAN WAGONER

Arno

Dan Wagoner and Linda Hodes in Acrobats of God, *1960.*

---●---

Dan Wagoner was born in Springfield, West Virginia, in 1932. He studied modern dance in Washington, D.C., with Ethel Butler, while serving in the United States Army.

Wagoner was awarded a scholarship by the Graham School and danced with the Graham Company from 1958 to 1962. He also danced with Merce Cunningham's company (1959-60) and Paul Taylor's company (1960-68). In 1969, he formed his own company, for which he choreographs.

Wagoner served briefly in 1989 as the artistic director of the London Contemporary Dance Theatre upon Robert Cohan's retirement. He is a member of the dance faculty of Connecticut College.

Dan Wagoner lives in New London, Connecticut and New York City.

---●---

I began to read about dance. I was absolutely fascinated by the photographs. My teacher, Mary Haberkon, mentioned a lot of names and then I went to the library and read. Most of the books [I read] were about ballet. I read about Antony Tudor, Martha Graham [and] the New York City Ballet. Some of the dance periodicals were also in the library.

The Korean draft was still on, so I joined ROTC. I took a degree in pharmacy at West Virginia University. When I was in the Army I was stationed in Washington, D.C., which is where I met Ethel Butler, who had been a dancer with Martha Graham. She introduced me to Louis Horst and got me a scholarship to the American Dance Festival, at Connecticut College. Martha Graham, José Limón, Doris Humphrey, Louis Horst and Alwin Nikolais were all there. I got a scholarship to Martha Graham's school in New York right away, and less than a year later she had me rehearsing in *Clytemnestra*.

For me, it was all about getting to New York—here was where all these

people I [had] read about and fantasized about were. Of course it is very theatrical. . . . It was thrilling for me to choose to come to New York, then to
choose to go to Martha Graham's school where she was teaching the class . . .
I was in the same studio with Martha Graham! Then, to be asked to rehearse
with the company was even more thrilling. It was with Martha that I became
aware of the fact that the only thing worthwhile is how you see [things] yourself. Otherwise, you are going to see it through somebody else's writing or
someone else's eyes—if you give up your identity [in order] to conform. The
only reason to be alive and to go on with life is that we have each been given
a uniqueness and a viewpoint. It is that viewpoint that illuminates and brings
everything to life.

Martha's image was athletic, virile men. She looked for those qualities rather
than multiple turns, high extension, all of that. I think her view of that has
changed. She is dazzled by virtuosic technique now. Martha couldn't quite figure
me out. I didn't quite fit the heroic mold. Martha looks at people—she gets an
image of someone in her own fantasy and then she choreographs them into that
mold. She found me rather fey, humorous and droll in a mysterious kind of way,
or this is what she told me. I think she saw me like [she did] Merce, in a way.

Martha couldn't quite figure out what I was thinking. The first time she did
try to scare [it out of] me I was so shocked. Martha had always been compli-
mentary to me in class. When it got to rehearsals, all of a sudden there was a
reversal of things: "You're not on the beat and da da dum." So I did nothing. I
didn't get angry. I didn't yell back. I didn't cry—which I felt like doing—and
retreat. I just stayed in the space. Afterwards, Matt [Turney] said to me, "Dan,
you handled that beautifully." I said, "Oh my God, Matt. I'm burning up inside.
I wanted both to beat the shit out of her and cry and run." Matt said, "No, no,
no. You are doing fine. Do it the way you are doing it." Finally, Martha and I
had an argument and I yelled back at her and that cleared the air. It may have
been my second season with Martha. But for me it was very brave to yell back
at Martha Graham. Paul [Taylor], for instance, had more of an idea of who he
was and what he wanted to do from the beginning. For me, it was very brave to
talk back and to let her hear what I was thinking and what I was feeling. But
the moment I did that, Martha understood.

Now, I try to trust my dancers once I've given them the movement, but I
must say I make [it] up every inch of the way. I'm interested in the dance. I
learned that from Paul, you see, which is why when it became a choice between

Paul and Martha, I chose to go with Paul. The allegro, the footwork of Paul's, was much more challenging than what was going on at Martha's. Temperament-wise I felt easier around Paul. I felt easier around a man than I did around Martha at that time. I admired Martha, and had learned so much from working with her, but fighting was not my way of working. To struggle in that way was against my theory of putting all my energy towards learning the steps and doing them.

When I started doing that movement vocabulary of Martha's I went home to a friend and I said, "I'm choreographing my own dance. Graham isn't doing anything." He said, "Dan, look. Martha got the studio, she wrote the scenario, she commissioned the music. You wouldn't have known what movement to use if you hadn't studied her technique and watched her dances." One forgets that the real touchstone in something like that is the person who then takes what you have done with her vocabulary of movement and edits it. Martha has that wonderful facility for compiling and arranging. Martha says in her own writing, "I'm a thief. I steal wherever I see things." She does do that, but she also pulls the best qualities out of the dancers.

If Martha didn't create those vehicles for herself no one else was going to create them for her. Bob Cohan said an interesting thing about Martha during a European tour. The producers wanted Martha to do lecture-demonstrations. Martha said, "I have never done that. I don't want to talk about the work or whatever." Finally, she had to do it. Martha said, "Rather than analyzing or knowing how I made these dances, I feel in a way I didn't make them but that I simply witnessed them." It is as if they existed and she brought them into focus, simply by going through them and doing them, but they were always there. It was almost like the modern physics, which is now almost a meta-physical patterning. Martha would introduce us to the path. She would open the thresholds. This is the direction—now go. You would look and say, "Can I?" And Martha would say, "Of course you can." That is inspiration, isn't it? When someone treats you in that way? They lend you the dignity that you are going to do something wonderful if you are challenged.

There was something smarter in me than my forebrain knew, and if I had not listened and trusted my instincts I would never had those experiences that I've had . . . that . . . allow me now to get excited about choreographing a new dance, rather than committing suicide. I think it would have been over before now if I had not allowed myself to trust myself.

Errand into the Maze is fearful and frightening, but at the same time it is liberating and exhilarating. The way of looking into the inner self. Martha Graham's journey into the maze. It is a beautiful metaphor and, of course, Martha performed it so beautifully. I saw how Martha Graham worked. In *Diversion of Angels,* I was alternating a part with Bob Powell and there was only one orchestra rehearsal before performance. I said, "If I don't do the orchestra rehearsal then I find that very difficult, and I would rather just let Bob do it all the way through." Martha said, "You will do what you are told. I'm getting tired of all these prima donnas around here." So I replied, "That is exactly it, Martha. There are a lot of prima donnas around here and I'm going to be one also." She looked at me, stunned, and said, "Well, I think we can work this out. I want my men to look well," and she put her arm around me. You see, that is what she was waiting for. I looked up to Bert [Ross], Bob [Cohan], Stuart Hodes, Gene McDonald and Paul, who really fascinated me more than any of the others. I imagine on the billing Paul was either a soloist or a principal. Paul was such a young upstart that Martha was very cautious about letting someone who was so new—even though she loved him because he was so good—get so much attention immediately. With Martha you often did arrange a lot of your own movement. Martha on other occasions would tell you what she wanted. Of course, Paul would make a whole dance.

I was in Martha's "Mary, Queen of Scots" section of *Episodes* (1959). She did her [section] and Balanchine did his. But it absolutely was an extraordinary event for the time. It was a very avant-garde thing to happen, even if it was done separately. Was that Lincoln Kirstein's idea? Balanchine . . . wanted Paul Taylor to join the New York City Ballet, but Paul didn't want to. Paul said, "That is not what I want to do. I want to choreograph."

Martha kept telling us the myths in the stories. I did go back and look at condensed material about the trilogy in *Clytemnestra* (1958). I didn't really take it and read it—which would have been wonderful for me at the time, if I had done that. It would have been good practice. Martha realized that the smart dancers would do it—go and read it. Helen McGehee already knew the classics, which was her major at Randolph-Macon, in Lynchburg, Virginia. Helen was very outspoken and very objective in looking at things. Helen could be quite sassy with Martha. When Martha would tell these classic myths, of course she would tell it from the woman's point of view. For example, [in] *Clytemnestra* [Martha] was not against turning things to make "Clytemnestra" stronger or more interesting. Martha would say then so-and-so happened and Helen would be there shaking her head, saying, "It wasn't that way. No. No." I thought Helen was very gutsy. Martha would look around and then go on with how she saw it. For Martha to take those universals and make them pertinent today was extraordinary.

I remember the rehearsals for *Clytemnestra*, and she was still moving around. To see Martha throw herself into the movement, in her mid-60s—and she was not afraid to look ugly in front of me and she wasn't afraid to fall down or make a mistake—who am I not to throw myself into it as completely and to look ugly and silly also if she is willing to do it? Martha was already a legend and the fact that she allowed us in the studio to see her working. . . . Image was very important to Martha. It was very real. I remember one day we were rehearsing and Martha said her knees were hurting. I said, "I have some knee pads. Would you like to put them on?" She said, "Oh, they would look terrible." I said, "But you're wearing that long skirt"—Martha always rehearsed in long skirts—"no one will know it." Martha said, "I will know it."

Martha was interested in image, but she wasn't interested in superficiality. She was interested in the image that came from deep inside her and she didn't care how anyone else saw it. She was going to paint every side of her house because that was what was beautiful for her, not just the front where the neighbors saw it, and she said, "Oh my, isn't that wonderful?" She was answering to a higher challenge within herself. That is what is touching, moving and also shattering. I think it refocuses what is important.

When Martha was onstage, one was convinced the Furies were there. You can see them, you sense them, you feel them. For Martha it was real and she brought all of that to life. One saw the truth of those Greek myths. Martha had done much of her work subconsciously. Martha was way ahead of her time, of course. I think it was simply that Martha took up the struggle, and she saw it from her own uniqueness, and she had the courage to see it through. Technology has outstripped all of the understanding that one must have and the experiences of ritual, the experience of entering humanity, the experience of a man becoming a man. That is how you become a human being—through those rituals, of course. It is through the acceptance of self and self-enlightenment and understanding. I felt that, in a way, for me, Merce was doing the same thing as Martha. Merce rebelled against Martha, but I think they are more alike than anyone has ever written. I think that would make a very interesting story.

Merce's dances were all vehicles for himself up until more recently.

There was a mixture of many feelings in [the] creation of *Clytemnestra*. I was so awed just being there. I was very young—emotionally, not maybe in years—but to experience the high-pressured world of the professional dancer, to be part of Martha's first full-evening dance—was overwhelming. It was so new that I was struggling to keep up with the steps. I would try to step back and look at Martha and the dance, but there wasn't much time for that because it was so difficult for me to keep up with the rest of the dancers. Martha does a lot by struggling. She lashes out at individuals to see how they will react. Are you going to snap? Are you going to cry and run out of the room? It was difficult for me to learn to deal with that.

Martha talked about us dancers being "acrobats of God," and I thought it was quite wonderful to be included in part of that—to be thought of as one of her dancers and to be thought of as being divine, simply because I had taken up dancing and was fortunate enough to have ended up with Martha Graham. It was reinforcement of the fact that Martha made sense to me and that what I'd done is right—by taking up dancing. The rehearsals for *Acrobats of God* were quite lively and fun. Of course, Martha was in the dance, and to see her in the studio working was amazing.

In *Phaedra* (1962), the older woman lusting after the younger man was very important to Martha Graham at the time I am sure. Martha had always represented to me the orgiastic. I remember Martha speaking about her dance *Embattled Garden* and when the woman, Eve, has all that chasing and rolling and bumping and grinding in it—the orgiastic experiences. The woman takes the man and rocks him, almost like . . . the Pietà, the Christ-like scene. Martha said that, for her, at the height of the orgy they reached their most spiritual moment, and this shocked me at the time because I never thought in that way. She said, "I think only by going through one's passions do you arrive at any kind of place of purity or holiness." It was the doing which allowed you to arrive at this other place. It is people who deny and never experience or strike out [who] can't reach that place. It was a metaphor for everything. Life is a process. Making a dance is a process. You go through it. Otherwise life becomes nothingness.

I did *Samson Agonistes* (1962), which was *Visionary Recital* (1961). That was interesting because Paul was in that too, and we both made a lot of movement. And that was the first place where Paul took movement that I had made. Paul saw me doing some movement and he said, "Oh, I like that step. I'm going to do that." I said, "But that is my movement. I'm going to do it, but go ahead and do it, too."

Martha did absolutely encourage the individualistic attitude. I think a lot of these things have come together for me in later years. When I was doing all that work with Martha, Merce and Paul I was so excited to be part of the work, which was so thrilling and rewarding that intuitively it made sense to me, and [it] was cathartic and a learning experience in an emotional way that I wasn't even aware of at the time I did it. But I followed my instincts. If I had not followed my instincts I would have listened to people who told me I was crazy— I was too old to dance, I have a good degree in pharmacy to fall back on, I can have a job, I can have money—I can have all the safety and security. But there was never a moment that I questioned why I was dancing, which I knew was a wonderful, wonderful world. It probably was a fulfillment of one's own sexuality through dance.

Martha was difficult and mysterious to me. Emotionally, she was way beyond the experiences that I had had to deal with it. I did do it, and through it I met Paul and [had] all of the other experiences that happened. It was an opening up for me. I think Martha has done that for a lot of dancers. The basic values were there if you wanted to see them and take hold of them. My work with Martha, Merce and Paul, I think, is a continuation in the sense that these three choreographers initiated me into my manhood, or into my individualism. It was a rite, it was a ritual I went through . . . I lived out those rituals through their dances and they allowed me to evolve into myself.

With Graham, it was a lesson in being an apprentice choreographer. What you learn with Martha is an incredible responsibility. You [would] go into a rehearsal and Martha would just start to indicate a phrase of movement, and there would be Helen McGehee and Mary Hinkson right behind her, adding movement as [they] went, figuring it out and making it work. One just did that, so you realized everyone took that responsibility. You didn't wait to be babied with was my foot here or back there and all of that. You did it, got caught up in all that energy, and then Martha would shape it, edit and arrange it, and use it. If you didn't, you got lost. It was exciting! Martha was fairly clear with directions: You enter there. I want you to get over here. You need to do this with that, or whatever. Then she would go back as if she were thinking, and she would be looking the opposite way of what everyone was doing, the "eyes in back of her head" syndrome. Everybody did contribute in a way. Martha's technique was so complete.

Martha was the matriarch. She talked to you even about herself . . . so that everyone referred to her as a legend. Most certainly, already, there was a mystique about her, and an acceptance of the fact that she already had contributed a tremendous amount, not only to American dance, but [also] to American theater and to design—what Martha had done with Noguchi, her way of using sculpture and space. . . .

She had a feminist attitude. Martha did talk to some of the women who were married. Bonnie Odar's husband was in California, and Martha would say, "All right Bonnie, what is wrong? Do you need sex? Do you need to have your husband come visit? Why don't you fly there and use him for what you need him for and fly back?" Martha did say, "Use the men." I think Martha had the feeling of the feminist survival plan. Of course, the traditional plan is that men use women. Martha was not about to use that nomenclature, or to think of herself in that way. Martha, instead, would use the men, like *The White Goddess* by Robert Graves, or even Frazier's *The Golden Bough.* All of that mythology about matriarchy. She thought she was a priestess who could control and give energy and power. The White Goddess is the moon goddess. She is poetry, which is the essence of life. It is the anima. And her consort is Dionysus, which is orgiastic. I was shocked by Martha's idea but it also made a lot of sense to me, that through deep, deep participation with the orgiastic—which also can be destructive—out of that will come renewal and life. If you deny it, it will destroy you. It will still demand its dues, but you won't have control over it. You eventually have to give in to the orgiastic. It is a very interesting concept.

Merce, Erick, Donnie McKayle, John Butler, Glen Tetley—those men wanted to dance with Martha. It was the challenge she presented to them. She was dealing with herself on that high level, so she challenged you in a way that made you really want to be part of that because it was exciting, fearful and difficult. At the same time, you knew if you wanted to be in on it that was the best available.

Men need to get in touch with their feminine, the anima in themselves, which we have denied for so long. Even women have denied their anima. That is one reason why we are in a lot of trouble . . . I think that is the reason we are in so much trouble now culturally. I think that is why fundamental religion is prevailing. These people are fearful. They want a "daddy" figure. There is no place for risk or discovery.

With Martha, dance is life for her and life is dance, and life, to Martha, is a struggle. You either take up the struggle and overtly say, yes, I'm going to struggle. . . . And for Martha, she takes up the struggle and she is determined she is going to win. She is going to be victorious. Martha is going to win over men, women, anyone else who is there. Martha is going to be on top.

GLEN TETLEY

Arnold Eagle.

Glen Tetley (jumping), Bertram Ross, Yuriko (middle), and Matt Turney in Embattled Garden, *1958.*

---◆●◆---

Glen Tetley was born in Cleveland, in 1926. He began his dance training on scholarship with Hanya Holm in 1946. He completed premedical training at Franklin and Marshall College, in Lancaster, Pennsylvania, under the Navy's V-12 program and thereafter enrolled in Columbia Medical School, in New York. To facilitate his dance training, Tetley transferred to New York University, where he studied modern dance with Holm and Martha Graham.

Tetley first danced professionally with Hanya Holm's company (1946-51). He was her assistant for the Broadway productions of Kiss Me, Kate *and* Out of This World. *He was a principal dancer with the New York City Opera (1952-54) and a leading member of John Butler's company for many years. Tetley was a member of the Graham Company from 1956 to 1958, creating "The Serpent" in* Embattled Garden *and "Apollo" in* Clytemnestra.

Tetley was a principal dancer with American Ballet Theater, Jerome Robbins' Ballet U.S.A. and the Joffrey Ballet, and a guest artist with many modern dance companies. He presented his first program of his own choreography in 1962 and he choreographs for companies all over the world.

Glen Tetley lives in New York City and Spoleto, Italy.

---◆●◆---

I was living down here in the Village in 1946 studying with Hanya [Holm]. I was traveling uptown to do my classical studies with Antony [Tudor] and Margaret Craske.[1] Hanya asked me whether I could demonstrate for her because she was teaching evening classes at N.Y.U. I did. There were also some classes

---

[1] Margaret Craske (1892-1990). English ballet dancer and teacher who worked in the United States beginning in the 1940s. She was trained by Enrico Cecchetti and became recognized internationally as an expert in performing and teaching his technical methods.

in the series given by Martha Graham. So I went and I took Martha Graham's class.

There was tremendous rivalry between Hanya and Martha. Hanya told me about a time when they were all together at Bennington. There was a studio which had a balcony that went around it and it was the only way to get to another studio. Martha was deep into something she was choreographing and Hanya had to traverse this balcony . . . Martha just stopped and glared at her until Hanya exited. Hanya resented Martha. She felt Martha's technique and theater were totally ego-oriented, whereas Hanya's concept of dance was more towards pure movement and discovery of space.

I went back to take another Graham class and I was awestruck by this woman. She had just lost Merce Cunningham, who had left her company in 1946. Martha asked me to come and see her in her studio, which was right over here on Fifth Avenue. I went the next evening and Martha took me into her office. She said, "I would like you to be in my company." It was a tremendous honor. I couldn't quite believe what she had said.

I felt overwhelmed by Martha. There was so much power there. There was Martha as a woman. There was Martha as a profound teacher, as a genius choreographer. Someone of physical, animal magnetism and [with] a hypnotic ability to convey seemingly ancient knowledge far beyond the Greeks. She absolutely hypnotized me. And I had been profoundly affected by seeing her on stage performing her own works. I had never seen dance that way—so stripped, so visually compelling and so profoundly psychological.

I was really torn apart. I would have given anything to be in Martha's company, to work with her creative genius. But after all of Hanya's generosity to me and her belief in me, I felt I could not just turn my back on Hanya and walk out. Hanya said to me, "I would rather see you dance on Broadway than with Martha Graham." That was ironic because I would be dancing on Broadway two years later in Hanya's choreography.

Decisions are so painful when one is 20 years old. I explained to Martha, lamely, that I was going to N.Y.U. and that I had promised my father that I would get my bachelor of science degree. I had to do my studies. Martha just stared at me in a silence that seemed to go forever. I felt she could see into every crevice of my soul.

I had a very big jump and I think John Martin had referred to me as "a young Merce Cunningham." That might have clicked in Martha's mind. I did begin then to study with Martha at her Fifth Avenue studio. Martha was teaching the old technique, which was very sparse and into the floor. Very percussive. No turn-out, no lyricism whatsoever. No spatial orientation. A very percussive contraction with body beats. It was very much earth-oriented, pelvic-movement technique. I felt a bit intimidated as I was often the only male in class and the women seemed like grim-faced Amazons. And the technique was very uncomfortable.

In the mid-Fifties, Agnes de Mille choreographed a solo for me in the musical *Juno.* It was based on the most ancient of Irish dances called the "slip-jig," with a soaring, leaping pattern of steps. When I danced it in the opening the critics called me "a show stopper." Martha came opening night and afterwards sent me a card saying "Thank you for a soul-stirring performance. Love, Martha." My heart leaped. Then she asked me to come to her apartment after the show the next night, and we sat up the entire night. She was eloquent. She was not drinking. It seemed to me she was imparting her personal code for survival. She touched something very deep within me. And again she asked me to join her company.

Lucia Chase had also been at the opening of *Juno* and had sent word to me that she would like me to join American Ballet Theater. Again, a difficult decision. But this time there was no hesitation. I chose absolutely to go with Martha. I totally committed myself to her, and it was the deepest, most satisfying period of study I had in my entire career. Just to begin each day sitting on the foot-polished floor with simple breathing exercises was an act of faith—a religious experience. I felt I was emptying out all that had gone before and filling with profound new sensations.

At that time, in 1956, I was there when Martha began to want more lyrical movement and air movement. She began to introduce things one could consider part of the classical idiom, such as tendu exercises in center and at the barre, and even battement frappé and a series of pliés, relevés, that lead into elevation. It was a distinct change from the earlier period when I had studied with her. One could see Martha's previous technique had not been a good technique for the male dancer—or for anyone—for air. Many of the dancers did not have well-articulated feet. They did not have an easy jump. Martha herself was never an air dancer. She had high extensions. She did not ever really elevate. But at this point, which was the point of *Diversion of Angels,* and the more lyrical works she was creating for the company, the direction was to a more lyrical technique.

They were wonderful, the dancers Martha had. Pearl, Mary, Matt, Linda, Helen, Ethel, Bert and Paul. Many of the dancers were taking classical training outside of Martha's studio. That was a bit of a sore point for Martha, which is when she started introducing these things which she felt her technique needed. But she was *always* transforming the technique. It was always growing. She never would teach a standard class. That is why it was marvelous to be there when she was teaching herself. She would sense when movement was becoming dead through repetition and break apart the form and make it newly unfamiliar and sensitized.

I began to learn *Diversion of Angels.* I loved every second of that choreography: the intense lyricism, the sudden stillness, the fugal, contrapuntal sections, the animal crescendos. A totally beautiful work. Then one day Martha said, "I have a role for you"—"The Serpent" in *Embattled Garden* (1958). She had begun with Robert Cohan in the cast. But he suddenly left. He actually just left a note on the piano. He couldn't take the atmosphere with Martha. It had been a claustrophobic situation. He had been there a long, long time. Martha had the ability to strangle.

Embattled Garden was in pieces when I stepped into rehearsal. Martha would come in, get into the choreography, but then there would be a block. She would leave it. Often we would be called for 7 o'clock, after evening class, to be ready for an 8 o'clock rehearsal. Martha would come by maybe 9:30 or 10 o'clock, and she would stand at the back and lean against the wall. She would say, "All right, start."

I remember one evening she came in and she was in street clothes, immaculately dressed. I was up in the Noguchi "tree of knowledge"—actually a large phallus, I discovered, when we were in the theater and I went out front and saw it from a distance. It faced a platform in the stylized form of a pelvis. Martha had me jump from this tree. She had me jumping from what seemed like an enormous height. Yuriko was combing her hair and I would grab Yuriko and pull her into a runaway rape. Martha yelled, "Stop! Stop!" She looked at Yuriko and said, "I will not have sentimentality in my theater." Martha said to me, "Get up into your tree." And she said to Yuriko, "I will be Eve. Give me the comb." Martha said to me, "You jump out of that tree and you embrace me. You don't kiss me on the cheek, you kiss me here, on the chest," slapping herself between her breasts. I thought, "Oh God. What is going to happen?" I had never physically touched Martha. So the music started. She was in her beautiful tailored dress and her famous bun. I thought to myself, "Here goes everything." I jumped out of the tree and I ran over and grabbed Martha, pulling her into the movement. Martha grabbed me like a tiger, pushing herself against me. It was all very ecstatic and spasmodic, and I remember her whole bun falling out and her hair falling down. Finally she stood up, completely flushed, and she said, "*That* is the Garden of Eden." And she strode out of the studio. I was very impressed and struck by all of that. It did temper what I did in *Embattled Garden* from then on and added megawatts to my performance.

Then we choreographed the entire end of the ballet, which was yet to be finished, and that was Martha's way. Very often the dancers more or less put things together. She would then come in at the very end and put her finishing touches on it, like an editor. We finished it and it was an enormous success.

I had early on the experience of choreographing my own roles. It was part of that period of contemporary dance. Actually, we did do great chunks of choreography. I was trained in improvisation by Hanya, even on the musical stage. I was in the original cast of *Kiss Me, Kate*. I was Hanya's assistant. I choreographed complete sequences of *Kiss Me, Kate*, of *Out of This World* and almost the entirety of *Where's Charley?* with Hanya in London. Hanya had bad knees and couldn't move. One got used to it being that way. It was the way it was done. Many dancers get very unhappy with this and resentful of it, especially in the musicals. But I just felt a dancer should create movement and it was a great experience.

One became part of Graham's family, the team. We interrelated and we all worked within her language. Just after that, Martha was working on *Clytemnestra* (1958). She decided to do a dialogue between Apollo and Athena. We were going to Israel. I guess because I had been in the competitive world of musicals that sometimes I was not such an easy person. I said I didn't want to got to Israel just to do *Embattled Garden*. It maybe was very presumptuous of me, but Martha respected that. She was having a problem with *Clytemnestra* and she said, "Through you being difficult I think I have found a way to solve for myself this part of 'Clytemnestra' and also to create a role for you." This was the beginning of the concept of a dialogue between "Apollo" and "Athena." I was very excited because she was starting from zero on this, not like with *Embattled Garden* where I came in the middle. I didn't know what it would be like. I was very nervous. Martha was pacing around the room and she said, "It is so difficult for me to find my way into male movement, to know what a male body should do." She was trying various things out. Then she went into her deep turns, and other elements which I knew very well from class. Gradually, as I began to follow her movement a structure came out of it. It was very exciting to have this thread directly to Martha.

Martha had a lot of blocks with *Clytemnestra*. One of the biggest blocks was at the very end—how to end it. Day after day for months we would be called and Martha would say when we got to this point, "I can't, I can't, I can't." And then she would dismiss everybody. One evening she improvised this marvelous sequence for herself at the end where the whole family was elevated in light with "Apollo" and "Athena"—everybody. Martha slowly exited the stage alone in darkness and defeat. I know how long Martha struggled with this, and it was such a powerful tragic ending. I thought, I would love to go over and tell you, Martha, how wonderful and courageous this ending is. [But] Martha didn't like that ending, which was the correct ending according to the myths and story. Then she did a very Martha thing. She *didn't* leave the stage in darkness when the action was done. Instead she put the family up on a sort of dais. We were standing on either side as "Apollo" and "Athena" and the scrim came down, leaving all of us in darkness upstage. Martha took the myrtle boughs and came running out toward the audience, to Hades, to death. But in full light. A very strong theatrical ending and very Martha. I think it was very indicative of Martha Graham. She has never been able to give over the keys of the kingdom to anybody. It was interesting and psychologically powerful, her first intuitive ending. She found it at that point of feeling defeated emotionally, physically, and choreographically. She did it for an instant. But the performer in her rebelled and Theater triumphed.

As long as I knew Martha, she was the goddess. She was also immensely physical. At the time I was in the company, she was still performing, doing back-falls. I remember in some classes with her company, late at night while she was setting movement for the Furies in *Clytemnestra,* she said, "You have no quality of madness of Furies." Martha herself did this whole diagonal of Furies' movement that was electrifying. The girls were like little sylphs. Martha was this figure out of ancient hell, antique hell, with all the incredible physicality and angularity and opposition and weight in the body.

When I first saw Martha perform, she was the most gifted technical performer I had ever seen. There was never an insecure technical moment. She had a brilliance of line, control, definition, especially in her famous deep turns in arabesque.

I had a feeling of competition with the men in the company because Martha placed the men in positions of rivalry for her affections. Martha had a very contrasted contingent of men. Martha could be very seductive and give favors and take them away. I remember telling Martha—and I don't think she liked suggestions like that—"I know you think of me as a lyric dancer, and someone who is built for the air, but I really want to dance some of the darker works. Some of the deeper dramatic roles."

One day Martha said to me and to Paul, "Would you remain after class because I want to talk to you about something I see in both of you?" We both stayed and Martha said, "Would you please go to the barre and stand? Put your right hand on the barre because I must see you from the left, the heart side." She said, "What do you think about the back of the neck? You must release the animal brain at the base and keep all of this tension out of it. The head must be elongated on the spine, and never do what they have done in classical ballet with the male, which was to castrate him by making him lift his head and squeeze the animal brain, in which the woman has been put on a pedestal and there is all of this artificial homage to an artificial woman." Then she went on and on in her most spellbinding manner. I was mesmerized and totally taken in by all of this. Martha had on one of her brocade Japanese robes. And she finished and she bowed deeply and turned. Paul said, "What a load of crap." Martha stopped dead. Without saying anything, she turned and went out. I thought, how can you say that? Outrageous, but very funny in retrospect.

Bob Cohan was a very sensual dancer, with a sleek, silky cat spring. In the Graham idiom he had his own unique quality. With the zeal of a disciple, he created a Graham-based school and company in London. The London Contemporary Dance Theatre brought Martha's technique to the U.K. And it was a very important influence.

Bert always had a theatricality that was a wild theatricality, that pulled things off into only Bertram Ross country. Of course his major experience, his total experience, his only experience was Martha. He was Martha from the use of his makeup to the use of the mouth, to the use of materials, to the imperious gesture. That was onstage. Offstage he was a very funny, humorous person, a warm and good friend.

I was there in 1956, 1957 and 1958. I did the Israeli tour and I came back. I had gone to the Spoleto Festival in 1958 and danced the lead in four ballets by John Butler. I went to Spoleto again the next year in a company put together by

Herbert Ross[2] and Antony Tudor. I was dancing in a work Herbie created for the festival to a Leonard Bernstein score, "Serenade for Seven Dancers." In it were Scott Douglas and Nora Kaye from American Ballet Theater. We just got along beautifully. Herbert wanted to take *Serenade for Seven Dancers* into American Ballet Theater. Nora had extolled my praises to Lucia Chase and said she should take me into the company, which she did. Lucia brought me in as she always brought everyone in, on a corps contract, but then immediately gave me a principal contract and cast me in the Tudor repertoire with Nora.

I called Martha up and I said, "I have a terrible decision to make." Actually, I didn't call her up. I went to the studio and I said, "Can I speak to you privately? I have this terrible decision to make and I hope you understand. I'm not going to be here with your company. I am going to join American Ballet Theater." Martha had her masklike face on, hooded eyes down. I said, "Artistically, I want to go. I want to dance the Tudor ballets. I want to work with these people." For the first time in my life I was being paid a major salary. In the three years with Martha I had never been paid, except for a few weeks of performance, so this seemed like more money than I ever heard of. Martha said nothing at that point; she remained completely silent. But for the next three months she would telephone me, sometimes at 3 or 4 in the morning. She would say, "You are destroying your career. You could have had with me many new works created for you. Now you are dancing other people's roles. You are wearing other people's clothes." Sometimes I would think I was dreaming this. A bad dream. And it broke my heart to leave Martha.

After we had our very difficult break, in several years we returned to being friends. Martha would call me up and say, "I have a wonderful new Japanese cook. Please come to dinner." I spent wonderful evenings with Martha. She came to my performances. She was always Martha Graham, but she was extremely generous.

When I was in Jerry Robbins' company, Ballet U.S.A., he made a ballet called *Events*. I danced *Faun, Moves, Cage* [and] *Concert* by Jerry. Anyway, *Events* was about all these things happening in the city. He made a pas de deux for two men which supposedly took place in Central Park. Talking with me Jerry said,

---

[2] Herbert Ross (1927-). American ballet, theater and film choreographer and director. His first wife was American ballerina Nora Kaye (1920-1987). His second wife is socialite Lee Radziwill.

"You are walking in this place and everything you see is beautiful. Everything is wonderful in a sensual marvelous light. There is beauty in everything you see." What he choreographed was a homosexual rape in which I was the aggressor and a young boy named Eddie Verser was the young street-tough kid who I raped. It was quite powerful choreography. It was quite stylized, but quite graphic at the same time. Martha walked out of the entire evening. She made a point of being seen walking out. Shortly after that, Scott Douglas, Mary Hinkson, Carmen de Lavallade and I were the four soloists in John Butler's *Carmina Burana,* with Leopold Stokowski conducting. Martha came to see that, and this time she came backstage and knocked on my dressing-room door. She struck me in the face as hard as she could, right after the performance. Martha said, "*That's* for Jerry Robbins." Then she took me in her arms and hugged and kissed me and said, "*This* is for tonight." I think she always had a chip on her shoulder about Jerry. Jerry had written some articles and done interviews about the non-necessity for modern dance. I think why she walked out of Jerry's homosexual rape was not the fact of the rape scene, but there was a lack of dignity of the human soul, in a spiritual sense, to the inner core of choreography. Martha would react very strongly when she felt it was not there.

When I was a dancer I wanted to be someone who was involved in the creative process. I didn't ever want to be a dancer who had everything stamped on them. I wanted to be involved in a give and take. There is a way the dancer can lead a choreographer and suggest movement. When I work now as a choreographer I like that interchange. I've never consciously said, "I am going to do a work that is based on my background in Holm technique, or my classical technique, or Graham technique."

When I began to choreograph, Martha was remarkably generous to me. She gave me more encouragement than any other single teacher or choreographer I had worked with. I was invited to the American Dance Festival at Connecticut College to perform with my new company I had formed with Linda Hodes and Robert Powell, two extraordinary Graham dancers. *Pierrot Lunaire,* to the difficult Schoenberg score, was my first choreographic venture. Voices at the festival wondered why I had used so much classical vocabulary—I hadn't—for a festival of American modern dance. But Martha embraced me and said, "You are dealing with very powerful and eternal themes that concern and touch all of us. And you are saying this in your own language." That was the only voice I needed to hear.

I don't think I ever did Graham choreography because I wanted to find my own idiom. That was one thing Hanya said to me in the very beginning. She said, "The most important thing as a dancer, as a creator, is to find your own individual being, whether it is performer, or creator, or performer-creator together." One must find their own uniqueness. Martha Graham made me realize my identity.

1960's

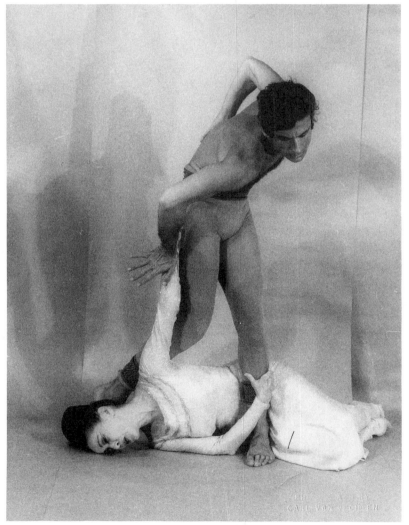

Carl Van Vechten.

Martha Graham and Bertram Ross in Visionary Recital, *1961.*

Takako Asakawa

Jack Vartoogian.

Takako Asakawa with the corps de ballet in Primitive Mysteries, *1982.*

Takako Asakawa was born in Tokyo, on February 23, 1938. In the Sixties she began her studies with Martha Graham. She has danced nearly every major role in the Graham repertoire. Since 1990 Asakawa has been a guest artist with the Graham Company, performing the title roles in Hérodiade *and* Clytemnestra *and the duet in* Acts of Light. *In addition, she has performed "St. Joan" in* Seraphic Dialogue, *"the Girl in Red" in* Diversion of Angels, *"Medea" in* Cave of the Heart *and "the Virgin" in* Primitive Mysteries.

Asakawa also has danced with Donald McKayle, Alvin Ailey, Bertram Ross, Pearl Lang, Lar Lubovitch and Louis Falco. She and David Hatch Walker formed the Asakawalker Dance Company in 1976 and performed their own choreographic works. Asakawa is a member of the Board of Directors of the Joyce Theater.

Takako Asakawa and her husband, Paul Richards, live in New York City.

I saw Miss Graham when she came to Japan in 1955 or 1956. Martha danced *Cave of the Heart* in Isamu Noguchi's set, which I will never forget—incredible. I didn't quite understand [it] then because my mind was not very advanced—I was still a child, [but] I knew it was something good. From what I felt on stage I said to myself, "This is real dance." I had never seen in my life dance like this. I wasn't that knowledgeable about dancing, but I liked the way Miss Graham performed. I thought this is the company I would love to go work with. [Of the dancers] I don't really remember anyone except Miss Graham. I do remember Donnie McKayle, though, because he was very tall and black. I also remember Matt Turney because she was very tall and elegant, and black also. I was fascinated by those two artists. I would stand outside the stage door in awe of these people.

At the time I just went to school, and I never saw that much dance. In 1955 there wasn't much communicated to Japan from other countries. Sometimes the

Bolshoi Ballet [came], but I am not a ballet dancer. When I was a child I studied "child dance," which is really like a game with children, and then I studied with Takaya Eguchi, who had studied with Mary Wigman. I studied jazz with Perry Parmisano and went to the Matsuyama Ballet to study a few times.

Somehow, Martha's dance talked to me in very dramatic terms. I like dramatic dance. Also, I thought *Diversion of Angels* was beautifully floating. I had never seen that much expressed in dance. I said, "I must go to study with Miss Graham," and my goal was to dance with her company.

When I came to study with Martha Graham, she didn't teach so much at that time. Bertram Ross was my main teacher, and a wonderful teacher. I learned a lot from him. Mary Hinkson, Helen McGehee, Ethel Winter, Donnie McKayle, David Wood [and] Dick Kuch were all my teachers. Whenever I had time I would sit outside the doorway of the rehearsal room and look in the little window at the advanced class or intermediate class. I couldn't stop smiling because I was so happy to be at the Graham school. I guess because I loved it every day.

Then I auditioned for the scholarship class. A very strange thing happened. I [had] ordered 10 classes and I couldn't follow anybody. Plus, I had only taken the beginners' class. My aim was to take the advanced class [but] I couldn't explain that to anyone. My name [was] not [on the beginners' audition list so] I couldn't take it. I had to take the advanced-class scholarship audition. The teacher didn't change clothes and show us the step. I couldn't understand anything. Since my name is Asakawa and "A" is the first, [I] had to be number one. Two people have to go [and] I was the first one. I was hysterical. One person steps and does [a] side jump. So everybody does step, side jump. I was so disappointed. I had never been scared in my life like then. Somehow I got a 10-class scholarship. I was so surprised. Everybody said, "It is so weird." [Martha] had put my name number one—I was only a beginning class student. A few months later I got in Miss Graham's company. . . .

My first performance in America [had been] with Donald McKayle's group, before I was in Martha Graham's company. Donnie had some performances at the 92nd Street Y. [Then] I danced in [Martha's] *Secular Games* (1962). I also danced with Alvin Ailey's company in 1965 and 1968. I danced with Pearl [Lang], Bert [Ross] and Donnie, who were all Miss Graham's disciples. Donnie was much more different, though. In 1962 we went on a State Department tour of Europe with Martha Graham. That was the first time I went to Europe.

Martha immediately created a role for me in her new dance, *Secular Games,* [when I joined the company]. I couldn't believe it! Helen McGehee was the star. Miss Graham created the choreography right in front of me. Everything was new. I was frightened [and] I still didn't speak English. I think Miss Graham put me into the high image of the Japanese doll. [The setting of] *Secular Games* is . . . like a beach, with all the young ones in the company together—except Martha, of course, made the choreography and Helen was in the leading part. All the young ones are playing games and throwing balls. Women are passing along the beach. Here I am, like a big blanket on the beach, rolling off and on. . . . Martha put me into it quite well. I eventually did almost every chorus role. I was also in the chorus in *Part Real—Part Dream* (1965). All those interesting artists were in that dance: Mary [Hinkson], Matt [Turney], Bert [Ross] and Bob [Cohan]. It was a remarkable time for the Martha Graham Company. Mary Hinkson and Matt Turney were the stars. I didn't speak so well—I just watched. In *Cortege of Eagles* I was in the chorus as one of the captive women of Troy—an incredible dance!

Martha created . . . *Dancing—Ground* (1967) for Bob Powell, me and Helen. Bob Powell and I danced *Dancing—Ground* and *The Plain of Prayer* (1968) together. [In] those two dances Martha didn't use a chorus. We were the leads in the duet. For me, it was more [of a responsibility] than if there [had been] a chorus. There was a lot of energy because it was a technical dance.

The Lady of the House of Sleep (1968) was the last role Martha choreographed for herself. I was in that dance also. In *The Lady of the House of Sleep* Martha was the leader, and she always wore capes. We dancers just fell in and out of her space. We only performed that once. *The Archaic Hours* (1969) was also a big piece, but we only performed it for a short time. Martha didn't even finish the choreography until the end, so we did our parts all by ourselves. At that point, Martha was really out of the dance world. All of us together—Helen, Ethel, Bert—had to come up with movement. All of those pieces were performed just once or twice—also *Mendicants of Evening* and *Myth of a Voyage,* [both of] which came in 1973. None of those dances lasted long. They didn't last.

Noguchi understood . . . Graham almost immediately. Martha Graham was lucky to have Noguchi's imagination. Noguchi was also lucky to have Martha Graham's space. Both had an intense light. Noguchi said he didn't know—he just felt. Sometimes I would get bumps on my arms because I would see

Martha and Noguchi fighting each other, the two of them, because they were so much into what they were doing. "Get out of here," they would scream. Isamu would come in the next day and they would make up. In art, they were like wife and husband. It was incredible. They were helping each other. Both Martha and Noguchi have a sense of Oriental architecture. You don't find this on the stage today. Picasso was much different. But Noguchi carried on the tradition. It is an Oriental texture in the air . . . I get goose pimples. Eventually I realized Martha was very influenced by the Asian sensibility. Martha Graham has a history of Asian women in her company. Yuriko (Kikuchi) was there. Yuriko Kimura came seven years after I did. Akiko Kanda was there, but only for a short while.

I left the Graham Company in 1976 to start the Asakawalker Dance Company. Then I came back to dance in 1982 or 1981. In 1990 I came back to the company as a guest artist. Martha tried to make a new dance for me with an opera of cats. "Meow, meow, meow, meow" was through the whole opera. It wasn't successful—it was only "meow, meow." Martha wanted to drop it and save the choreography. We were only three people.

It was very difficult for Martha to trust anybody to do her roles. Martha performed till her early 70s, but then she couldn't take it anymore. It was difficult in the beginning for people to take over her roles. Gradually she learned how to [let them do the roles] but in the beginning she got sick. Later we were lucky because Martha grew with us and we could put our own feeling into it.

I danced *Cave of the Heart, Seraphic Dialogue, Clytemnestra, Dark Meadow* [and] *Hérodiade*—one of the most gorgeous dances. Miss Graham's heroines are ageless. I put my imagination into Miss Graham's imagination and come up with my own interpretation. The flexibility and freedom I received from Miss Graham was unusual because most choreographers don't give that to you. Miss Graham was not that way before, when she was dancing. Now each one of us is respected by Miss Graham to interpret her creations. I am able to use Martha Graham's technique, choreography, everything, to put in me with my past—put together—and that is why I am always alive onstage, because of that freedom. Also, I feel so much into those dances. It is a great and difficult responsibility. I realized my identity through Martha Graham—I think so—as an artist and as a woman.

I could never be a copy of Martha. She hates a copy. A copy will never be as great as the original. That is one of Martha's greatest accomplishments as a leader: [letting us] express our feelings well. That is why I have more responsibility—because Martha gave it to me and now I have to give it to the audience. That is growing, give-and-take. Martha's main key is that the interpretation comes from inside of you, not outside. With Martha's dances the women are as strong as the men. Male [and] female are the same for Martha. Sometimes the women are stronger than the men, too. That is the thing: There is no difference between male [and] female for Martha. Also, Martha Graham knows the place of the erotic in relation to the sexes. I watched [Rudolf] Nureyev quite a bit when he danced with Martha. I didn't dance with him. He was a real artist, though. I learned lots from him. He comes on the stage like magic. Not too many people have that. After she began working with Nureyev, Martha told everyone, "Finally, I found a man who has the courage to do a contraction."

Martha Graham created her own technique. Her root is from Ted Shawn, Ruth St. Denis and herself. I think it has something to do with the deep root of human beings. It goes way, way back, even though she created it for herself. It comes from history through the ages. The construction of her dances is somehow connected to her genius, which is why her creations are so great. Everything is combined into her sketch—not only movement, but also music, décor, costumes. She is very intelligent. Martha's main quality is being able to pass on the drama through her knowledge of dance.

Now I like to concentrate on how much greatness Martha has had in her choreographic past. I like to go into the dances more, and to express myself onstage, rather than create a new dance which wasn't really concrete yet. Without Miss Graham, today's modern dance in America wouldn't be the same. We all know that.

Gus Solomons Jr.

Martha Swope © Time Inc.

Gus Solomons Jr. and Bertram Ross in
The Witch of Endor, *1965.*

Gus Solomons, Jr. was born in Boston, in 1938. He graduated with a bachelor of architecture degree from the Massachusetts Institute of Technology. While at M.I.T. he studied dance with Jan Veen at the Boston Conservatory of Music and Graham technique with Robert Cohan at his Boston studio.

Gus Solomons Jr. danced with the companies of Donald McKayle (1961-64), Pearl Lang (1961-68), Martha Graham (1964-65) and Merce Cunningham (1965-68). In 1972 he formed his own experimental concert dance troupe, The Solomons Company / Dance, for which he has choreographed many works. The formal organization of his work reflects his architectural training; he also experiments with indeterminacy and site-specificity, and regularly collaborates with architects, visual artists and new-music composers.

From 1976-78 Solomons was Artistic Director / Dean of the Dance School at the California Institute of the Arts. A frequent arts council panelist, he teaches and choreographs as artist-in-residence at universities throughout the country. He is a contributing dance writer / critic for Dance Magazine *and* The Village Voice, *among other publications. In 1994 he joined the full-time dance faculty at the New York University Tisch School of the Arts.*

Gus Solomons Jr. lives in New York City.

I am trying to think when and how I really learned about Martha. I remember coming to New York City as an architecture student in 1958 for a weekend of looking at new buildings. I walked by the 54th Street Theater, where the Martha Graham Company was premiering *Clytemnestra.* I didn't get to see it then, but that was the first time I had seen Martha Graham's name in lights. I think at the time I was also reading the Barbara Morgan book, [*Martha Graham: Sixteen Dances in Photographs*], as a general artifact of dance, my main avocation. . . .

When I was a sophomore at M.I.T., I started to study dance with Jan Veen[1] at the Boston Conservatory. He was trained by Laban[2] and Wigman. He taught us well about movement in space and time in that scientific, German way. It was a wonderful way to learn dance, because it was so organized. Shortly after that Robert Cohan came to Boston and opened a studio, where I took every class he gave. Cohan had recently left the Graham company and was reteaching himself the Graham technique at that point, taking what he had learned from Martha and making it his own. Those classes were intense!

I was a quick study and in demand in the tiny Boston dance world because I was tall and there weren't many male dancers around. Because of Veen's training I had no trouble picking up different styles easily. I mean, I could dance in Graham style, Cunningham style, Donnie McKayle's jazzier style and Pearl Lang's version of Graham. Being versatile kept life interesting.

I really never did aspire to dance with Martha Graham until I got asked. I thought: That's cool; that might be fun. I'll do that. In 1964 we did a lecture-demonstration at Lincoln Center: "An Evening with Martha Graham," hosted by dance critic Walter Terry. We did a demonstration class at Avery Fisher Hall, but that was just a single shot. The following year Martha asked me to join the company; 1964-65 was my only season with the Martha Graham Company. Martha always made a point of having an interracial company: Yuriko, Matt Turney, Mary Hinkson, Donnie (McKayle), Takako Asakawa, Yuriko Kimura. I appreciated that, because at that time most Broadway shows weren't integrated.[3] Martha and I got along very well.

---

[1] Jan Veen (1903-67). Born Hans Weiner in Vienna, Veen was a concert dancer who worked in the Boston area after the late 1920s.

[2] Rudolf von Laban (1879-1958). Slovakian pioneer of modern dance and dance notation. Originally interested in "plastic rhythm"—motion for its own sake—he later tried to find a physical expression of the coordination of mind, nerves and muscles and believed that the quality of movement had to have its own psychological motivation. He also developed ideas relating to space patterns and harmonies, ideas which led to expressionism in the modern dance. He divided all people into 3 physical types and, believing that people react kinetically according to their physiological and psychological make-up, found that certain styles of movement corresponded to each physical type. In addition, he delineated the importance of "Anspannung und Abspannung," the range of dance movement between extremes of utter tension and complete relaxation. He is best known for inventing "Labanotation," a written system used to record, and thus preserve, choreographic movement.

[3] When Graham's *The Witch of Endor* was performed in 1965, half of the male cast were people of color, an extraordinary casting decision for its time. Each of these dancers—Gus Solomons, Jr., Clive Thompson, Dudley Williams and William Louther—all went on to make his individual mark in modern dance history.

From Bob Cohan I learned more about Martha's technique more than from the teachers at her school in New York. Fortunately, I learned the real Graham contraction from him—that it wasn't just a rounded spine but a total muscular, emotional and spiritual commitment. The Graham floorwork is limited by one's physique: If you don't have hyper-flexible hips like Martha, or if you have legs as long as mine, you just can't really do the floor exercises properly. Oh, you can screw yourself into those positions, but you really don't learn a thing except tenseness that way. I used to teach a floor section in my class, but it was based mostly on Ruth Solomon's anatomically/kinesiologically based exercises. That's one big benefit of Merce Cunningham's technique: Standing up, you can learn to dance with whatever anatomy you own. You don't have to be a certain way physically. You can learn to play your own physical instrument in the most eloquent, most efficient way.

With Veen we learned that dancing and choreography were inseparable. But Martha didn't teach choreography. She taught her vocabulary, then she composed it her way. The rehearsal process I recall as being unique: First everybody got angry—at each other, at the dance, at Martha, whatever. Then, when they were all at a full peak of rage, we'd run through the dance. Merce, on the other hand, worked from inner stillness. We'd get totally calm and serene and see how few muscles it took to move a leg or arm. During Graham rehearsals I'd always be running off into a corner to meditate, until everyone else was worked up enough to dance. Anyway, that's how it seemed. With Merce's approach I could do technical feats I didn't even believe I could do.

Ultimately, Cunningham's approach better suited my temperament. Working with Graham was fascinating and enjoyable in a theatrically indulgent sort of way, which satisfied the "ham" in me. But I wasn't as besotted as some with the Martha Graham mystique. To me, she was a smart, funny little woman who sometimes drank too much and digressed frequently but had a flawless instinct for epic theatricality. She was present at rehearsals for a new work, but rarely oversaw the repertoire. (The company would put that together, and then Martha would come look and give it the OK.) Anyway, when she was creating a new dance, she would plop down on the studio floor and chat with us dancers about, for instance, the deli around the corner, where you had to watch out for the chicken because it sometimes wasn't good. When she'd eventually get to the work at hand, she'd say, "In this piece [*The Witch of Endor*, in which I played the ghost of Samuel], I have a vision of Samuel as an enormous presence." That is what I had to work with: an "enormous presence." But that was part of her genius. The dancers were all steeped in her movement, so whatever they improvised was stylistically right. Then Martha would just watch and edit what the dancers came up with: "Yes, do that, dear!" Her aura and her vision gave her the ability to produce amazing results, despite sometimes being detached or distracted.

What I did to make this "enormous presence" that was Samuel was devise a stool, bolted to the floor, which had boots bolted to it. Laced into the boots, I could lean with my whole body out into space, like a 10-foot-tall ski jumper, making my whole body into the gesture that Martha wanted. Being attached to the stage, I was onstage the whole time, looking through the big hinged gate (by Ming Cho Lee, who designed the set) that descended like a drawbridge to reveal me behind it. Consequently, I could watch Bert [Ross] and David Wood, I think, steering Martha around the stage. By 1965 Martha could only do about three steps herself: a high kick (always with the left leg) and descent to the knees, an emotionally fraught heel-walk and a still-fierce contraction. And she couldn't always remember what came next or where she was supposed to be. The men would literally move her from place to place, where she'd do her three steps.

Graham's work demanded a lot more creative input from her dancers than Merce's, but all the input was, of course, Martha's own movement vocabulary. When Paul Taylor came to her, he didn't know all her steps, so he did a lot of his own movement, and everybody said, "Ooh, look how Martha has stretched her vocabulary!" Well, Paul Taylor was just doing what he knew how to do, and immediately it became Martha Graham's property. Remarkably, in the eyes of the dance world any movement Martha touched became hers—even an arabesque—so great was her force as a creative genius.

One Christmas—or Thanksgiving, I don't remember—I was sitting alone at home, when the phone rang. It was Martha. She called up just to chat, because she was lonely. As she said, "We are all profoundly alone." I thought, Wait a minute! This is Martha Graham, calling *me* up, because she's lonely and just wants someone to talk to. That was very moving to me. I would see Martha occasionally over the years after I left the company, and she always remembered me. I treated her informally, like "my friend Martha," not worshipfully, like *Miss Graham*; that always seemed to faze her entourage of attendants—and delighted me.

Yes, I am glad, and increasingly grateful, to have had the chance to dance for Martha Graham. In fact, I have been incredibly lucky altogether in my career: I have been able to make a living doing what I most enjoy—dancing.

THE
1970's

Louis Peres.

Pearl Lang and Rudolf Nureyev in El Penitente, *c. 1975-76.*

PEGGY LYMAN

Max Wald

Peggy Lyman as "Phaedra" in Phaedra, *1979.*

Peggy Lyman was born in Cincinnati, in 1950. She began her dance training in Cincinnati and has appeared with the Cincinnati Ballet, the New York City Opera Ballet, the Contemporary Dance Theater and the Radio City Music Hall corps de ballet, as well as in the Broadway musical Sugar.

Since becoming a member of the Martha Graham Company in 1973, Lyman has performed many principal roles, including the title roles in Judith and Clytemnestra, the central Joan role in Seraphic Dialogue, "Jocasta" in Night Journey, "Ariadne" in Errand into the Maze, Andromache's Lament, "Cleopatra" in Frescoes and the duet, "Conversations of Lovers," in Acts of Light. In addition, two classic dances, Frontier and Lamentation, were re-created for her by Miss Graham.

In addition to having been a member and a coach of the Graham School faculty, she was the rehearsal director of the Graham Company and the artistic director of the Martha Graham Ensemble, the student company. As an authorized Graham reconstructionist, she has set Diversion of Angels at the University of Michigan and on the Dutch National Ballet and Panorama at the University of Illinois.

Lyman has made guest appearances, presented her own company in the U.S. and abroad, developed dance programs and taught throughout the United States and Europe. Her television credits include a guest appearance with Rudolf Nureyev on the Julie Andrews' CBS special, Invitation to the Dance.

Currently Lyman is the chairman of the School of the Hartford Ballet's four-year Bachelor of Fine Arts Degree in Dance program at the University of Hartford's Hartt School.

Peggy Lyman lives in Connecticut with her husband, Tim Lynch, a writer, and their son, Kevin.

My first 10 years of training was in classical ballet. I had no interest in modern dance at all. When I first came to New York City, I went right to Joffrey Ballet and studied there for 1 $^1/_2$ years. As Bob Joffrey's esthetic was changing he told me I was too tall (5' 9-$^3/_4$") for his ballets, but he arranged auditions for me. I even studied at S.A.B. (School of American Ballet) for about a month. Mr. B. (George Balanchine) came in to look at me and he said, "You're a beautiful dancer, but you are not trained in my style at all. You are 19 years old. You are too old to retrain."

At that point I returned home to Cincinnati. In fact, I didn't hear about Martha Graham until I began to study with a modern dance company that was just forming there. It was directed by Jefferson James, a woman who had studied at Juilliard. She introduced me to Martha Graham's name and technique. She said that when I went back to New York City I should study at Martha's school, which I did, beginning in 1972, while I supported myself performing in the Broadway musical, *Sugar.*

About 1973, Martha took me in her company. Martha loved that Broadway background of mine. It reminded her of her "Follies" days, I think. My legs would kick up all over the place, and she would love that. Martha's attraction to me was pretty immediate. I was taken into her company way before I felt I was ready, I mean technically ready. I was more than willing even though, I suppose, I wasn't ready. Right away, Martha put me into really difficult Graham choreography like "The Furies" in *Clytemnestra.* Then she entrusted me with the lovely solo for "Athena," which was originally danced by Mary Hinkson, one of my first Graham teachers.

Mary Hinkson and Ethel Winter are two of my favorite Graham teachers—I was talking about Mary Hinkson in my class today. Mary was at Graham when I first got into the company. It was an amazing time . . . because of Mary and Bert [Ross] and Matt [Turney] and Takako [Asakawa]. Bill Carter was around then also.

I feel fortunate to have been preceded by Matt and May [O'Donnell] [because they] set the path for dancers of my size in Martha's "Mother Earth" roles, such as when she cast me as the lead in *Chronique* (1974). Martha just re-worked the dance from *Mendicants of Evening* which she had choreographed the year before. In *Mendicants* I was in the chorus. The next year, I went into Matt's part and Bill Carter came into Bert Ross' part, so Bill and I danced together. That is when it became *Chronique.* I [had] forgotten that one dance evolved into the other. Martha was just getting back into working with her company. She was choreographing for the first time without dancing. This was a transition period for Martha and she was not very happy not dancing, not being able to show things. She had a whole new young company that wasn't familiar with the way she worked. It was not an easy time.

My Graham heroines are Mary Hinkson, Yuriko Kimura and Takako Asakawa. I think every moment with Martha is such a learning experience for anyone who wants to be a choreographer. Just watching Martha work over the last 17 years, I keep learning. Whether or not you want to use the movement that Graham codified, it is so fantastic and intense to see Martha's way of approaching material. One of the most valuable things I've learned from her is that part of what choreography entails is just literally being in the studio every day with your dancers, whether you have an idea or not—being in a space with your dancers and allowing yourself the vulnerability of emptiness so that you're receptive. You are ready to receive, whether you want to think it is the gods stimulating you or your own subconscious feeding you the necessary material. After all, it is all stored up [within] us. That is the luxury of being empty, so that you can receive from yourself and from your dancers. It is a really nervous place to be, the studio, and you must allow yourself the freedom to experiment. Maybe you don't produce anything for a day or a week, but still you are together—you experiment, you talk, you listen to music. Also, you let the dancers participate in that process. Martha says, "I hypnotize you. I bring you to the studio. We listen to music. I tell you the theme. If it is a narrative, I explain the story." What she is saying is [that] part of her job is to hypnotize the dancers onto her wavelength so [that] all . . . our energies [are] going in the same direction.

Martha demanded [that] you draw a lot [from] your own growth. Through the growing process of working with Martha, I realized my identity as a dancer, performer and woman. When you work with Martha, you don't stand there and wait for her to tell you what to do. A lot of it is researching your own life's experiences and [finding] what you [can] bring to the story that Martha is trying to tell. I could go down the line of dances, starting with *Frescoes* (1979)—which was very archaic, and very flat and linear—to *Judith* (1980), where Martha tore me apart. Everything was jagged and angular and twisted and taut. Martha needed to challenge me for that role of "Judith" in order to achieve a physical density and contrast between Judith as "the austere widow" and Judith as the "seductress" she must become to save her tribe. I believe Martha took a great deal of interest in watching me struggle through the choreography to successfully develop this character. Once Martha tore me apart like that for *Judith,* in the next dance, *Acts of Light,* she let me be soft again. In rehearsal one night, Martha told me to take my hair down and wear it long in order to allow myself the not-often-called-for romantic feelings of the duet. I went from being legendary to being human.

Over the years of growing with Martha, every time I would work with her it would be in a larger role, in a greater capacity. A lot of the movement actually comes from our own bodies. We are trained in Martha's technique so it is her expression, although a lot of the movement goes beyond the classroom shapes. Martha loved breaking me apart. I was very lyrical and classically lined. Martha loved twisting that up and making me find ways to twist it up. Martha outlines and suggests, and then lets you feel it through the movement. Martha always said—and she said it again the other day—"Really what I do is coordinate the movements that you give me." Martha is an editor. She will say, "No. Do two of those," or "Only do one of those," or "Do it to the other side," or "Do it in that direction." I am told that even earlier, when Martha was more mobile and working with the other soloists, those dancers choreographed a lot of their solos. The chorus choreography Martha always did herself.

I believe Martha's technique is the best modern technique for training a dancer. From my own point of view, Graham and ballet are the two most important techniques in training a dancer—a combination of both. I used to teach a summer workshop where first we would do a ballet class, then I would teach a Graham class, back-to-back. I learned a lot, and the students learned a lot, because there are a lot of technical elements that cross over from one to the other. When I started with Martha, I didn't take any ballet for three years. I cut it off completely. When I finally had what I felt was "Graham" under my belt, I started going back. There were many aspects of ballet technique that were so much easier—balance, turns—because of Martha's use of the spiral. My back was much stronger.

Martha's contraction can be used architecturally or dramatically. Of course, choreographers use different contractions than Martha does, [but] their contractions are not our contractions; Merce does a body curve. We, at Graham, wouldn't call that a contraction. At Graham we do work a lot on the floor, and teaching those students to get up off the floor and not look like old ladies is very difficult. One has to use one's stomach muscles and thighs. My understanding is that Erick Hawkins is the total opposite of Martha Graham. Martha is the center of the universe. You, as the dancer, are the center. For Erick, you are at one with the universe at peace.

Adorations (1975) is one example of Martha's contractions being used architecturally; another is *Frescoes,* which Martha choreographed for me and Tim Wengerd in 1978. Originally, the first section was Janet Eilber and Peter Sparling who were "Cleopatra" and "Anthony," and [in] the second section, Tim and I were "Anthony" and "Cleopatra." When Janet and Peter left the company, Martha combined [*Frescoes*] with just one couple who did both sections. That was 1979.

As I said before, *Judith* was the complete opposite—the contraction was danced very dramatically. For this *Judith,* in 1980, Martha used a different score, replacing the Schuman with Varèse. The dance had a stunning set by Noguchi, especially the piece of cloth where you see "Holoferne's" severed head after "Judith" beheads him. *Andromache's Lament* (1982) was the last dance Martha choreographed for me. *Andromache's Lament* was a turning point for me because that particular solo I choreographed almost all on my own and Martha barely changed a step. It was right after that that I choreographed my first solo for my own program of solo concerts. I began choreographing for my own company in 1984.

In 1986, knowing that I didn't have too much longer to perform—I had arthritis in my hips—I asked Martha if I could be the next "Clytemnestra." Initially she thought I might be too tall, but she said that when I was ready to show her the prologue she would make her decision. I performed the role of "Clytemnestra" in 1987. I am so glad I got to perform Martha's role of "Clytemnestra" before my hip gave out. It is an amazing role. I could get through the performance of *Clytemnestra,* but it got to a point where I couldn't walk afterwards. I consider having danced "Clytemnestra" the pinnacle of my performing career. Without writing a book on the role I can't put into words the depth, research, learning and performing of that particular character.

I would have loved to dance Martha's "Medea" in *Cave of the Heart.* That is one role I didn't get to do that I would have really loved to do. I did "Joan." It didn't bother me as much that I didn't get to do *Appalachian Spring.* But "Medea" I would have really loved to perform. I loved dancing *Night Journey, Seraphic Dialogue* and *Errand into the Maze*—I loved doing them all. Especially

Johan E

Peggy Lyman and David Brown in Andromache's Lament, *1982.*

dear to me are the two early solos of Martha's that she revived for me, *Lamentation*[1] and *Frontier.* These two dances we re-created off of silent films with Martha dancing. We had to work from the written musical score to put the dance to the music. That Martha entrusted those two roles to me and Janet Eilber at such an early time in our own Graham careers was instrumental in creating that strong trust I had with Martha from that point on.

This mutual respect is what allowed me to come and go so frequently from Martha's company. Martha does encourage the individual quest. I never got the feeling I wasn't allowed to go away and work and then come back. I always felt I could go and teach, or choreograph, and come back and my place would be there for me. But that is not true with everybody. Even now, you have to get to a certain point in your relationship with the management before that freedom is offered to you.

Although I was performing solo concerts of other dancers' work, I didn't want to choreograph until 1982. That was 9 years of Martha until I felt strong enough to get out there myself. Elisa Monte and Pascal Rioult are the strongest choreographers to come out of Martha from my generation.

We have a joke with the men in Martha's company about how emasculated they really were as men in this Graham repertory—all of these strong women beheading them, banishing them, killing them. For the women it was great. As women we got to explore a huge range of vivid emotions by acting out our characters' angers and fears and ecstasies. Where else could one do that except with Martha Graham? Not just experiencing the turmoil of life, but creating a solution out of it. There is the stumbling block, the struggle and salvation. And Martha's narratives usually included the conflict, struggle and salvation. That is why the women stay in the company with Martha for so long. From this we've learned incredible amounts from Martha, and the next step is to go on and try it ourselves. I think we all feel that.

---

[1] After Peggy Lyman danced *Lamentation,* Martha Graham autographed a photograph of her in this solo: "From one Lamentation to another. Love, Martha." Later this image was used as a Martha Graham Dance Company poster.

ELISA MONTE

Jack Vartoogian.

Elisa Monte and George White Jr. in Errand into the Maze, *1980.*

Elisa Monte was born in New York City on May 23, 1946. She made her pro-
fessional dance debut at the age of 10 in a 1956 revival of Agnes de Mille's
choreography for Carousel, *and worked for de Mille in later productions. Al-*
though she has danced with Pilobolus, Pearl Lang and Lar Lubovitch, as a dancer
she is best remembered for her work with the Martha Graham Company
(1974-82).

Monte's first choreographic work, Treading *(1979), immediately identified her*
as an important innovator and contributor to contemporary dance. In 1982,
Treading *was taken into the repertory of the Alvin Ailey American Dance The-*
ater and a commission from Ailey quickly followed, resulting in Monte's dance,
Pigs and Fishes.

Her company, Elisa Monte Dance, was founded in 1981 and immediately gained
an international reputation in the field of modern dance after winning first
prize for Best Company at the International Dance Festival in Paris in 1982.
Over the past decade the company has performed 20 original works by Monte,
as well as those of her husband, David Brown.

Elisa Monte lives in New York City.

Pearl Lang was using Graham technique when I was dancing with her, so it
was a very strong introduction for me into Graham. I've always been the kind
of dancer who has enjoyed learning dance through repertory and not through
technique. Later, I learned the technique in detail, but it was more the repertory that intrigued me and caught my interest [when] I started to become interested in Martha Graham. The first piece I saw with her was *Cave of the Heart.*
With "Medea," I went absolutely out of my mind. I thought she was fabulous.
It caught my imagination: "I would just love to dance 'Medea.' This is it!"

I heard Martha had begun teaching again. Well, if I'm going to study at Graham, then Martha is certainly the person to study with. Martha had great changes going on, and she changed her company and started her apprentice program. At that point, I went to the Graham school to take classes with Martha Graham. I had known Robert Powell, who was the rehearsal director of the company then. We became great friends and I loved him dearly. Martha was teaching, and I took class with her and right after the first class—things are luck and timing, but also being able to see the opportunities being there, and recognizing what is going on is another issue—I heard a rumor Martha was looking at women. They needed a new woman, or two, perhaps, in the company. I said to Bob Powell, "I know it is my first class here, but will it be possible for Martha to take a look at me?" He said, "I'll try to get you in." Martha was looking at specific, regular girls she knew, and here I was begging . . . to have her take a look at me. So, I was at the audition. She looked at us after the class and she didn't look at me. I got furious. I said, "I know if she would look at me she would want me because I know her repertory. I know I can dance her repertory. And she hasn't looked at me." I was determined to get her to look at me. So I went back the next day because she was teaching the entire week. I put myself much closer than the day before and I got her to look at me during the class. And once again, they were doing final looks at the girls they had chosen. Bob said, "Come back to the audition. Martha wants to look at you again." As a result of that, she invited me to join the Graham Company. That was 1974.

Martha was a very strong woman, so there was always something to deal with. Nothing was ever "just fine." There was never the easy answer to any of it. But that was part of the excitement of working for her, that was part of the growth that was possible in taking all of Martha's criticism. . . . If you could stand up under it, you could triumph. I've seen Martha cut so many heads off!

Martha did develop her own technique—so at some point she was very interested in it—but it was always a means to the end. She wanted the repertory. The technique came out of the repertory. She would do a piece and people couldn't do a step very well, so [the step] would come into classes. People would then practice it so they could do it well.

I think Martha developed the technique, but she had a long line of artists coming into the company who were very fine teachers, who were interested in passing on what she had started, which was the core of her soul.

With Martha, it was always from an emotional point of view. An impulse to demonstrate Martha's technique was so codified that she, in fact, didn't even remember most of it. I'm not a historian. There is a place for history and there should be historians . . . I'm just not one of them. The minute something gets passed on, all I can see is the original personality. I'm very much into individuality and not into the larger grouping of individuals, which is for someone else to deal with. All I see is the loss of the individual within something getting codified. However, one has to pass information on. If it were up to me, everything would disintegrate as soon as the originator passed on.

I think Martha knew I was going to leave and start my own odyssey of choreographing. I knew at some point in my future I would choreograph. I wanted a situation in which it would be possible. Actually I had [my own] studio, and organized it about 1976. I could use it just as a dancer to work myself. So when I did choreograph I used my own studio, whereas most of the other people had to use Martha's studio to work in. But I could stay at home and work. I didn't want to be psychologically in that atmosphere with Martha's influence. I do believe in spirits. The spirit is there within the presence of that strong woman—Martha.

There always is room for interpretation as a dancer with Martha. That is the incredible thing about dancing and why I love it so much . . . it is very formal and very structured. Certainly Martha's work is. Certainly classical is. But within that structure you realize the freedom a human being has and the choices they can make. To me, that is intriguing, that something so final, so elusive, can make such a huge difference within the interpretation of a role. Just a change of breath, the change of an eye, the change of the direction of the structure of the skull . . . slight little things can make a huge difference. You see, Martha is not a technician. The work is there, and a lot of her solos especially are very idiosyncratic. They are very personally Martha. And I think a lot of dancers have made the mistake of trying to imitate those specific characteristics of Martha Graham. They are Martha specifically, and not the role. They are Martha performing the role. It is always a mistake for any performer, or choreographer, for that matter, to try to imitate someone. All one can do is see what the basis is, what the real core is—where was the starting point—and then take it from there, and look at what they were trying to do in the role perhaps. But one can't ever imitate someone because it will just be a cheap imitation of what that person is and it is not going to read honestly because it is a shell of what it is supposed to be. As a performer, one can only hope that one can surmise what was intended as a performer of a role or as interpreter of a role.

It went rather quickly with me at Martha's. I knew I was right for the repertory. I mean, all those characters, Martha's women, they were fascinating to me. Having the opportunity to play Jocasta, Medea, Electra, Ariadne . . . I had read these plays. I was already in love with these characters. It was kind of a perfect opportunity.

They were in and out, all those former dancers. Mary Hinkson was not, actually. She had already had her falling out and left. Bert and Matt had also left. Ethel was still around. The people that still are, were, and the people that aren't, weren't. There was a lot of change going on. Martha was resurging because she hadn't taught in years.

All of Graham's women are romantically involved. It is all about love. Maybe the hate that resulted from the love, but it was always a love affair. Martha did a duet with Tim Wengerd and me, that Marisol designed, called *Oh Thou Desire Who Art About to Sing* (1977). Later, she choreographed another duet for my husband, David Brown, and me, called *Dance of the Golden Horn*. *Oh Thou Desire* was quite daring for Martha because it was a romantic dance. I felt that was a departure for Martha.

Whatever Martha's desire was, she was entirely entitled to that privilege. I mean as long as she gave me the freedom onstage to perform her treasured roles she had every right to all of her opinions, even if I perhaps thought differently. It wasn't my studio, it wasn't my company. It was completely up to Martha to make all the choices, whether they are right or wrong. I didn't feel that was a problem. Certainly Martha is a very strong personality. In the day-to-day interaction there would be moments where I had had it. I couldn't take one more comment, but it wasn't for me to change. It was my problem. All of Martha's company had that problem to deal with in the end. But she has the prerogative to do as she wishes in her studio as far as I'm concerned.

There is a lot of room for interpretation with Martha's choreography. Everyone goes through that with Martha. If you look at Martha choreographically, [her dances] are a series of solos. All of them. The better the dance, the more that specific form is there. She absolutely left it up to the individual. Medea would come and do a solo. Then Medea goes back and the chorus comes and . . . Jason goes back. The chorus comes again. They have a little interaction, they go off and come back and do solos. It is always in solo. Even the choruses she does are really one big solo. It is more people doing the solo.

When I did Martha's *Errand into the Maze,* she said it was completely different than the way she did it. But she said, "It was good." I can only honestly do [a role as] I interpret it. What I felt it was, and who I felt the woman was, and what she was coping with. The only way I could perform it was to see how it related to my life. Martha, as a director, would say, "It can't be that," or "This is what it should be at this moment." Martha would push you further, but basically she would let the interpretation be yours, because she realized the person performing had to be herself if she was going to have any kind of performance for the audience. She would push you further, but she would never specifically be a technician, in the sense that "your foot has to be in *this* position." Martha was trying to get the emotional response in you and didn't bother with the shape being the important thing. She was trying to get at some deeper thing by her corrections, which were never just form. They were never pure form.

In 1982, I left. I did the taping for television of *Clytemnestra,* performing "Electra," which was one of the last events I participated in with Graham. We were feuding by then.

On the one hand, it was always from Martha's point of view. Helen McGehee, on the other hand, is a purist. She knew the classics and is a historian. I always felt Martha used things as an excuse. She would always come in to start her new piece . . . I mean, to start a new piece for anyone is frightening on the first day. It is a horrifying moment and one has to get courage from somewhere to start. Anyway, Martha would come in with books and pictures and say, "Look at these, dear. Look at this sculpture, dear." It never had anything to do with anything. We would start. I mean, maybe it had something to do with the epic, but it was an excuse for Martha to start working. For me, it was very comforting. I mean, you don't come into the rehearsal room knowing. The best thing to do is come in not knowing. That is what really takes courage and that is when you can really discover something. I think the only way one learns to choreograph is to apprentice with choreographers. To be a child and sit, watch and look.

It was my responsibility to bring these great Graham prototypes to breath and pulse. Martha always personalized the archetype. She made the broad concept specific. I wanted to bring these classical truths of our existence to present-day realities, to make them current and personally relevant for the audience.

Martha threw my husband, David, and myself together very often. I think she enjoyed being a part of our strong emotion for each other. Martha would never shy [away] from people's personal interactions. She would keep up on all the gossip and use it!

I'm trying at this point, actually, to have the ability to be able to set up a situation and manipulate someone within more of their freedom. I want to have more freedom within my technique as a choreographer, so that is why I'm pushing to do something that is against my instinct or my natural inclination. It is the same. . . . A dancer has to try to do the things they can't do as well as the things they can do, even if you chose not to use them. Choreographically, I'm trying to expand and use more of the improvisation and a looser structure for a dancer to work with. I'm having a lot of trouble because I ultimately say, "Do this." As with Martha, I found it very hard to work with her as her tool because I didn't want to imitate her way of moving. If I was going to improvise, it was going to be from my standpoint. And I could never just put myself in her technique, and improvise within her technique because then I was giving my soul over to her. I was saying, "This is my impulse to move in your movement, Martha." I would resist that completely. It was really torture for me to work with Martha on a new piece because of that resistance. I wanted Martha to do it. I would always try to get more from Martha, and she would resent that, but in a sense, I think it would get her further because she would have to take more responsibility. You see, I wasn't going to give Martha my soul because I didn't trust her with it. Again, it is not imitating. I'm talking about base instinct that is right, about the past. That is what survives.

❖ THE ❖
1980's-90's

Jack Vartoogian.

From left to right: Floyd Flynn, Steve Rooks and Terese Capucilli in
Maple Leaf Rag, *1990.*

TERESE CAPUCILLI

Nan Melville.

Terese Capucilli in Deep Song, 1986.

Terese Capucilli was born in Syracuse, New York, in 1956, the middle child in a family of seven children. She received her B.F.A. degree from the State University of New York at Purchase in 1978 and in 1979 was asked to join the Martha Graham Dance Company. That same year she was one of four performers to dance in honor of Martha Graham in the CBS-TV presentation of the Kennedy Center Honors. The following year, in the featured role of "Young Clytemnestra," she was partnered by Rudolf Nureyev in Clytemnestra *at the Metropolitan Opera House in New York City.*

Performing principal roles since 1982, she has danced a wide range of classic roles, among them over twenty-five originally performed by Martha Graham. Capucilli has become known for her interpretation of lead roles in nearly every revival presented by the Company since 1983. These include the "Principal Sister" in Deaths and Entrances, *"She Who Dances" in* Letter to the World, *"The Empress of the Arena" in* Every Soul Is a Circus, *"One Who Seeks" in* Dark Meadow, *"Hecuba" in* Cortege of Eagles, *and "Mary, Queen of Scots" in* Episodes. *Other classic roles include "Joan" in* Seraphic Dialogue, *"Medea" in* Cave of the Heart, *"The Bride" in* Appalachian Spring, *"Jocasta" in* Night Journey, *"Mary" in* El Penitente, *and those in* Errand into the Maze, Heretic, Primitive Mysteries, Judith, *and* Phaedra. *Graham choreographed on Capucilli the role of "The Chosen One" in* The Rite of Spring *in 1984, "The Crescent Moon" in* Temptations of the Moon *in 1986 and the lead role in her final ballet,* Maple Leaf Rag, *in 1991.*

Deep Song *was reconstructed for Capucilli in 1988 and in the years to follow she has become instrumental in the research and reconstruction of many early Graham solos, including* Salem Shore *and "Spectre - 1914" from* Chronicle. *Capucilli also assisted Sophie Maslow in the reconstruction of "Call to Action," the final section of* Chronicle. *She has become the first dancer other than Graham to perform* Deep Song, *"Spectre - 1914" and "Call to Action."*

On film, she danced Errand into the Maze *in* An Evening of Dance and Conversation with Martha Graham, *and later again in the Company's filming in Tokyo, Japan, and she also filmed* Maple Leaf Rag *at the Paris Opera. In 1987 she performed "The Bride" in* Appalachian Spring *with Mikhail Baryshnikov as "The Husbandman" and Rudolf Nureyev as "The Revivalist." Later, she was partnered by Baryshnikov in Graham's* Night Journey *and* El Penitente. *She was subsequently invited to perform* El Penitente *with Baryshnikov's White Oak Dance Project in Paris and London. She has had roles choreographed for her by Twyla Tharp and Robert Wilson in works created for the Graham Company.*

Capucilli was the recipient of a Princess Grace Fellowship in 1986 and in 1987 she received the Princess Grace Statuette Award. She is an Associate Founder of Buglisi/Foreman Dance, a company formed with Graham colleagues Jacqulyn Buglisi, Donlin Foreman and Christine Dakin.

Terese Capucilli lives with her husband, actor Bill Randolph, in New York City.

———————————— ✦ ● ✦ ————————————

I did everything. I did study dance when I was young, but it was tap, jazz, ballet, acrobatics. . . . I started in second grade for a half an hour each week in the church basement. I was in Catholic school, and my parents put me in all of these classes. I continued with the same teacher throughout high school and became very involved in musical theater as well, studying voice and performing a great deal. I really had no idea what "modern" dance was until I met my first "Graham" teacher, Joni Consroe. She knew Bill Bales when he was dean of dance at SUNY Purchase, and in any case, she choreographed a little solo for me, wrote my letter of recommendation, I auditioned for Purchase and was accepted.

Carol Fried was very much my mentor at Purchase, along with Mel Wong. They are from very diverse schools—Graham's and Cunningham's. Carol, a very strict Grahamite, was complemented with a more lyrical side of Graham from

Kazuko Hirabayashi. Both [were] so solid and pure. I was surrounded by many wonderful teachers from assorted backgrounds and these years became extremely important for me. I spent every hour in the dance building, from 8:30 in the morning—I remember doing Graham class that early—until late at night. I was like a sponge, absorbing all I could. If doors opened I stepped into them. Consequently, I performed continually while I was there, in many works by Wong, Hirabayashi, Limón, Humphrey and Graham. I also had the opportunity to work with Anna Sokolow, who influenced me greatly. I was so into it that there was no time to think about why I was doing it, or where I would end up. Before I graduated Carol arranged a scholarship for me at the Graham studio. Another door opened so I stepped in.

Martha has said that mediocrity is the greatest sin. I believe that. After all these years of working with Martha, I am more aware of what this means now, artistically, than ever before. A lot of times the opposition that people experience in their lives can either foster or deny them the confidence to move forward. For me, the opposition has always been within myself. I am never fully satisfied with anything, and that is what continually drives me forward. Martha recognized that inner struggle and [that] is why I believe she entrusted me with her roles and allowed me the opportunity to find my own way through them. I can take these roles onstage with me hundreds of times and still be able to go deeper into them. I've danced *Errand into the Maze* since 1983, and each time I take it onto the stage there continues the never-ending process of learning and discovering new approaches, new solutions. Like a beautifully terraced garden, through the years you begin to layer what you learn. It is full of resources I continually add to and draw from. Who I am as an artist is a direct result of being able to work with Martha's diversified repertoire of incredible masterpieces and because Martha allowed *me* to live in each role. This is something that has become uniquely mine, that no one can ever know in the same way or ever take away from me. This was Martha's gift to each of us.

In many ways, with Martha's work you prepare for a role as an actor would prepare. You are given a script, you read it, you make your choices. I would be studying the video, playing it through many times, and then I would go back and write down every step from beginning to end. You are also able to see different interpretations with different dancers in three or four different films, so by the time you've gone through that process, well, it is like seeing a play many times. You begin to understand where the threads are leading, what

Martha was trying to say. Technically, the movement can stand by itself. But you must be able to add something dramatically—*your* inner dialogue—putting yourself in a certain place and time which add this other important dimension. For example, in *Night Journey,* not only does the beginning foreshadow the end, but the ballet also takes you through the lives of "Jocasta" and "Oedipus" in a very short time. As difficult as it is, the only way to link the threads is to be willing to take the risk in finding that inner dialogue. There is so much depth in Martha's work that you have to move far beyond any comfortable place in order to explore its limits.

Martha appeals to audiences' emotions—and it is really as simple as that—because of the enormous figures, the myths, the legends, the types of poetic and heroic themes she deals with. There is always something to grasp onto that has a strong validity and vitality to it. Working with these characters of archetypal stature—the men and women of Martha's work, like Jocasta and Oedipus or Medea and Jason—you discover that they are so tangible to an audience. They speak about gut-level truths.

Martha said one time about audiences, "It is not just the technique. It can't be just the technique that reaches an audience. There has to be something behind it. An emotional climate." The emotions come out of the movement itself. She didn't believe there had to be a reality to what you were going through onstage. She often said that we could be writing our grocery list for all the audience knew. She said you can never *really* allow yourself to be out of control—it is in the acting, being able to bring that back on will, to do it again the same way. The consistency, within spontaneity. Often, though, I actually get caught up in that—in that feeling of nearly losing control. For me, it has been these moments where I have felt the most vulnerable and yet so fearless.

It was very frustrating for Martha not to be able to readily produce choreography. The choreographic process was so grueling—you would see and feel the frustration. But Martha drew fresh inspiration from her surrounding world and lived for those hours in her studio with her dancers. She was a vibrant person, intuitive, alive, exciting, perceptive, intense and uncompromising. Just Martha sitting in that chair—she did more movement than I have ever seen anyone do sitting down. Rehearsing a ballet in 1989, one she never finished, Martha said, "I'm doing something I've been dreaming. . . . Sitting in one place is very difficult for me." You knew she was itching to get up and show you. Instead, she had to tell you verbally. It had to be a collaboration with the choreographer and the dancer, what Antony Tudor called his "sympathetic family." We had to be in cahoots with what Martha was thinking. You are her instrument. If you think she wanted one thing, you'd try it out and show her. If that was not what she was looking for, you'd try something else. Some days she'd come into the studio and be at your throat.

With *Rite of Spring* (1984) being the first major role choreographed on me, it was a very big deal for me to work in this way in Martha's hands. The "Chosen One's" solo was choreographed by a constant provoking and it wasn't necessarily personal. In fact, it wasn't personal at all. Martha wanted to get something out of me. She was on the edge of her seat glaring at me, Stravinsky blaring, and she was yelling things for me to do: "Twist your body! Leap! Fall!" She had me in a bit of a frenzy, but when I couldn't give Martha what she asked for immediately, I became angry, and she came over and wrenched my body far beyond where I thought it could go, and through the pain of it I heard Martha say, "That's it." Then it was there . . . and I realized 150 percent would never be enough.

When Martha spoke about the use of music she would say, "You should *be* the beat, not *follow* the beat. Pluck the beat out of the air," which is a perfect image. Physicality alone can say so much, but her use of the music to create a dramatic pulse can be so incredible to work with.

Martha ventured into the reconstruction of *Deep Song* in 1989. She said very early on to me in the rehearsal process, "It is very difficult to do a solo with another person. I find it increasingly difficult. It's easier for two or three people or a dozen people, but one solo, to try to transfer to another person . . . it has to be a constant exchange." I felt a tremendous responsibility during that time to be a constant inspiration for Martha. I spent many hours in Studio 3 with Barbara Morgan photographs splayed all over the floor, working out movement phrases in order to be well-prepared before my rehearsals with Martha. In 1991, after Martha died, Carol Fried and I would begin researching other solos of Martha's. *Salem Shore*, reconstructed in 1992, and "Spectre - 1914," [reconstructed] in 1994, both dealt with war themes as *Deep Song* had, but in very different ways. This particular experience of working with Martha on *Deep Song* was instrumental in preparing me for the frightening process of reconstructing these other solos without her. What I had learned from her I realized gave me the courage and the insight to trust what I know.

Knowing Martha, I think what was extremely important to her—or devastat-

Beatriz

Terese Capucilli as "The Chosen One" with George White Jr. in
Rite of Spring, *1984.*

ing to her—was that her roles can go on without her. It is a beautiful statement of her genius that her roles will survive without her performing them, but at the time when she started giving them up it must have been terrifying for her to relinquish them to other dancers. She was still struggling with not being able to dance or being able to dance only a little. By the time I came to the company Martha had resigned herself to this and although she could be utterly ruthless, she could also be extremely generous. I had the luxury of Martha herself coaching me through a tremendous amount of roles and she gave me the opportunity to perform them again and again. This is where I feel the importance lies with the last generation that worked with Martha. Martha was extremely vibrant during this time *not only* as a choreographer, but as a mentor and teacher as well.

The "Golden Era" generation of Ethel, Helen, Matt, Mary . . . was different than mine. The old company was not necessarily allotted these luxuries simply because Martha could not deal with others doing her roles so [she] would leave them to fend for themselves and also because performance opportunities were not as abundant. There has been a lot of change since then. I don't know if Martha ever thought about what she had done, but rather what she was about to do. She needed to be in the studio working. She never dwelt in the past.

I have probably danced over 25 of Martha's roles. From the beginning I knew that Martha really wanted me to make them my own. I never felt that she was comparing me to anybody else, [either] to herself or anybody who had performed the roles. Martha had always insisted on having individuals in her company. It has helped immensely to have people like Pearl Lang and Yuriko [Kikuchi] around in helping to bring back some of the older pieces. Linda Hodes also had been there all those years constantly at our side, and Martha's, as well. Of course everyone has a different idea about what something should be, but I feel what is important is not whether a step is this way or that way, but to continually hold onto what Martha has given me, molded on me and created *in* me.

There is a certain amount of giving up of yourself in the commitment to Martha Graham. I am amazed when I look back and see the dances that I've performed and dedicated my life to. I am very fortunate to have been chosen.

TWO

Guest Artists

Nan Melville.

Terese Capucilli and Mikhail Baryshnikov in Appalachian Spring, *1987.*

MARGOT FONTEYN

Louis

Margot Fonteyn and Rudolf Nureyev in Lucifer, 1975.

Margot Fonteyn was born in Reigate, Surrey, England, on May 18, 1919. She studied dance as a child in Shanghai, and later with Vera Volkova at the Sadler's Wells Ballet School in England. She began her professional career in 1934 as a Snowflake in The Nutcracker. *Her first major creation was "The Bride" in Sir Frederick Ashton's* Le Baiser de la Fée *for the Royal Ballet in 1935. Thereafter, she created a long line of roles in Ashton ballets. She went on to become the quintessential English Prima Ballerina Assoluta. In 1955, she married Dr. Roberto Arias, the former Panamanian Ambassador to the Court of St. James, and in 1956 she became a Dame of the Order of the British Empire, the first dancer to be awarded such a title.*

At the age of 60, Fonteyn danced in Le Spectre de la Rose *and* L'Après-Midi d'un Faun *with Rudolf Nureyev at the Nureyev Festival in London. In 1981, she danced the role of "Lady Capulet" in Nureyev's production of* Romeo and Juliet, *starring Rudolf Nureyev and Carla Fracci, with the La Scala Ballet. They were her last performances.*

Dame Margot Fonteyn died in Panama in 1992.

I would have felt it would have been very ungracious to refuse Martha Graham. But it is not very easy to do modern dance suddenly. In fact, it is exceedingly difficult.

To me, modern dance in America really started with Martha Graham. I just can't go along with Isadora Duncan being the founder of modern dance. All she did was bang open doors. However, Isadora didn't do anything choreographically, in my opinion. Ruth St. Denis did even less. Also, even before Isadora started liberating the body, a great deal of society women were dressing in robes and posing about in that period. It was very much in the air at the time. Isadora wasn't the only one.

Modern dance was in the air before World War II because of the Central European artists like Mary Wigman, but the German modern dance pioneers lost it all because of Hitler and the world falling to pieces. So Martha does seem to be the one who progressed—codified modern dance technique and established a school system—and put it all together.

In the classic ballet, we dance out for the public. We are brought up that way. To Martha, it is all inside. I always loved what Martha used to say about the interior landscape. Her dances are like seeing inside the head—seeing all the emotions. All of these were ideas which I read and [I] found [it] incredibly interesting to be working with Martha Graham, who actually said them. Of course it was totally different, at least to what we were all doing in the classic ballet. At one point, Martha turned and flexed the foot instead of pointing the foot to be contrary to ballet.

I compared Martha Graham's way of choreographing to that of Sir Frederick Ashton's way of allowing one to contribute in order to get the best for the artist. I do think they are a great deal alike.

I don't think I danced exceptionally well in *Lucifer* (1975), because I did not have training in the Graham technique. You don't suddenly go into it and do it well. For *Lucifer*, Martha was very nice and tactful with me. She would leave me in the rehearsal room with the other dancers to help me and adapt or change anything I didn't like. She wanted me to feel free to do anything that I felt able to do, or not to do something I didn't feel able to do. Martha would try to teach me and help me and leave me alone. Then Martha would come in and look afterwards. Martha would sometimes rearrange things with her wonderful eye.

Martha is very clever the way she makes other things part of her choreography. The snake in *Lucifer* was part of her choreography and also part of my costume.

Martha sees the interior landscape and then she feels that her choreography is with space and movement in space. I never thought about space being my partner until I worked with Martha at that late age.

Incense was a Ruth St. Denis solo that Maya Plisetskaya actually danced for Martha Graham instead of me. I thought, well why not do Martha's choreography, which is much better than Ruth St. Denis' choreography? I mean, Ruth St. Denis' choreography must have been all right for her in that period. And the music was so terrible. Ruth St. Denis choreographed the solo for herself. She never did anything for anybody else except herself. The dance I could see. In fact, I saw a film of Ruth St. Denis doing the solo and she was wonderful. But I couldn't possibly have done it, and if I were going to do something new, I would have had Martha do something for me.

After I danced *Lucifer* in 1975, Martha wanted me to dance *Primitive Mysteries*. I just felt I wouldn't be able to do that anymore, you know. I mean, it was quite a late age to dance modern choreography.

Martha's sense of theater is extraordinary: The way she used Noguchi and his sculptures; the way she uses costumes, fabrics and cloaks is tremendously theatrical; the way she uses music that is contemporary to what she is doing. She doesn't go back and use an old score from the last century. Her works are very unified with the music, the décor, the style of movement and the costumes. What is so great about Martha Graham is she is so theatrical.

RUDOLF NUREYEV

Courtesy of Rudolf Nureyev.

Rudolf Nureyev and Christine Dakin in Phaedra's Dream, *Paris, 1984.*

--- ◆ ● ◆ ---

*Rudolf Nureyev was born in Ufa, Bashkiria, Russia, on March 17, 1938, and
had his first dance lessons there. He found his way to Leningrad's Kirov Ballet
School when he was 17 and passed the rigid course under the guidance of his
great teacher, Pushkin. Within three years, he won first prize at the National
Student Dance Competition in Moscow and was immediately invited to dance
opposite the Kirov's prima ballerina, Natalia Dudinskaya, in* Laurentia. *Thereafter, he danced most of the classics, as well as the contemporary productions,
in the Kirov repertoire.*

Rudolf Nureyev defected to the West in 1961. In London, he saw Graham's film,
A Dancer's World, *starring Helen McGehee, Mary Hinkson, Ethel Winter, Yuriko,
Bertram Ross, Bob Cohan, Gene McDonald and David Wood. Immediately, he
wanted to work with Graham and eventually he did for 13 years (1975-88),
learning the principal male roles in eight of Graham's dances:* Lucifer, The Scarlet
Letter, El Penitente, Night Journey, Appalachian Spring, Clytemnestra, Ecuatorial
and Phaedra's Dream.

*On January 25, 1984, Rudolf Nureyev, then artistic director of the Paris Op-
era Ballet, invited Graham and her company to appear at the Palais Garnier,
the first American dance company ever to do so. For the occasion Nureyev made
his debut in Graham's* Phaedra's Dream. *Later that evening Graham was named
a knight of the French Legion of Honor by France's Minister of Culture, Jacques
Lang.*

When Graham was asked if she had choreographed Phaedra's Dream *(which
premiered in Athens, Greece, in July 1983) with Nureyev in mind, Graham
replied that the gifted Russian* "is seldom far from my mind."

Martha Graham was quoted by The New York Times about the creation of Lucifer *in 1975 for Fonteyn and Nureyev:* "I'd much rather be dancing than choreographing. I'll always miss it. This is the only time that I've ever lived through

another person in movement. Rudolf is not a substitute for myself, but working with him gives me a very definite identification."

Graham also wrote in the gala program for Lucifer:

> Tyger Tyger burning bright. In the
> forest of the night.
> Lucifer suffered all the terrors
> a man suffers.
> It is part of nothingness, part of
> Lucifer's life,
> my life and part of Rudolf's life.

Rudolf Nureyev died in January 1993.

———————◆ ● ◆———————

I went in 1963 to see Martha's company in London. It was very foolish of me because I had just landed, then I went to [the] theater and started to fall asleep. I couldn't wait till the end when Martha came out on stage. However, I did see Martha in London at the Charlesbury Theatre, when she was still dancing. She had a strong presence.

With Martha, I was learning how to waste less energy with her steps. I was hammering away. I was plunging, going crazy. I just wanted movement. Martha had movement and I was stealing it. Martha said, "Yes, I'm a thief. I steal from the best." So I was there also stealing.

I had to show the world that I was not retiring to modern dance, so I choreographed *Raymonda* for Cynthia Gregory[1] at the American Ballet Theater simultaneously while I was dancing with Martha. Well, Martha defends herself with words very well. And she had to sell her company, remember. The whole event really was a publicity stunt with me and Margot, Martha, Betty Ford, Woody Allen and Halston.

---

[1] Cynthia Gregory (1946 -). American ballerina with the American Ballet Theater, now retired.

Absolutely! It was all like an MGM promotion.

I never took private classes with Martha Graham. I took two private classes with David Hatch Walker, who Martha sent to teach me. Then my knee started to swell because of her fourth position. Martha saw it and said, "Oh, that is nothing. You already know how to do that. Go directly to repertoire." But we went through the syllabus of Graham's. They taught it to me quickly, what was going on. Martha wouldn't let me go and take class with the company. I would have felt more comfortable being behind someone copying the exercises and seeing what they do. It is very difficult when all the attention is on me.

Erick [Hawkins] was the first to break away from Martha. Then Merce and Paul made what Martha was doing more palpable. They translated Martha's language to our day.

One must have a rock toward which people gravitate or reject, rather than a nebula, or nothing.

Martha demanded from her dancers so much energy. Of course without energy it doesn't look like anything at Graham. When you do a dance with so much energy you can't survive for the next segment. And then you begin to lose balances.

It is wanking with Martha. You see me trying to play Bach [on the piano or organ or harpsichord]—the goddamn same thing. It doesn't want to play easily. You have to build up your stamina by wanking. When I got to Graham, I figured out that everyone was cooking up their own thing. What I did like of Martha's was her corps de ballet work in *Primitive Mysteries*. That was the best of Martha Graham. *El Penitente* . . . I liked that one, although I can't remember nothing. I can't remember what I did to myself, not even flagellating and whipping myself in *El Penitente*. But I liked that ballet. I remember there was a cross of Noguchi's.

Martha would begin something, start talking and then say, "I'm going to leave it to you, dears." And she goes back to her hovel to have a drink, take a nap, whatever. Martha said, "I want action." Well, good. That is ballsy. You could see Martha devouring people, undress and devour. A real vampire. She devoured not their blood, but their flesh. I asked one of the male dancers, "What you do in *Night Journey*, what is that for? How can you do this, and that, and something else?" So they fixed it for me.

I think *Appalachian Spring* is the ideal ballet. Very well done. It is intricately composed. Bill Carter was there sometimes. He danced "The Husbandman" in *Appalachian Spring*. . . . Pearl Lang was a very great artist. I liked the two Japanese women (Yuriko Kimura and Takako Asakawa). And there was another Japanese, an

Beatriz Schill

Rudolf Nureyev and Yuriko Kimura in Ecuatorial, *1980.*

older Yuriko [Kikuchi], who danced *Diversion of Angels.* She was setting the Joan of Arc dance, *Seraphic Dialogue.*

Halston designed golden mesh to put on my dance belt in *Lucifer,* which is why some people thought the dance was pornographic. He put some diamonds and rubies and I don't know what else. He wanted to stitch these things on my crotch himself. After I had rehearsed all day long, he wanted me to stand for him while he sewed up my crotch. I said, "Here is my dance belt, sew it on. Let me have one hour." My foot was enormous because I had twisted my foot.

Rehearsals were nonstop with Martha. That is where Martha spent endless money. She had rehearsal onstage full-out: overtime, lights, costumes, with orchestra. I danced for five weeks, eight performances a week with them, and it was all sold out. They should have made enormous amounts of money. I refused salary. I danced for free. Those people were extraordinary. I only asked them to bring me chicken devil lai and borscht from the Russian Tea Room. They didn't. It came, but I had to pay myself.

[In] *Clytemnestra* I danced the role of "Aegisthus" to Yuriko Kimura's "Clytemnestra." I liked the four boys. They come and rape Troy. The dance of four gorillas. It was strange and yet pathetic, slapping girls on their hips—and that is supposed to be the rape. Gosh. Martha has done over 150 dances. She could have done *Sacre.* . . . Great with her technique. There are some moments that are good and then it is so pathetic.

Martha choreographed for me *Scarlet Letter.* It was quite a good story . . . Martha couldn't tell the story, though. She wanted me to kvetch all the time. I said, "What about?"

It was a good set. Marisol did a second floor on top but it wasn't enough space to do something on two different levels. No, I thought it was a very clever set for *Scarlet Letter.*

I also danced a new creation of *Ecuatorial* with a set—a rock formation—by Marisol. I had quite a confrontation one time with Anna [Kisselgoff] who came to have an interview; she wanted me to gibber-jabber, by repeating words Martha was saying. I said, "I am not interested in mimicking Martha. Martha has a dance vocabulary and that is what I am after." I didn't want to sound like a monkey repeating Martha's verbose pronouncements. Later, I wasn't surprised at all that Erick [Hawkins] said he created the male movement for Graham. What were [the men] supposed to be? Big dummies? I saw Bertram Ross with Martha and I didn't like him very much because he was jumping like a big

William R.

*From left to right: Rudolf Nureyev, Christine Dakin and George White Jr.
in Phaedra's Dream, New York City, 1984.*

dummy with Martha's steps. Big wooden dummy! Then I saw him with Pearl Lang when she choreographed *The Dybbuk* and he was very good there. He had nice good movement.

Once I was driving in a taxicab with Martha in Japan. I said, "Takako [Asakawa] danced well tonight." Martha hissed, "She didn't dance from her vagina."

Martha created for herself. That is what she can speak, so they were heroines, not heroes. Why should one make them masculine? That is what Martha was saying. That was what was strong for her. To just stand there, like in the Japanese theater, while the rest surrounded her.

Martha Graham didn't give up anything. Nothing. She was Martha Graham, and that already was great. Great satisfaction! This is a terrible thing with everybody, not having exact profession, not being pulled anywhere, not deciding. Martha knew she is Martha Graham. No dancer sacrifices anything for anybody. Because they have satisfaction that no other people have.

Balanchine didn't give up anything either. He poured all the money into his company. He had the most expensive toy. Those 100 dancers were for him only.

Look at Paul Taylor. He curses every other ballet he has to do. Yet he has to do it. He feels it. He needs it. Paul was attracted to Martha's language so he had to go on. Martha had the complete alphabet!

From the very beginning Martha did very few performances. They were wanking in front of the mirror for hours and hours and hours. Martha had very few people, and the dance theater she developed was always centered on her. So she had a knack. It is not difficult. It is difficult to train yourself at the beginning, and the moment it is going, there it is. Martha wouldn't think nothing of it to go into the studio after breakfast until lunch and then again in the afternoon. Self-glorification. Endless self-glorification!

She was longing, longing for it. For whom? For what? For God? Longing to come back into the glory eternally.

The End

INDEX

Page numbers in **bold** refer to subject interviews
Page numbers in *italics* refer to illustrations

PHOTOGRAPHIC ACKNOWLEDGMENTS

First and foremost, grateful acknowledgment is made to Mrs. Arnold Eagle for the use of photographs by Arnold Eagle, and to Lloyd and Douglas Morgan for the use of photographs by Barbara Morgan.

Special thanks to Cris Alexander and to Shaun O'Brien, Brooks Jackson, and Randy Crocker. Also, I would especially like to thank Ms. Diane-Bouchard for the use of her father's photograph of Martha Hill. Thank you to Robert and Reiko Sunami Kopelson for permission to use Soichi Sunami's photograph of Martha Graham in *Heretic*. Thanks to Steve and Jane Halsman Bello of the Halsman Studio for permission to use Philippe Halsman's photo of Martha Graham's *Cave of the Heart*. And special thanks to Joseph Solomon for permission to use the Carl Van Vechten photographs as well as to Carol Greunke of the Max Waldman Archives for use of the Max Waldman photograph of Peggy Lyman. Thank you to Milton Oleaga for permission to use his photograph of Graham's *Visionary Recital*.

I am grateful to Madeline Nichols and the staff of the Dance Collection of the Lincoln Center Library and Museum of the Performing Arts for providing the reproductions of the photographs on pages 6, 16, 118, 138, 144, and 202.

Finally, I would like to thank all the contemporary dance photographers who generously lent their images for this oral history: Johan Elbers, Nan Melville, Louis Peres, William Reilly, Beatriz Schiller, Jack Vartoogian and to William Waters for permission to use his photograph of me in Central Park, NYC.

Pages ii, 82, 92 and 146: © Cris Alexander. Courtesy Cris Alexander.

Pages 1 and 2: Courtesy Betty MacDonald.

Page 10: © Thomas Bouchard. Courtesy Diane Bouchard.

Page 16: Soichi Sunami © estate of Soichi Sunami. Courtesy Mrs. Reiko Sunami Kopelson, Executor.

Pages 21, 22, 43, 50, 59, 62, 72 and 76: © Photographs by Barbara Morgan,

Courtesy Willard and Barbara Morgan Archives, 45 Dochester Avenue, Hastings-on-Hudson, New York 10706, (914) 478-0132.

Pages 28, 40, 68, 81, 86, 118, 122, 128, 142, 144, 153, 154, 172, 176, 189, 191, 216, 236, 246 and 256: © Photographs by Arnold Eagle. Courtesy Mrs. Arnold Eagle on behalf of the Estate of Arnold Eagle.

Page 100: Philippe Halsman © estate of Philippe Halsman. Courtesy Steve Bello and Jane Halsman Bello of the Philippe Halsman Studio.

Page 108: Courtesy Yuriko.

Pages 112, 164, 168 and 186: Anthony Crickmay © Theatre Museum, Victoria and Albert Museum, London, Courtesy Sarah Woodcock.

Page 131: © Jaacov Agor. Courtesy Helen McGehee.

Pages 138 and 269: © Photograph by Carl Van Vechten. Courtesy Estate of Carl Van Vechten, Joseph Solomon, Executor.

Page 166: Courtesy Bertram Ross.

Page 213: © Milton Oleaga. Courtesy Milton Oleaga.

Page 228 and 234: Courtesy Donald McKayle for the two Y. Hayata rehearsal photographs.

Pages 270, 292 and 301: © Jack Vartoogian. Courtesy Jack Vartoogian.

Page 276: Martha Swope © Time Inc.

Pages 283 and 312: © Louis Peres. Courtesy Louis Peres.

Page 284: Max Waldman © Max Waldman Archives. Courtesy Carol Greunke, Executor.

Page 290: © Johan Elbers. Courtesy Johan Elbers.

Pages 302 and 311: © Nan Melville. Courtesy Nan Melville.

Page 308 and 320: © Beatriz Schiller. Courtesy Beatriz Schiller.

Page 316: Courtesy Rudolf Nureyev.

Page 322: © William Reilly. Courtesy William Reilly.

Author's Photograph © William Waters. Courtesy William Waters.

ACKNOWLEDGMENTS

First, I would like to thank all of the artists who participated in this oral history project. My thanks to Christine Dougherty who has been involved with this project since the beginning—from typing the transcripts to editing, shaping, refining, and tightening the text.

Special thanks to the Edward F. Albee Foundation and the William Flanagan Memorial Creative Persons Center, Albee's artist colony in Montauk, New York, especially to Rex and Diane for their generosity. Thank you to Merce Cunningham and to the late Rudolf Nureyev for writing recommendations for this Albee writing fellowship.

In addition, I am grateful to: the Rudolf Nureyev Dance Foundation, Barry Weinstein, Executor; the late Jacqueline Kennedy Onassis; Isabel Brown, my first dance history professor at Skidmore College—close to twenty-five years ago she screened Graham's film *A Dancer's World* and I have been hooked on Martha Graham's drama ever since; Steven Saltzman, who copy-edited the manuscript; and my extended family, friends, and teachers, including Nile, Phyllis and Jamie Wyeth, Hannie Gillman, David Israel, William Behr, Jr., Eddy Edwards, Wendy Battey, Duncan Cooper, Janet Soares, Cynthia O'Neal, Nick Siano and Scott Berliner and his staff at Estroff (Daveda, Eric, Howie, José, Roma), for their continuous support of me and my dance projects.

Finally, thanks to my publisher Mel Zerman, the staff of Limelight Editions, and to Bryan McHugh for their terrific work.

AUTHOR'S BIOGRAPHY

Robert Tracy received an Edward F. Albee Foundation writing fellowship to complete his oral history, *Goddess: Martha Graham's Dancers Remember.* While a student at Skidmore College, where he earned his Bachelor of Arts degree in Classical Studies and Dance, he studied the Graham modern dance technique with two former artists of Graham's company, Mary Hinkson and Ethel Winter, under the aegis of the Artist in Residence, Melissa Hayden. After graduating, he danced for one year with Maria Tallchief's Chicago Lyric Opera Ballet. He then was awarded a three-year scholarship to George Balanchine and Lincoln Kirstein's School of American Ballet in New York City. Tracy appeared in Balanchine's recreation of *Le Bourgeois Gentilhomme,* for Rudolf Nureyev and Patricia McBride, and later in the same production with Suzanne Farrell and Peter Martins. Thereafter he danced professionally, most frequently in Nureyev's productions on Broadway and around the world. From 1989 to 1991 he studied dance with choreographer Merce Cunningham.

As a journalist on dance since 1977, Tracy has written for such magazines as the French, Spanish, German and English editions of *Vogue, Vanity Fair, Mademoiselle, Architectural Digest, Elle* and *Mirabella.* From 1989 to 1991 he wrote a monthly column for *Paris Vogue* about culture and fashion in New York City, titled *New York en Parle.*

His first book, *Balanchine's Ballerinas: Conversations with the Muses,* published in 1983 was recognized by the Wall Street Journal as "this year's great ballet book." In 1986 he edited Nigel Gosling's *Prowling the Pavements: Selected Arts Writings from London, 1950-1980.* Tracy researched and compiled Rudolf Nureyev's Introduction for Alexander Pushkin's *The Golden Cockerel and Other Fairy Tales,* published in 1990. His dialogue, *Collaborating with Graham,* was published in Isamu Noguchi's 1994 anthology, *Essays and Conversations.* In 1995 Oxford University Press commissioned him to write the entry on modern dancer Bill T. Jones for the *International Encyclopedia of Dance,* edited by Selma Jeanne Cohen. He is the 1997 recipient of the Skidmore College Alumni Association's Distinguished Achievement Award.